THE KORAN
IN THE
LIGHT OF CHRIST

THE KORAN
IN THE
LIGHT OF CHRIST

*A Christian Interpretation
of the
Sacred Book of Islam*

by
GIULIO BASETTI-SANI O.F.M.

FRANCISCAN HERALD PRESS
CHICAGO, ILLINOIS 60609

Library of Congress Cataloging in Publication Data

Basetti-Sani, Giulio, 1912-
  The Koran in the light of Christ.

  1. Christianity and other religions—Islam.
2. Islam—Relations—Christianity.   3. Koran—Criticism,
interpretation, etc.   4. Jesus Christ in the Koran.   I. Title.
BP172.B327   297'.1226   76-28786
ISBN 0-8199-0713-8

Nihil Obstat:
  MARK HEGENER O.F.M.
  Censor

Imprimatur:
  MSGR. RICHARD A. ROSEMEYER, J.D.
  Vicar General, Archdiocese of Chicago

November 10, 1977

Gratefully
dedicated to
the cherished and
revered memory of
my teachers,
Monsignor
Paolo Mario Mulla
and Louis Massignon

List of Biblical Abbreviations

The Books of the Old and New Testaments and Their Abbreviations

The Old Testament

Genesis	Gn	Proverbs	Prv
Exodus	Ex	Ecclesiastes	Eccl
Leviticus	Lv	Song of Songs	Sg (Song)
Numbers	Nm	Wisdom	Wis
Deuteronomy	Dt	Sirach	Sir
Joshua	Jos	Isaiah	Is
Judges	Jgs	Jeremiah	Jer
Ruth	Ru	Lamentations	Lam
1 Samuel	1 Sm	Baruch	Bar
2 Samuel	2 Sm	Ezekiel	Ez
1 Kings	1 Kgs	Daniel	Dn
2 Kings	2 Kgs	Hosea	Hos
1 Chronicles	1 Chr	Joel	Jl
2 Chronicles	2 Chr	Amos	Am
Ezra	Ezr	Obadiah	Ob
Nehemiah	Neh	Jonah	Jon
Tobit	Tb	Micah	Mi
Judith	Jdt	Nahum	Na
Esther	Est	Habakkuk	Hb
1 Maccabees	1 Mc	Zephaniah	Zep
2 Maccabees	2 Mc	Haggai	Hg
Job	Jb	Zechariah	Zec
Pslams	Ps (s)	Malachi	Mal

vii

The New Testament

St. Matthew	Mt	1 Timothy	1 Tm
St. Mark	Mk	2 Timothy	2 Tm
St. Luke	Lk	Titus	Ti
St. John	Jn	Philemon	Phlm
Acts of the Apostles	Acts	Hebrews	Heb
Romans	Rom	St. James	Jas
1 Corinthians	1 Cor	1 St. Peter	1 Pt
2 Corinthians	2 Cor	2 St. Peter	2 Pt
Galatians	Gal	1 St. John	1 Jn
Ephesians	Eph	2 St. John	2 Jn
Philippians	Phil	3 St. John	3 Jn
Colossians	Col	St. Jude	Jude
1 Thessalonians	1 Thes	Revelation	Rv
2 Thessalonians	2 Thes		

Acknowledgements

The trans-Atlantic journey of *The Koran in the Light of Christ* from Italy to America has been long and difficult. That it is finally over is completely due to the fraternal, professional and financial support of my Franciscan confreres of the New York-based Holy Name Province.

The journey began with the initial translation by Fr. William Russell Carroll O.F.M., of Paterson, N. J. At the other end of the world, Fr. Bede Dauphinee O.F.M., then stationed in Hong Kong, completed the revised translation.

Without the financial support of Fr. Seraphin Priestley O.F.M., director of the Far East Procuration Office in Hong Kong, the journey might have been aborted. Fr. Roy Gasnick O.F.M., director of the Franciscan Communications Office in New York City, and Mr. James C. G. Conniff, president of Megadot, Inc., Upper Montclair, N. J., handled all the details of the publication of the English edition. Fr. Cassian Miles O.F.M., did me the great service of proofreading and correcting the galley sheets.

Finally, I must acknowledge, with heart-felt gratitude, the fraternal support of my Provincial Superiors, first Fr. Finian Kerwin O.F.M., and now Fr. Charles Finnegan O.F.M. Though I was born in Italy and still work here, the American Holy Name Province is my adopted community. Because of the Christian love and concern of these two gentle superiors. I have never felt "adopted" but rather have experienced the joy of being a true son and brother.

G. B-S., Fiesoli, Italy, March, 1977

Contents

PART THREE

THE MEANING OF THE KORAN'S MESSAGE: MOHAMMED'S
PROVIDENTIAL MISSION REINTERPRETED IN THE
LIGHT OF CHRIST

PART FOUR
Vatican Council II, Dialogue Between
Christians and Muslims, and Conclusion

PART ONE

THE HISTORY OF
AN INTELLECTUAL AND
SPIRITUAL PILGRIMAGE

Before beginning our study of the holy book of Islam and the character and personality of its "prophet," I would like to trace the intellectual and spiritual evolution I underwent during a period of more than twenty-five years. This preliminary sketch will serve a twofold purpose: first, it will shed light on my present position; second, it will enable me to share with others a very valuable experience I had. Of necessity, then, the first part of this work will be of a highly personal nature. This departure from the impersonal character of a theoretical study can be justified only by its value to others, of which the reader must be the final judge.

A Missionary Vocation

As does every high school and college student, in my studies of European history I encountered the name of Mohammed and was given a more or less accurate description of the religion he founded and its rapid progress and expansion. I also beheld the magnificent epic of medieval Christendom, girding itself to defend Christian civilization by means of the Crusades. The Crusades! What a word to fire the imagination with thoughts of adventure and heroism! Horsemen, Arabs, the crescent moon, scimitars, Saracens, the Holy Land! So many names to conjure with — names that not only stir the heart of a young man but evoke a marvelous generosity.

My vocation as a Franciscan and a missionary began to take shape with a reading of the life of St. Anthony of Padua, with its accounts of the martyrdom of the first Franciscan saints, slain by Muslims in Morocco for publicly insulting the Arab prophet. There arose in me at that time the dream and aspiration of being martyred for Jesus Christ by becoming a missionary to the Muslim world and, like St. Anthony and the martyrs in Morocco, a son of St. Francis.

First Contacts with the Muslim World

After my theological studies were completed and I had worked for several years in the priesthood, praying all the while for a missionary assignment among the Muslim, in 1935 I finally arrived in an Islamic country — Egypt. All my dreams and enthusiasms were threatened with disillusion as the harsh light of reality flowed in from all sides. I seemed to be face to face with what has been accepted as an indisputable fact, proved by centuries of experience and continually asserted and repeated by all the missionaries who had preceded me: "You can do nothing with the Muslim. These Arabs will never be converted!" Those to whom the truth of this axiom had been painfully brought home smiled at the simplicity of the novice missionary, an inexperienced dreamer, and remarked: "Just wait a little. When you have found out what a strange bunch they are, you will lose your enthusiasm."

and the talent and interest of Fr. Jouin, a Lebanese Maronite priest, by which I slowly overcame the great difficulties of pronunciation, reading, and grammar, many years were to pass before I had a good grasp of the language — although I still could not claim to have mastered the "language of the angels" and the desert prophet.

The knowledge of Arabic, however, while it is a necessary condition for understanding Islam and the soul of the Arab, is not sufficient in itself for this purpose. Many other things must be studied before one can claim that he has penetrated the secrets of Arab and Muslim psychology or regard himself qualified in any minimal sense to talk about Islam.

Nevertheless, this difficulty in uncovering, penetrating, and evaluating the Muslim world increased my interest and study — and finally my understanding. After one year in Cairo, at the end of which my knowledge of Islam was restricted to external contact with the Muslim world, I was sent to Paris to undertake more advanced studies.

Study of Islam in Paris and Rome

In October 1936 I arrived in Paris to begin my studies at the Catholic Institute. Even apart from the course of studies, my stay in Paris proved to be a wonderful piece of good fortune, for at that time I met two people who profoundly influenced the evolution of my intellectual and spiritual appreciation of Islam.

First, there was a fellow Franciscan, Fr. John Mohammed Abd-el-Jalil, whom I had known slightly at Alverna in 1929, before he entered the order. He was a native Moroccan who, as a young Muslim, had come to Paris to do his university studies. The help of Professor Louis Massignon and the warm, kind, understanding, and brotherly atmosphere of the Franciscan friary in Paris, where the young man was made a welcome guest, greatly contributed to his discovery of Christianity and led to his conversion to Catholicism. This likewise fostered his vocation to the order and to the priesthood. Keeping his former name, Fr. John Mohammed Abd-el-Jalil was able to provide background and make suggestions for my research. In conversation, by letter, and especially through his publications he became the source of a continual flow of information on the religious soul of Islam.

The other person in Paris who had a profound impact on the direction of my studies and on my interpretation of Islam during that period, and until his death (his last letter to me was in July 1962), was that outstanding Catholic Oriental scholar, Professor Louis Massignon. I was introduced to him by Fr. Abd-el-Jalil almost as soon as I arrived in Paris.

Taking his course at the Ecole des Hautes Etudes at the Sorbonne that year was a real hardship. He was giving lectures on the Kharijites and an analysis of the eighteenth sura of the Koran. To grasp the matter, a linguistic and historical foundation was presupposed, and at that time I had neither. Despite the fact that the style of teaching, as well as the terminology, formed an insurmountable obstacle, I soon found myself captivated by the magic Professor Massignon exercised over his students and I stayed to listen. I learned, if nothing else, the importance of the subject he was dealing with. The study of Islam was not just a light intellectual exercise, a trifling thing mastered with the reading of a few pages about Mohammed and the Koran!

Massignon's influence on my thoughts came about through many personal conversations and the study of his writings. During this period, when I had the good fortune to be with him, I became aware that he was not just a great and learned man but also a holy one. While listening to him, one always had the feeling that his words came from the depths of a soul in continuous contact with God.

It was only after those first personal contacts with him that I discovered the special meaning of my Franciscan vocation in regard to Islam. It was he who, from the first, repeatedly advised me to meditate upon the mystery of the stigmata of St. Francis and their mysterious signification for Islam. It was he who made me understand the necessity of a profound love for Muslims, following the example of the Seraphic Father, and of suffering for them. This great influence on my life had its beginning in Paris, but it was not until later years, after 1947, that I began to imbue myself with his spirit and his deep intuitions concerning the mystery of Islam.[1]

My studies of Islam continued in Rome during the two-year period, 1937–1939, at the Pontifical Institute for Oriental Studies. The course was Institutiones Islamicae, given by Msgr. Paul Mary Mulla. What fond memories I have of this mentor: his goodness, his discretion, his shyness — the difficulty he had teaching the course in Latin (many times he unintentionally lapsed into French to communicate more freely). Mulla, who was of Turkish and Muslim origin, had studied in Aix-en-Provence under the guidance of the great scholar Maurice Blondel. It was through the Blondelian dialectic that he discovered the supernatural faith of Christianity. After his baptism, he consecrated himself wholly to Christ and his Church in the priesthood. Later, Pius XI appointed him to the newly established chair of the Institutiones Islamicae at the Pontifical Institute for Oriental Studies. (The Pope recalls this occasion in his encyclical on Oriental studies, *Rerum Orientalium*.)

Those two years under Msgr. Mulla were of great profit. New horizons appeared and the missionary enthusiasm, which had already lighted a flame for the salvation of the Muslims, burned with renewed vigor. The problem of Islam became a personal problem and, simultaneously, began to appear to me as one of the most urgent of the Church's missionary problems.

Up to this point my curiosity was concentrated on the figure of Islam's founder and on the meaning of his message, but as I listened to Msgr. Mulla I found him extremely reluctant to hazard any kind of definitive judgment concerning either the person of Mohammed or his work: Islam. He confined himself to giving what he considered to be the "results of scientific criticism of Islam." The intensely critical works that he valued the most were those of Prince Leone Caetani and Fr. Lammens S.J., as well as (at that time) the most recent studies of Tor Andrae and Michelangelo

Guidi. Even so, at times his ex-Muslim soul showed through in profound uneasiness when he was faced with certain outrageous judgments of Mohammed's person by some Orientalists or Christian apologists.

A number of times, in private, I tried to sound out Mulla to get his opinion of the personality and mission of Mohammed. At these moments he reacted as if he were faced with an unpleasant decision. He would shut his eyes, as though to recollect himself interiorly, and after a short silence would voice his usual conclusion:

> God alone can judge a man's conscience. Without doubt Mohammed was one of the great religious figures in history. He was most surely in good faith and, as with each of us, without being conscious of it, may have been an instrument of God. But on the other hand he could just as well have been an instrument of Satan, meant to oppose the kingdom of God. It is extremely difficult to add anything else.

He would then close his eyes, bow his head, and withdraw into silent prayer — his favorite prayer: for those of his brethren who were "still outside the house of their Father," but were, just as much as ourselves, "sons of Abraham."

I remember only once when he had occasion to express himself somewhat more explicitly about the function of Satan's instrument, which each of us more or less consciously can be. He liked to quote a text from St. Gregory the Great: "Caiphas and Annas were ministers of Satan, as were Herod and Pilate. So too were the Jews who shouted: 'Crucify Him!' So too were the Roman soldiers who carried out the execution of Jesus." This was in 1938, the year of those ephemeral triumphs of Hitlerism and the increasingly dangerous activity of communism in Europe.

Mulla viewed the development of history as a prolonged struggle between the kingdom of God and the kingdom of Satan. This struggle began with the rebellion of the angels and is still going on, here on earth, in the struggle between good and evil. The great historic fact which came out of Mohammed's activity,

Islam, which so profoundly marked not only Christian history but that of all mankind, in his mind had to be situated in this context. He repeated to me: "It is in the theology of history and not in the philosophy of history that the deep causes of this religious phenomenon must be sought."

If Mulla never desired explicitly to declare his personal judgment on Mohammed and Islam, it seemed that he was indicating a line of research which would lead me in the direction I desired. Thus he gradually stirred in me a compelling need to seek a theological solution to this question which was now in the foreground of my consciousness: What is the meaning of Islam in the story of mankind — mankind created to become conscious of and enter into the mystery of Christ?

Initial Attempts at a "Theological" Answer

In July of 1939 I was back in Egypt, where I had been appointed a professor in the Franciscan Oriental Seminary of Ghiza (Cairo). I was still preoccupied with the problem of finding the formulation of a theology of history which included Islam. That text of St. Gregory, so often repeated by Mulla, remained the point of departure in the search for a satisfactory answer: "Minister of Satan, Mohammed; kingdom of God, the Church; and the reign of Satan, or Islam."

Because of my Scholastic education, I had a fondness for dialectic between "opposites" and "contrasts." It was along these lines, then, that I searched for arguments to prove that Mohammed, a servant of Satan, had founded a diabolical religion, Islam. In the mission's ancient library, which had been transferred to the new seminary of Ghiza, I came across the great work of Fr. Ludovico Marracci (1612–1700): *Prodromus in refutatione*

Alcorani (Padua, 1691) and the *Refutatio Alcorani* (1698). I
had paged through it previously at Rome rather superficially,
where it had been presented to me as "an extraordinary work,
noted for the exactness and scientific care with which he goes
about examining the life of Mohammed, his constant references to the Arab sources, which he examined critically, and
useful especially for the force of the arguments with which he
rebuts the falsity of the Koran and the other Islamic doctrines. A
colossal work!"

Along with Marracci's book, I found that of Fr. Filippo Guadagnolo, a book just as heated in its anti-Islamic polemic.

These authors became the principal sources for my knowledge
of Islam. Perhaps this will explain why, after being in the com-
pany of these and similar "professors" — men of such different
spirit from that which I had known, even so slightly, at Paris in
Professor Massignon — the results of my researches were a bit
confusing.

It is interesting to note the conclusions I had come to at this
time, through the guidance of Marracci and Guadagnolo, regarding the significance and worth of Mohammed's mission and Islam.
During World War II when I was interned in a concentration
camp, I had the opportunity of giving lectures on the conclusions
of modern research on Islam to my companions. They were Italian
religious of several different orders and congregations who were
missionaries in Egypt. At the end of the series, desiring to express
my judgment of the person of the Arab prophet and the religion
he founded, I made the following observation on the necessity of
postulating a "preternatural" cause for the origin of Islam.

The judgments given by experts on Islam to explain the personality of Mohammed seem insufficient to me, though they
may help to some degree to understand how much Mohammed
contributed to his work. I question whether it is really possible
that a man of this type, quite sincere in the beginning, endowed
with real genius and ability, though perhaps culturally limited,
could have set in motion a movement so terrible, a movement
which was to influence so greatly the course of human history.

I think not! It seems to me that the personality of Jesus as it appears in the gospels, the sublime doctrine taught by him, and the work founded by him can have no adequate human explanation, but require, if they are to be fully explained, the intervention of "preternatural" causes, of divine causes. Analogously, then, Mohammed as an active and influential personality and his achievement, Islam, both as a historic fact and as a doctrine, cannot be attributed solely to human and natural causes as a total explanation. They need a reasonable explanation: the intervention of "preternatural," superhuman causes. Neither the history of religions nor the philosophy of history can ever furnish us with the profound reasons that adequately account for this historic fact. Hence, any judgment on the activity, personality, and achievement of the Arab "prophet" has to be sought within the context of a theology of history.

I was convinced then that only the theology of history could answer the questions "Who is Mohammed? What significance did his mission have? What is Islam's place in the story of mankind?" And the following answer was the only one, the only sufficient one that I could formulate then, in October 1941.

MY FORMER JUDGMENT OF MOHAMMED AND ISLAM

Mohammed was an instrument (we shall not judge whether consciously or not) of Satan. His purpose was to bring into actuality another aspect of the reign of Satan in the history of humanity: an antichurch in opposition to the Church of Christ. Jesus applied the frightful expression "sons of the devil" (*vos ex diabolo estis* [Jn 8:44]) to those obstinate Jews who were obstructing the reign of God. St. Gregory the Great, along with all of Christian tradition, calls Annas, Caiphas, Herod, Pilate, and all those who work with Satan for the destruction of Christ's reign "members of Satan." In Christian tradition, Satan is called the *simia Dei,* the "ape of God," because he attempts to bring about his own reign on earth in opposition to the reign of God. He tries to set up his own antichurch against the true and only Church, his false religions against the one and true religion. The works of all the heresiarchs are humano-diabolic, but no heresy and no antichurch has the mark of Satan so prominently as Islam! Mohammed is one of Satan's "prophets" and Islam is a form of Satan's pseudo-religion, the most anti-Christian because it is the most contrary to the gospels.

Let us recognize the natural merits of Mohammed — something that medieval Christianity refused to do: his religious character, his sincerity at the commencement of his prophetic career, his imaginative powers, his genius for organization, and all the latent talents that modern Orientalists (sometimes too generously) have recognized in him. Still, all these "positive" characteristics are not sufficient to explain the effects that followed.

Mohammed was of course an Arab merchant, in no way educated in literary or religious matters. Suddenly, his personality takes over Arab literature, and his Koran is considered the ideal of literary perfection. An unexpected "human wisdom" appears which is seen as a gift of God by his followers, an unusual religious spirit which experiments with unusual phases of religious experience — visions which, unless one wishes to make their explanation even more complicated, must be recognized as real. All these things are phenomena which must be classified as a false mysticism by which Satan, the ape of God, attempts with unction, pseudo-spiritual feelings, visions, and prophecies to imitate the supernatural action of God. The words of St. Peter concerning false teachers (2 Pt 2:10–18) can literally be applied to Mohammed. The "virtues" of the sons of Satan shine brilliantly in Mohammed: pride, lust, love of earthly riches — all these in opposition to the evangelical virtues.

I should like to dwell a little longer on the second conclusion: Islam is the actualization of the kingdom of Satan and functions as an antichurch. The Church of Christ is always faithful to her own image. The church of Satan does not have a positive and consistent unity of teaching but only a negative unity that is always dissolving into thin air. The kingdom of Satan is actually everything which the Church of Christ denies and combats, and it varies with time and place. The point of division between

Church and antichurch is always dependence upon God or independence from him — through faith in the only mediator, Jesus Christ, the God-Man. He who is not with Christ is against Christ (cf. Mt 12:30).

Islam functions as an adversary of God's kingdom; therefore it must be Satan's work. It is enough to glance at its doctrinal content to see how much it is the antithesis of Catholic doctrine. No man, not even the most learned rationalist, could have elaborated a doctrine and a spirit so essentially antievangelical as that of Mohammed. This too can have no adequate explanation unless we admit that Satan is the author of Islam.

Allah, the "god of the Koran," is anti-God, the enemy of the one true God, the God of the gospels. The Trinity of the Christians has no point of contact with the Koranic Allah for he is excluded absolutely and explicitly from the Trinity, from the divine natural paternity (the generation of the Word, Christ, the Son of God) and from adoptive fatherhood. The fatherhood of God has no place in Islam. The concept of the God of love is denied. The god of the Koran bears all the personal characteristics of Satan. He *is* Satan, clothed with pseudo-divine light, who has managed to attract a cult of divine adoration from a part of the human race. The awesome conclusion to all this is that millions of Muslims, without knowing it, adore Satan himself in their false god.

After the Holy Trinity, the center of Christian dogma, comes the Incarnation. Islam denied the Incarnation, both by its teaching on God and its teaching on Jesus Christ. It explicitly rules out the possibility of any such teaching. The "Jesus" of the Koran is the antithesis of the living and true Jesus of the gospels. To remove divinity from Jesus is to remove Jesus himself, because the human nature of Christ has no person other than the person of the divine Word. Whoever says that Christ is not the Son of God "is not from God," as St. John puts it: "Every spirit which will not say this of Jesus is not from God, but is the spirit of Antichrist" (1 Jn 4:3). Islam bears the Devil's mark in its Christology as well.

The Koran claims to be a successor to and a substitute for the gospel. Therefore it can be nothing other than an antigospel. Christ said that his words would remain forever (cf. Mt 24:35; 1 Pt 1:25), but the Koran, in Satanic wisdom, announces that it supersedes and completes the gospel, thus becoming its substitute.

To the concept and teaching concerning the Church, as taught by the Catholic Church — namely, that the Church is the mystical body of Christ, a visible, monarchico-hierarchical society, with authority and assistance given by Christ himself, the prolongation of his Incarnation — Islam is opposed as an antichurch organization, saturated with hatred for Christianity, in which there predominates, in function of a unifying chain, a very lively feeling which is basically racial and national — something quite the contrary of the universality and catholicity of Christianity. Islam is conscious of having a pseudo-vocation as a witness-bearing and missionary people of Satan's action, in opposition to the consciousness within the Catholic Church of a divine mission to bring salvation and redemption to souls.

Islam is an antichurch assembled about a "book," the Koran, in antithesis to that Church which is centered upon and unified in the person of Christ.

Islam's naturalism, so loudly proclaimed by the Encyclopedists and Rationalists, absolutely excludes any supernatural order. There can be no doctrine of grace in Islam because there is no "divine filiation." Its "divine predetermination" (*taqdîr*) cancels out free will; nor does it leave any room for the doctrine of original sin. The Christian struggle between spirit and flesh is quietly resolved by the compromise of sensual materialism. Still another antithesis is the absence in Islam of a priesthood and sacrifice, whereas the very life of Christianity is Calvary, the Mass, and the eternal priesthood of Christ.

The diabolical doctrine of the "holy war" teaches that no mercy is to be shown the unbeliever (sura 8:58–60; sura 47:4, 22, 37, etc.). "Do not show yourselves weak with your enemies, nor invite them to peace, while you have the advantage of them" is a direct contradiction to the meekness and sincerity of the gospel.

Islam knows no pardoning of enemies nor good people's power

of intercession in favor of sinners. The Allah of the Koran has no mercy for the non-Muslim. Moreover, it denies the dogma of the salvific will of God and the universality of the redemption. Since Islam lacks the dogma of redemption, it also lacks the Christian attitude toward suffering and the expiatory and redemptive role of suffering.

The absence of the divine imprint upon Islam and the presence of Satanic activity is attested by its fruits. Against the creative activity of God, Islam puts a destructive activity which hinders the religious, intellectual, and moral development of the individual and society. To the spiritual force that flows from the message of Christ, a force that has raised up monuments of wisdom, science, and holiness, Islam sets in opposition the abasement of the intellect and the decay of morals. These are fruits of Satan. The Muslim family can never know the peace of the Christian family. For the Christian, matrimony is hallowed by sacramental grace. Islamic society will never know the providential social works of charity that issue from the evangelical spirit. Nor will it ever have a conception of the state as a human society distinct from the Church. The theocracy which is Islam is in opposition to "Render Caesar the things that are Caesar's and to God the things that are God's" (Mt 22:21).

Islam's fruits are the Satanic convulsions of fanaticism, alternating with a lethargic torpor — a passing prosperity followed by a long decadence. Islam is motionless and lifeless; it flees from any kind of development or progress. That is why, between the teaching and work of Christ and the teaching and work of Mohammed, there is the difference between life and death. Christ is life and Satan is the adversary of all life, the author of death (cf. Jn 8:44). There is the difference between love — for God is love — and giving, and Satan, who was the first one to envy and the first egotist.

If we leave aside the question of personal responsibility, which God alone can judge, Mohammed was an instrument of Satan. In Islam Satan organized an antichurch in which all the opposites of the gospel message are gathered together with an energy which transcends all human natural activity. Islam is, therefore, one of the gravest, most baneful and dangerous actualizations of Satan, an attacker and destroyer of the reign of Christ.

These were the results I arrived at in 1941, when my sole purpose in studying Islam was to disprove it, to destroy an enemy. It was an enemy because I could not understand it and, hence, was unable to love it. This was the result of my study of Marracci. So I was scarcely surprised at a remark made by someone who said that he had been struck by the resemblance between nazism and Islam; when he read Hitler's *Mein Kampf,* he felt as though he was reading the Koran!

This incapacity to comprehend Islam is a heritage of most Christians. It goes back, in part, to their childhood study of history. It is not easy to free ourselves from the tangle of prejudices which envelops our minds and of which we are not even conscious.

My Conclusions Today: Rethinking and Rejecting My Old View

When I was released from internment and resumed daily and personal contact with Muslims of all classes, I entered a period of agonizing self-doubt. This torment was accentuated by the sight of so many Arabs prostrate on the ground in devotion at the hour of prayer. This moving and edifying spectacle invariably caused me to reflect on my ideas and reactions. My conclusion that these people were in reality adoring Satan began to seem a great outrage to charity and truth. Was it, perhaps, because my insight was bad that I blackened every Muslim action, even the best? Several years were to pass before I emerged from this anguished frame of mind.

Once, when Professor Massignon was in Cairo, I went to see him at the French Institute of Oriental Archaeology with the purpose of discussing my view of Islam and asking for his comments. Only someone who has known Massignon can fully imagine his reaction to my ideas. His usual grave expression changed to a smile like the lighting of a lamp and his eyes twinkled. He said:

"The medieval Christian world taught that Mohammed was a messenger of Satan and that the Allah of the Koran was not the God of Abraham. We should not do to others what we would not have them do to us. The apologetic skepticism of the critics and supercritics of the type of Marracci, Caetani, even good Fr. Lammens, can become a weapon that cuts both ways." Massignon was to repeat this to me on many other occasions. He was motivated by the principle of charity, a principle indispensable for finding the truth.

He continued:

Why reserve to Islam, to Mohammed and the Koran, degrading explanations of psychological or social fraud? Why apply all the principles of an acid critique that believing Christians would refuse to apply to the Bible? Do they not accuse the Rationalists of doing precisely this when they say that the latter employ false science to dissect the Bible? It is hypocritical for honest and scientifically minded Christians to apply these same methods — as if this were true science — to the Koran. This un-Christian and unscientific attitude has done nothing for the conversion of the Muslim. Rather, it has pushed the Muslim into a polemic of self-defense. As a result, they have translated into Arabic every writing from Lessing to Couchoud which presents the Bible as a great hoax, Jesus as a mythical person, and his Church as an ecclesiastical conspiracy for the exploitation of sorrow and misery. [Massignon repeated this principle of charity and scientific honesty in an interview that was published subsequently in *Rhythmes du Monde*.][2]

Massignon advised me to read his study, *Les trois prières*

d'*Abraham-Seconde prière* (Tours, 1935), a very difficult work. A profitable reading is possible only if one is familiar with Massignon's premises and his peculiar style. After spending a great deal of time with these pages, I found myself beginning to move in a totally different direction toward the solution of my problem. Before deciding what could be done for the Muslim, I had to know what Islam represented, what its function was. Massignon had alerted me against an unjust condemnation of it that precluded any sincere and productive dialogue between Christians and Muslims. Islam is a mystery linked with the blessing obtained by Abraham from God for his son Ishmael and Ishmael's progeny. This line of thought, derived from the Bible, is the one to take in order to grasp the significance of Islam.

Before we parted, Massignon gave me two thoughts meant as guidelines in my reorientation. One was from Augustine, *"Amor dat novos oculos"* ("Love sees with new eyes"), and the other was from John of the Cross, "Where there is no love put love, and you will find Love Himself." It was true: my eyes had seen badly and so I had perceived only the darker aspects. Later, when my eyes were to see clearly, I would discover in Islam and the Muslims the reflections of the infinite goodness of God.

An Hour of Grace

On a hot and radiant June evening in 1947 I was on a raft, crossing the Nile in Upper Egypt. I was the only European on it. The other passengers, a group of *fellahin,* poor Arab farmers, were prostrated in silence on the deck, adoring God. Their black-clad women stood aside in silence, while the ragged children, eyes almost covered with flies, stared at me and smiled at one another. They remained silent, however, aware that their fathers were speaking with God. But their smiles and their glances held a

message for me. The words of Jesus came unbidden to my mind:
"I have compassion on the crowd" (Mk 8:2).

For more than a year I had been a member in Cairo of a group
started by Professor Massignon and called the Badaliya. This
was a movement whose purpose was to manifest Jesus Christ in
the land of Islam by means of fraternal understanding and profound love. The members offered prayers and works in "substitution" (*al-Badaliya* means "substitution"), the idea being to make
up for whatever defects there are in the prayers and works of the
Muslim. I have to admit that, up to that moment of grace, though
I had made up my mind to love according to the spirit of *badaliya,*
the Muslims were still strangers to me. I no longer despised them,
but I still did not have real love for them.

That is why I look upon that summer sunset upon the Nile as
a moment of special, divine illumination. I seemed to see the
crowds of Palestine following our Lord — the children of the
Holy Land suddenly became those of Jesus' words, "Let the little
children come to me" (Mk 10:14). I saw them as very little
different, in their poverty and filth, from the staring and smiling
huddle in front of me. This miserable group of Arabs, who stood
or prostrated themselves before me, again brought to mind the
expression of Jesus, "I have compassion on the crowd." God was
listening to their sincere prayers. These Muslim men, women, and
children, whom many despise, are also the objects of divine love.
Jesus died on the cross for them also. If Jesus, if God, loved
these poor and ragged Arabs, could I continue to refuse to love
them — notwithstanding the repugnance their external appearance
stirred up in me at first? How could I refuse, even for another
moment, to recognize them as my brothers? That moment of grace
suddenly awakened me to the reality of the absolute command of
God: You must love the Muslim, they are your brothers.

That was a significant moment in my life. I must love the
Muslim. I must strive to love them with the same love that Jesus
has for them, the same love that Francis had for them. From that
moment, I began to experience a great change of mind. The new
vision of Islam which meditation on the pages of Massignon gave

me, formed by the light and fire of true charity, stirred a need within me to relate all of human history to Jesus Christ. That love which God poured into me, all at one moment, had given me the new eyes spoken of by Augustine, and at the same time I felt urged to communicate my new-found truth in Francis' name to everyone: They too must love the Muslim.

It is true that only love can uncover the secrets of the heart. People who love interpret the facts about the one they love much more accurately than those who do not love, as John Chrysostom said. Love had given me new eyes to look upon Mohammed, the Koran, and Islam. My study of Islam, which had practically ceased after meditating on Massignon's works, now became an essential part of my vocation. From then on my contacts with Muslim friends became more fraternal, more Christian and Franciscan. I had a strong desire to reach the new horizons, to see Islam in an entirely different light. I was on an altogether different road from the one I had traveled with Marracci.

Toward a Christian-Islamic Dialogue

This interior transformation, this rediscovery of the meaning of charity and of living in the land of Islam in the spirit of *badaliya,* made me want to spread the message far and wide. I wanted to tell my fellow missionaries about it. I spoke about it to my students at the seminary: More respect for the Muslim and for what the Muslim honors! Meanwhile I began a serious study of Muslim doctrine and history with Muslim-Christian understanding as my ultimate goal.

In 1947 Egypt set a Muslim precedent by establishing diplomatic relations with the Holy See. This was a most important event, though it did not look like it at the time. During this period there were also evident signs of a renaissance all over the Arab world. This was seen not only in the rise of Arab nationalism (a term fondly used by Westerners) but in a real rebirth of the Arab soul and a new religious-political consciousness concerning Islam. Islam was not, after all, a dead religion; on the contrary, it was showing signs of a new ferment.

Was a religious fanaticism about to burst out as a reactionary movement or an anti-Christian persecution? Would the new social ideas moving through the Middle East, that were bringing about a profound transformation of life and past customs and spreading the revolutionary ideology of communism, as well as an Arab racism patterned after Nazi thinking — would this thrust the Arab world into the communist orbit? Or was it possible to begin a new phase in Christian-Islamic relations which would lead to the building of a new world?

A stay in Lebanon during the summer of 1949 convinced me that great spiritual, cultural, and social transformations were already in evidence in that postwar period. The Christian Arabs were the first to take note of this transformation and to realize that they had an important part to play in a new spirit of collaboration with their Muslim brothers. New political situations, and the war psychosis brought on by the creation of the state of Israel, introduced new problems. Here, perhaps, was a chance for Christian mediation between the Muslim world and the new Jewish world.

These manifold problems stirred me and other missionaries to seek new methods and a new mentality to cope with the needs of the day. Most important, I could see the necessity for a greater understanding of Islam as both a religion and a culture, if we were to begin a sincere fraternal and effective cooperation between Christians and Muslims. For some years I had been involved in personal contacts aimed at a deeper and more edifying collaboration among the different Christian denominations in Egypt. With this in mind, some friends and I organized an ecumenical commemoration of the sixteenth centenary of the great Egyptian St. Pachomius, founder of monasticism. I gradually became aware of the intimate relationship between the ecumenical movement for Christian unity and the missionary problem of Christianity in the Muslim world. The Muslim considers Christian divisions the visible sign of God's curse upon the churches' unfaithfulness to the message of Christ's love. A good Muslim once remarked to me, "You do not love the Muslims. But then you do not love one another. Just take a trip to Jerusalem and see how you war upon one another at the Holy Sepulchre." I began to see, ever more clearly, that every missionary in the Orient had to have, first, an ecumenical vocation for the reunion of Christians and, second, a missionary vocation to uncover the true visage of Christ for the Muslims.

In January 1950, Msgr. Igino Cardinale, then Secretary of the Apostolic Nunciature in Cairo and new Apostolic Nuncio to Belgium, introduced me to His Excellency, Mohammed Taher el Omari, Egyptian Minister to the Holy See. From this meeting was born the resolve, upon returning to Italy, of working in Italian Catholic circles to spread greater comprehension of Christian friendship with the Muslim world. In 1950 and 1951 I began giving lectures, not just in Franciscan and other seminaries but in cultural centers of a number of cities: Rome, Naples, Florence, Como, Milan, Genoa, etc. The idea, of course, was to sound the possibilities for collaboration between the Muslim and Christian worlds, which naturally raised suspicions and misunderstandings on occasion. I could see how much prejudice lingered in the Christian soul, a heritage of distant centuries. I sometimes got the impression that not only were most Christians unprepared for a sympathetic presentation of Islam and its prophet, but they somehow thought that even talking on the subject was an attack on the Catholic faith.

I still recall the statement of a confrere, now a bishop in South America, after a series of conferences in the seminary where he was spiritual director: "In the eighteen years I have been in Rome I have met most of the missionaries when they returned from China, India, or Japan. They always spoke with great sympathy for the people. But I have hardly ever heard a missionary returning from a Muslim country speak well of the Muslims. You can understand, then, why many are a little surprised to hear you speak so highly of Mohammed and the Muslims."

I began to see that a difficult road lay ahead, before the Catholic world would become interested in the world of Islam. The danger of atheistic communism seemed an unworthy motive for a new interest in the Muslim, and in any case it appeared insufficient. There is a very positive duty in justice, as well as charity, for every Christian to love his Muslim brother, independent of the threat of atheistic communism.

Mutual understanding of the Christian and Muslim worlds could only come about through a consideration of strictly religious values. To many Catholics at the time this was treading on dangerous ground. John XXIII did not yet sit in Peter's chair, nor had Vatican Council II yet initiated its "opening of windows."

No comprehension of Islam and the Muslim, either religiously, socially, or politically, is possible unless we start with the Koran. To this day, the Koran is in some sense the essential factor in the formation of their spirituality and conscience.

Toward a Deeper Study of the Koran

In October 1952 I was transferred to the Franciscan mission seminary in Lyons. While there, I was able to take courses at the Theological Faculty of Lyons (1952–1954). The course given by Fr. Albert Gelin on the Old Testament was immensely useful to me, notably for its tracing of God's plan for mankind through a long evolution and the constant aid of prophetic revelation until its supreme manifestation in the Incarnation. But in addition to this, Fr. Gelin introduced me to a method of exegesis of the Old Testament that I subsequently employed in studying the Koran.

Pius XII, in his radio address to the Indian Congress in Ernakullen on December 31, 1952, had this to say: "Make it clear that whatever is just and good in other religions finds its deepest meaning and its final perfection in Christ." I took these words as a divine command for the orientation of my study of the Koran. The works of Massignon, Fr. Abd-el-Jalil, and Fr. Moubarac had already enabled me to perceive a way of transcending the usual interpretation of the Koran.[3] If Islam is really the Abrahamitic mystery of the descendants of Ishmael, then it had to have an actual, though mysterious, relationship to the mystery of Christ. The words of the Pope set me on the way. In what way does the Koran conserve and conceal elements which could recapture their profound meaning in the mystery of Christ?

Over eighty years ago, when Leon Bloy's *Destiny of Israel* appeared, Catholic theology reoriented its interpretation of the continual survival of the people of Israel through a more biblical solution in the light of St. Paul's writings. After that and one by one, all the old terms, in use for centuries concerning the Jews, were gradually dropped from the liturgy and from the solemn pronouncements of popes and councils. Gone were such expressions as Jewish perfidy, blindness, stubbornness. Analogously, I reflected, might not this be the time to attempt new and more Christian, more genuinely theological, ways of interpreting the fact of Islam's existence as a religious phenomenon closely interwoven in mankind's history?

At that time, Fr. Moubarac kindly sent me his unpublished thesis that had been presented some years before at the Catholic Institute of Paris, on Abraham in the Koran.[4] His analysis of the texts, his presentation of a theory of the "prophetology" of the Koran, the vision of sacred history in the Koran, all combined to suggest a far better opportunity of passing a really Christian judgment on the book of Islam. From 1953 on, my studies and analyses of the Koran — always keeping in mind past history — led me to a theological explanation of the phenomenon which was entirely different from my position of ten years before, when I was under the influence of Marracci. The same methods which modern theology uses for the "mystery of Israel" could start, as a foundation for a solution to the problem, with biblical data and Christian tradition and arrive at the conclusion that Islam might well be the Abrahamitic mystery of Ishmael, as Massignon and Moubarac continually insisted.

I began, more and more, to concentrate my exegetical and historical research upon this central point. Is it not possible that a mysterious design of Providence — which the Christian is only beginning to become aware of — is at the origin of Islam? Could we not, perhaps, find mysterious connections between the appearance of Islam in history and the universal unfolding of God's plan for mankind in history? Can we seek a historico-theological explanation which would take into account the providential development of the salvific plan of God for humanity and, at the same time, explain the prophetic mission of Mohammed and his religious message, directed to a section of humanity, as being "relatively" authentic? And if they are, the next question is: How do they fit into the supernatural design of history which centers upon Christ?

These were the problems that bothered me then — and still do. But I consider them essential if we wish to have a sincere and effective dialogue with the Muslim world of today. The presentation of these problems, I knew, involved a whole complex of most difficult theological problems. Some people considered anyone who undertook this task to be extremely rash. They thought it dangerous, and a waste of time, to concern themselves with the Muslims, who are a "hopeless case." They might concede a certain academic value to such studies, but they were fraught with doctrinal dangers. However, I felt that it was a workable hypothesis which deserved much more interest on the part both of Islamic scholars and theologians who deal with comparative religion. So I set to work with confidence.

Islam, an Abrahamitic Mystery

Is Islam the fulfillment of the promise made to Ishmael? If we start with the biblical data of God's blessing given Abraham on behalf of his son Ishmael, may we not find in those divine words the key to the understanding of Islam's providential significance? I had actually attempted such an inquiry — at first for a short time and then resumed in later years — regarding the traditional Christian understanding of chapters 16 and 19 of Genesis, which relate the expulsion of Agar and her son Ishmael and, likewise, the blessing Abraham asked of Yahweh for his son. I determined that these words, once Islam appeared on the scene, must be referred to the Muslims. Moreover, the bulls the popes issued to proclaim crusades usually had the expression *Ejice ancillam et filium ejus:* "Cast out the maid servant and her son." Commentators of Genesis, from the time of Rhabanus Maurus and Strabo, explained the warlike character attributed to Ishmael and his descendants by the Bible as that of the Muslims, whom they called Agarenes or Ishmaelites.

Unfortunately, right up to the present the Christian conscience, which has consistently recognized and affirmed a connection between Islam and the words of Genesis regarding Ishmael: "He shall be a wild man. His hand will be against all men and all men's hands against him" (16:12), has emphasized only the negative aspect. More reflection is needed on the meaning and force of the words of blessing obtained by Abraham for his son Ishmael and the Ishmaelite progeny stemming from him. Their implications bring us to the discovery of Islam's place in the evolution of salvific history.

This Abrahamitic-Ishmaelitic consciousness is very vivid in Mohammed. He is concerned with having his own people rediscover it. Moubarac's book has demonstrated — in contradiction to the usual thesis of Orientalists — that Mohammed discovered Abraham at Mecca and not later in Medina, where he underwent

Jewish influence. All Muslim tradition points to the words of Genesis to prove, to both Christian and Jew, the fulfillment of God's promise to Abraham in favor of Ishmael in Mohammed and Islam. This convergence of Muslim and Christian thinking on the significance of an Abrahamitic-Ishmaelian origin of Islam also has importance from a theological point of view and merits special attention in assessing the authenticity of Mohammed's message.

I felt that an entirely new study of the Koran was necessary, and it had to be done in a spirit free of prejudice. In the past, Christian students were hampered in their appreciation of the real worth of Islam's sacred book. An intelligent, sincere, and open-minded study will yield a more historic and realistic figure of Mohammed himself.

I set to work to trace, by means of the Koran, the development of Mohammed's spiritual journey in chronological order. Fr. Moubarac had already indicated some directions to take, which could be developed in greater detail. These appear in the last pages of his volume on Abraham.[5] (Admittedly, this inquiry is not an easy one.) I then took as my criterion the psychological study of the religious behavior of the messengers and prophets presented by the Koran.

As Professor Massignon and Fr. Moubarac have insisted on a number of occasions, the Koran is one of the most complete syntheses of the Semitic mind which can be found. Therefore it simply cannot be studied except with serious and specific preparation and a knowledge of the psychology and mentality of the Semite. This is why the courses I had under Fr. Gelin, and later ones as well, were invaluable to me. It is not enough to study the Koran with rationalistic critical methods, as did Geiger, Sprenger, Caetani, Lammens, Tor Andrae, and others. These men sought only the influences which shaped the Koran, the different sources of isolated elements. The Koran has to be looked at as a whole and as the expression of the progress of a religious experience. Evidently, today's Muslim exegesis and theology cannot accept this point of departure. Yet we hope that the day is not far off when Christian collaboration will have made it possible.

How I "Rediscovered" Mohammed

A first study of the different figures of the prophets the Koran speaks of seemed to show me the path to follow if I were to grasp, even tenuously, the mind of Mohammed. It is in the suras of the second Mecca period that the personages (*Rasûl*) sent by God to the various peoples begin to appear. Here the Koran points out that their message from God is rejected. But whether it is the biblical story of Noah, the stories of the missions to the Thamudite peoples, to the "Adites," or the sending of Lot, they are all sent to call men back to the worship of the One God, the Creator, who speaks through the "signs" of cosmic revelation which manifests the presence and activity of the Provident God.

With the story of Abraham (sura 37) the history of God's message is begun. God speaks directly to mankind through personal revelation (to Abraham, Moses, Aaron, etc.). The personalities of the New Testament come on the scene in sura 19, and, in my opinion, it is the very modest figure of Mary which introduces the mysterious mission of Jesus.

A careful analysis of the spiritual comportment of all these personages, studied in chronological order (as far as modern criticism is able to ascertain), seemed to lead to important conclusions. The various divine messengers seemed gradually to be enriched in spiritual content. I gathered this from the Arabic expressions used to describe the attitude of these personalities with regard to God and with regard to men. I could see in this gradual development the image of Mohammed's spiritual consciousness. I felt that Mohammed was mirrored in these figures, as aspects of his own religious experience, of his own psychology. He projected into their figures and their actions some facet of his own soul. He, in turn, through meditation on these personages, deepened the consciousness of his special religious message. Moreover, the figures of Mary and Jesus, as is recognized by all, occupy a very special position in the Koran.

The figure of Jesus has ever increasing importance, though it never unfolds all the mystery of Jesus. The Koran stops with sura 5, where the presentation of Jesus remains a "mystery." From that time on I felt one had to maintain that the Koran has no acquaintance with the precise presentation of the Christian mystery of the Trinity, nor of the Incarnation as formulated at Chalcedon. It had not come this far. The formulas of the Koran deny and refute heterodox formulations of the mystery of the Trinity (such as God, Jesus, and Mary) which have nothing at all to do with the Trinity of authentic Christianity. The Koran rejects the Nestorian formulation of the Incarnation ("to take a son to oneself") as well as that of the Monophysites ("God is the Messiah"). From that time on I was convinced — as I am today — that when Muslim theology exploited the different Koranic texts against Christian dogmas, it did not comprehend the precise meaning of those denials and went beyond the objective meaning of those rebuttals. Thus I saw the "problem" of Christ in the Koran in terms quite different from the way it was seen either by Muslim theology, with its anti-Christian polemical ends, by Christian apologists, or by Orientalists.

I was convinced, as I am today, that I had grasped a true insight into this religious journey of Mohammed. Though it is contrary to the common opinion of Orientalists, I no longer could see the alleged split between the Mohammed of the first period at Mecca, a sincere and religious man, and the Mohammed of the second period at Medina, an imposter and, at very least, a man who was exploiting his position for political and personal advantages. As a consequence, I felt that the spiritual tone remained consonant and, under some aspects, even became more profound, though the expression of it no longer carried the accents of primitive fervor.

It is undeniable that one comes in contact with a greater theological and spiritual depth, which has escaped the analysis of many Orientalists. Contrary to the manner in which I perceived him ten years before, Mohammed now appeared as a man in the grip of a profound religious feeling and taken with the idea of establishing the reign of God among the idolatrous Arabs. In the footsteps of Massignon and Moubarac, I more and more narrowed the gap between Mohammed's psychology and spirituality and those of Abraham in regard to faith and of David in regard to the defense of God's rights — by means of a holy war. In the light of Old Testament morality, or more exactly that of patriarchal morality, it is easier to understand his deuteronomic kind of religion, his moral life, and his ideas on marriage with the limitations imposed by the development of his moral consciousness.[6]

Following this line of research, it seemed to me, from then on, that a surprisingly real though slow progress toward the knowledge of God and of Jesus Christ could be discovered in the Koran. This knowledge, without doubt, is embryonic and, as it were, limited. It needs development and enrichment. This is what Islam has lacked, and that during thirteen centuries of contact with Christianity.

Is Islam Waiting for Christ?

It also seemed that some prominence must be given to the fact that there is a feeling of expectation in the Koran. Mohammed is constantly exhorted to "wait." Islam is thus oriented toward the second coming of Christ the Judge. The last sura of the Koran, in chronological order, is the fifth. I had the feeling that it deserved a very careful analysis in depth to uncover just what the final spiritual position of Mohammed was. He has now decided to give up Judaism and a form of Christianity he had come into contact with, but which was no longer an authentic Christianity. Mohammed never knew the doctrine of the Catholic Church, of orthodox Christianity; hence he was unable to reject it. He rejected *distortions* of Christianity. This, I think, is an essential point which must be given prominence in order to end a regrettable misunderstanding which has lasted for centuries.

His systematic refusal to accept a heretical Christianity and his combating its two forms condemned by the Church (Monophysitism and Nestorianism) should allow us to see, at the bottom of his soul, a longing and desire for a true, genuine knowledge of Jesus Christ and, hence, an orientation toward Christ. In the Koran, Mohammed is invited to state that if God had a Son, he — Mohammed — is the first to adore him. This interior disposition of Mohammed must be admitted, based on a text Professor Massignon called to my attention many times. It is an interesting text, which Christians have not sufficiently appreciated and Muslim exegesis interprets as a negation of divine generation. "Say: 'If the All-merciful has a son, then I am the first to serve him'" (sura 43:81).

Furthermore, this refusal to accept Judaism and heretical Christianity is accompanied by a protest against Jewish and Christian exclusiveness, against the claim that they alone are the chosen ones of God. Say the Jews and Christians: "We are the sons of God, and his beloved ones" (sura 5:21). This refusal has to be aligned with the dramatic request for the integration of Abraham's sons through Ishmael's branch, who were excluded from the promises through the exclusion of Agar and her son from the family of Abraham (cf. sura 2:105/111–107/113). Sura 5 closes with a mysterious presentation of Jesus, who causes the "heavenly table" (the Eucharist?), a foretaste of the eternal peace of Heaven (*rida*), to descend. The proclamation of the unfathomable mystery of God, transcendent and inaccessible, proclaimed by Christ at the general judgment, is intended to place into relief the absolute freedom of God's election. It will be at the Last Judgment that Islam will know who Jesus Christ really is. The Koran's emphasis on waiting may signify that some day the mystery of Christ will be unveiled even for Muslim eyes.

This beginning of a progression in the direction of knowledge and acceptance of Christ as Son of God was arrested for centuries, and perhaps turned aside, in the development of Islam after the time of Mohammed. This happened because there was no one to help Islam continue on the right path to the house of the Father and fulfill its role as a catechumenate for the sons of Ishmael.

More and more, I have been convinced that the Christian apostolate, over a period of thirteen centuries, has always been unsuccessful because it never found out who the Muslims really are. It has never been able to help them retrace their steps to those first miles of the arrested march and lead them toward the complete encounter with Christ, the Son of God, sole Mediator, sole Savior.

The Special Place of St. Francis of Assisi in Helping the Muslims Take Up Their March Toward Jesus Christ

On several occasions Professor Massignon encouraged me to think out the expiatory significance of the stigmata of Alverna in relation to the salvation of Islam. He had discovered in Cairo, in 1951, an Arabic text which referred to the visit of St. Francis to the Sultan of Egypt in Damietta, and he was happy to communicate this information to a son of St. Francis. Massignon suggested that I meditate upon and attempt to understand just why Francis went to see the Sultan, and this in the context of the crusading atmosphere of the time. The episode was not just an accident. It had to have a profound meaning: Approach Islam not with violent arms but with gospel holiness composed of goodness and mild-ness.

With my gradual discovery of the Koran, I set myself more and more to understanding the special vocation God had con-fided to St. Francis: to guide Christianity toward a more evan-gelical treatment of the "Muslim brothers." I expressed these ideas in an article titled "Muhammed et S. François: pour une compréhension plus chrétienne de nos frères les musulmans" published in *Nouvelle Revue de science missionnaire.*[7]

After spending time in Egypt again, from October 1955 to April 1956, doing research at the Dominican Institute of Oriental Studies in Cairo as guest of the Dominican fathers, and still fol-lowing the direction indicated above, I received an invitation from the Institute of Islamic Studies at McGill University in Mont-real, Canada, to continue my research on the Koran and Islam. During my stay in Montreal I learned two important "things." For the first time I met the non-Arab Muslim world — the Muslim of Pakistan, India, Indonesia, and even China, who were stu-dents at the institute. The other thing I learned was how much our Protestant brethren are interested in the study of the Muslim world for the sake of evangelization or dialogue. (They were far ahead of Catholics.) The resulting confidence of Muslims in Protestants should give Catholics something to think about. Here, in Montreal, are Muslims who have come to a Christian institu-tion to study their own religion scientifically.

This atmosphere gave me a sense of urgency. I had to do some-thing to arouse the interest of our own people, and especially the Franciscan friars, who because of their founder have a special vocation to work with the Muslim. Francis' role was prophetic. He called the Church back to its duty of proclaiming the Good News to the Muslim. From Francis, too, the friars have the task of suffering vicariously, as he did on Mount Alverna, on behalf of Islam.

I took the ideas I had expressed in my article in *Nouvelle Revue de science missionaire* and wrote, while in Montreal, my study called *Mohammed et Saint François* (published by the Commissariat of the Holy Land, Ottawa, Canada, in 1959). I hoped to stir up interest within my order for this urgent missionary problem, because it has missions in a score of Muslim countries. Unfortunately, one of my confreres felt he had to write more than a hundred pages of denunciation. He thought that my sympathy for Islam had led me into a maze wherein the history, the doctrine, and even the psychology of the Orient, as well as the Catholic Occident, became distorted and falsified. The conclusions I had come to were "hazardous." Comparing Mohammed with Francis was not merely "shocking" but had no foundation in history, doctrine, or psychology. My work was, through and through, a double hoax: a historical fraud and a doctrinal fraud. My paralleling of the figures of Mohammed and Francis was not only fictitious, without historical evidence, but an irreverent, if not blasphemous, attack on the sanctity of St. Francis. My confrere must have had in mind the Mohammed of Marracci, not the one I had discovered.

The unfortunate reception the book received, which I had intended to be a call and a manifesto, was a serious blow to my priestly and missionary life.

Toward a New Interpretation of the Koran in the Light of Christ

These setbacks did not deter me from continuing to seek a solution to the problem of Islam's orientation toward Christ. Pius XII's statement that good and just elements must be sought in Islam became my watchword. From 1952 onward it had guided and accelerated my exegetical study of the Koran. Together with the scriptural method I learned from Abbé Gelin and the line of thought suggested by the studies of Professor Massignon, Abbé

Ledit,[8] and Fr. Moubarac, it had brought me to the presentation of Mohammed's person and mission, which I gave in my book. In the conclusion I took up ideas that had been traced some twenty years before by the saintly Abbé Jules Monchanin in an article titled "Islam et Christianisme," which appeared in *Bulletin des missions.*[9] This was an effort to place Islam within the plan of salvation.

In a fraternal correspondence, Abbé Ledit repeated several ideas I had heard him speak about. On August 25, 1958, he wrote:

As regards Islam, with or without *prophetia directive,* it will be necessary sooner or later to find a formula taking into account either the lateness in time of Islam in relation to Christianity or its theme of expectation. This formula will then furnish the Church with a key to the interpretation of the Koran (though this sounds paradoxical) just as she possesses the key to the Bible. This is not possible unless Islam is recognized as a path which leads in the direction of Christ (but not an economy of salvation parallel to that of Christ). This is the Muslim's position, and, believe it or not, it is accepted by Catholic theologians who accept only the interpretation of the *Ulêma.* This is the reason for our present impasse on the subject.

In another letter, of May 15, 1959, he wrote:

Some day the right of the Church to interpret the Koran just as she does the Old Testament will have to become an accepted thing. If Islam in reality represents a special case in the history of religions, by reason of its Abrahamitic origin, its challenge to Israel to review its judgment on the Messiah, its spur to the Church to rid herself of her divisions, and her orientation toward the construction of the Church, then it is up to the Church to judge her *intersignes.* To leave this to the *'Ulêma,* as some insist, is to prevent any solution.

In March 1960, as a visiting professor in the Department of Religion at Columbia University in New York, and again in the same capacity at the Muir Institute of Edinburgh University in May of 1962, I had the opportunity in my lectures to attempt an interpretation of the Koran "read with a Christian key." This seems to me the only avenue of research that could prove useful for a dialogue with the Muslim. My conviction was greatly strengthened by a most revealing and interesting experience I had at Dropsie University in Philadelphia. I had received a grant through the kind interest of Professor Theodore Gaster of Columbia University and Rabbi David Neuman of Brandeis University. The purpose of the grant was to enable me to study Judaism, its history and its relations with both Islam and Christianity. I noticed that the interpretation of the Old and New Testaments, made with a rabbinical "key," was quite different from one made with a Christian "key." I thought it must also be possible to read the Koran with a Christian key, even if the Muslim is unable to accept this in principle. Apropos of this, I recalled an exchange of ideas some years ago with a noted Islamologist who found it impossible to admit that, after thirteen centuries of reflection on the Koran, the Muslim could not have understood its actual sense or that, today, we might be able to "open" it with a Christian key. Now that I have seen how Jews, after twenty centuries, read the Old Testament and reproach us Christians for claiming to understand it better than they, I am even more convinced — against the contrary opinion — that it is not only possible but that it is a duty to read the Koran with a Christian key if we want to help the Muslim relinquish a position which hinders a sincere dialogue between us and him.[10]

In 1956 two books came out under the pen name of Hanna Zaccaria, one with the offensive title *L'Islam, enterprise juive, de Moïse à Mohammet.* The author argued that the "real" Koran was written by the rabbi of Mecca, who had converted Mohammed to Judaism in order to spread Judaism among the pagan Arabs of Arabia. (Indeed, the dependence of Islam upon Judaism is a thesis sustained by all of Jewish tradition, from Saadia [892–942], Maimonides [1135–1204], and Simon Ben Semah Duran [1361–1444] to Abraham Geiger [1810–1874], Ignaz Goldziher, Goitein, Katsh, and others. Christianity and Islam supposedly, are only two "daughters" of Judaism.) Hanna Zaccaria, nevertheless, does nothing but heap abuse on Orientalists and "Koranizers."

Anyone with even a passing acquaintance with rabbinic literature and the history of Jewish thought will realize that Zaccaria
is completely ignorant in these areas. It was the reading of such
a work, in which every page breathed a French nationalist, anti-
Muslim resentment, that led me to completely opposite conclusions: It is not Mohammed who learns from the Jews; rather, it
is Mohammed who teaches the Jews, both from Mecca and from
Medina. It is Mohammed who teaches the doctrine of the Resurrection, of the Last Judgment, and the messiahship of Jesus.

It was to these conclusions that I came, as I shall point out in
Part Three, by attempting a reading of the Koran with a "Christian key."

If I have been a bit long in describing my intellectual journey
of some thirty years' study of the Koran, it is because, as the
development of my position indicates, it is very difficult to make
a definitive judgment on the nature of the Koran and the person
of its herald. I consider the clarification of these two points by
Christians to be an urgent necessity if we are to engage in sincere
and effective dialogue with our Muslim brothers. As long as the
traditional Muslim interpretation is the only feasible one, a
Christian dialogue starts with the prejudgment that the Koran has
a purely human origin and that its doctrine is incompatible with
Christian revelation, that the "Arab prophet" may have been in
good faith but simply had no real mission from God. And so
Islam remains immobilized in the position it has occupied these
many centuries.

But if the language of Christians who today are trying to con-
verse with Muslims is indeed purged of offensive phrases, particularly in regard to Mohammed, this appears to Muslim eyes as only
a tactical move. As a Muslim friend who had lived in the Christian
environment of Europe for some time told me:

You Christians have not changed your opinion of the Prophet

at all. During the Middle Ages, your missionary confreres were more sincere and courageous. They came to Egypt convinced that Mohammed was a false prophet and Islam a false religion. They went into the mosques and announced their convictions. And because they "blasphemed" the Prophet they were put to death — not, mark you, because they were Christians. Muslim law has the death penalty for anyone who blasphemes either God or the Prophet. As a matter of fact, your own Inquisition burned heretics and apostates who became Jews. Today your missionaries are just as much convinced that Mohammed is a false prophet and Islam a false religion. You teach this in Europe. You write it openly in your magazines and books. Then, when you come to Egypt or any other Muslim country, you show external signs of respect for our Prophet, for Islam, but we know that you still are inwardly of the same opinion, that your language does not correspond to what you really think. And so we must continually suspect your sincerity and conclude that you have simply changed tactics. I personally prefer the brutal sincerity of your missionaries of the Middle Ages, who got themselves killed for their convictions. They were at least honest with themselves and with us!

It is possible for us to commence a revision of our judgments upon the sacred book of Islam and its prophet. We must use all the methods of the biblical criticism of our age, which have helped us deepen our understanding of the Bible, in the service of the truth. Analogously, we must apply these methods and criteria to the Koran and discover a way of reinterpreting Islam's book from a Christian standpoint, at the same time inviting our Muslim brethren to undertake a similar study.

I am convinced that dialogue between Muslims and Christians will truly bear fruit only if it takes as its point of departure a new spirit and a new orientation in interpreting the Koran and the person and mission of the prophet. For centuries, every Christian author began with the conviction that the Koran could not be a revealed book and that Mohammed could not be a messenger from God. Likewise, all the apologists, Jews and Christians, with these same convictions, thought they could convince the Muslim.

Why is it not possible to start from a different position, a position which takes into consideration the deep faith of millions of Muslims, who for centuries have believed in the divine origin of the Koran and in a genuine mission of Mohammed? I asked myself why it would not be possible, therefore, to start from two suppositions that are recognized as hypothetically possible. Let us suppose that the Koran is actually a revealed book and that Mohammed is a genuine messenger of God. Let us apply the methods of criticism and history, and keep in mind, too, the "analogy of faith" which we use in the study of Sacred Scripture. What results can come of such a realistic and honest approach?

Jewish exegetes still interpret the Old Testament without the Christian key. If, by using this key, Christian scholars arrive at a whole new interpretation of the Old Testament, might it not likewise be possible to use this Christian key in studying the Koran? Perhaps reading it in this way will permit interpretations that are quite different, and far removed, from those that have resulted from thirteen centuries of both Muslim and Christian study.

It might just be, then, that the light of Christ and of Christian revelation is the only light that permits the accurate understanding of Islam's sacred book. It might turn out that Mohammed's mission will look different to Muslim and Christian alike.

Of course, the final judgment is not mine to make. But if so many formerly held positions are being abandoned today, it might be useful to try this method and give more serious attention to the conclusions that may be drawn by or from it.

In Part Three, as an introduction to the "new way," I shall set forth the lines and principles of my investigation.

PART TWO

INTRODUCTION TO THE
STUDY OF THE KORAN
THROUGH A CHRISTIAN
REINTERPRETATION IN THE
LIGHT OF CHRIST

Introduction to the Koran

The Koran (in Arabic *Al-Qur'an*) is the holy book of the Muslim religion of Islam. Etymologically it means "reading" or "preaching." It is shorter than the New Testament and is divided into 114 suras or chapters. Each sura is divided into verses, or *ayat*. In the text as we have it, the order of the suras is not chronological, but was practical at one time for joining them together into scrolls, according to their length. Thus, with the exception of the first sura, titled *Fâtiha* "The Opening" (i.e., that which "opens" the Koran), the suras are arranged according to length, the latter ones being the shortest. In the Arabic text, the number of each verse is placed after the text because, according to Muslim doctors, it is not permitted to put anything in front of the "revelation."

At the beginning of some of the suras, certain letters of the alphabet are found; most frequently these are *alef, lam, mim*. What they mean has never been satisfactorily explained, either by commentators or Orientalists. The rest, with the exception of sura 9, begin with the verse: "In the Name of God, the Merciful, the Compassionate."

The etymology of *sura* or *chapter* has been explained variously by the Muslim commentators. The great Islamic scholar Nöldeke derives it from the Hebrew word *shûrâh*.[1]

The Koran is written in Arabic, and probably in the Arabic which was in use in Mecca in Mohammed's time. As Professor Massignon has always insisted, its grammatical structure brings us back to the most ancient origins of the Semitic languages.

Further, the Koran is the first Arabic text (known to us) which was composed in prose and not in poetry; but the prose is rhythmic and often rhymed or with final assonance. Its Arabic reading is musical. As in other Semitic languages, the rhythm is born of the harsh sounds of the gutturals, which are clarified by the sounds of the vowel *a* and combined with the feeling of severity of the lugubrious sound *u* (*wai*).

The style is varied, and it is from this variety that Orientalists have tried to determine the chronology of the suras. Thus a vividly imaginative style is considered the sign of an early Mecca sura and a more prolix style that of Mohammed's period of activity in Medina. The reading of the Koran is an art called *Al-tajwïd*. Tradition has crystallized the rules for its reading and singing, musical intonation, contraction of sounds, and the like.

Muslims consider the Arabic language of the Koran to be "most perfect." *I'jâz al-Qur'ân,* or the "inimitability of the Koran," constitutes Mohammed's miracle, based upon the texts of suras 2:21–23 and 59:21. Muslim theologians have developed a whole theory (which does not seem to be demanded by the text) that seems entirely alien to the mind of Mohammed.

Difficulties in Interpretation of the Koran

Muslims deem the language of the Koran perfect because the grammar of literary Arabic was constructed after the pattern of the Koran, which in turn is the "model of perfection" because it is "God's language." But like all the other Semitic languages, it has words that often have more than one meaning, and some have many meanings. To determine the exact meaning, one must compare samples of the same expression in different texts, a great obstacle to understanding the precise meaning intended.

Another difficulty arises from the fact that at times the Koran makes allusion to persons and deeds that are no longer known, and even Muslim tradition cannot always explain the meaning of such allusions. Even the Muslim commentators do not have a unanimous interpretation, and, as Goldhizer has shown, they have not always been free of bias in favor of the theological schools to which they belonged. Thus it is difficult to find good translations of the Koran in European languages.

According to the testimony of Ambrogio Teseo in his *Introductio in linguam Chaldaicam,*[2] the first printing of the Koran in Arabic was by the Brescian, Paganini, in Venice in 1530. All the copies were ordered destroyed by Paul III. The oldest Italian translation is supposed to have been made from the Latin translation of Robert of Ketton and published at Basle by Bibliander in 1543 — that of Andrea Arrivabene of Mantua.[3]

English Translations of the Koran

The first translation of the Koran into English was done anonymously, but probably by Alexander Ross. Probably, also, it was done not from the Arabic text but from the 1649 French translation by Ryer [The Alcoran of Mahomet, translated from Arabic into French by the Sieur du Ryer . . . and newly Englished for the satisfaction of all that desire to look into the Turkish vanities (1649)]. It was only later, in 1734, that a translation into English was made directly from the Arabic, by George Sale, and published in London by the Society for the Promotion of Christian Knowledge. A new edition was reproduced in 1929 with an introduction by E. D. Rose. Arberry writes:

Sale's translation was not supplanted for some 150 years. Its influence was thus enormous. . . . But with the nineteenth century came the rise of oriental studies in the scientific meaning of the term; and the interpretation of the Koran inevitably engaged the interest of scholars eager to apply the methods of the higher criticism to this as yet virgin field of research. Thus it came to pass that in the next translation of the Koran to appear, the work of the Rev. J. M. Rodwell, the order of the Suras — the chapters of which the Koran is composed — was completely changed, with the object of reconstituting the historical sequence of its original composition.[4]

Rodwell's translation was published for the first time in 1861 and is still to be had in Everyman's Library.

The translation of Edward Henry Palmer appeared in 1880 in a collection of sacred books of the East and still enjoys wide authority, especially for its literal faithfulness to the text. It is reproduced in World's Classics.

Marmaduke Pickthall, an Englishman who became a Muslim, published his translation, *The Meaning of the Glorious Koran*,[5] from the Cairo edition of the Arabic text. Guillaume observes with justice: "It is often an interpretation rather than a translation." Since he used the Arabic text of Cairo, Pickthall also follows its numbering of verses, whereas Rodwell and Palmer followed the numbering of Fluegel's Arabic edition. (Since I follow Blachère's system, I usually give a double numbering. For example, "no. 93" is a chronological classification given by Blachère and is equivalent to "sura 2:80/86." The first verse, number, 80, is that of Fluegel's edition, and hence also of Rodwell and Palmer, while the second number, 86, is that of the Arabic edition of Cairo and of Pickthall.)

Richard Bell has attempted, with much exaggeration, to analyze each text and to track down its origin in his *The Qur'an*, a translation and critical rearrangement of the suras.[6]

The recent English translations by A. J. Arberry (*The Koran Interpreted*)[7] and N. J. Dawood (*The Koran Classic* [1956]) follow the late orthodox interpretation, though the former attempts to suggest the rhythmical style of the original in English. Arberry says: "My chief reason for offering this new version of a book which has been 'translated' many times already is that in no previous rendering has a serious attempt been made to imitate, however imperfectly, those rhetorical and rhythmical patterns which are the glory and the sublimity of the Koran" (p. 25).

Chronology of the Koran

Muslim tradition, long before the Orientalist critics, bequeathed us a rough classification of the suras of the Koran according to the two periods of Mohammed's preaching at Mecca and Medina: Mecca suras and Medina suras. After the minute and critical analyses done by Nöldeke and continued by Schwally, this can be accepted as rather well founded. Other Orientalists have also tried to discover the chronology of the suras, following other criteria, and thus we have the classifications of Grimme, Hirschfeld, Barth, Bell, and Blachère.

The period of the suras' composition is certainly not irrelevant to understanding the Koran. The Koran, in fact, must be a communication that was made in definite, particular circumstances. Mohammed's preaching covered twenty years.

Mohammed's religious activity was spread over two periods: one, preceding the Hegira, in Mecca, beginning at the end of the year 612 and lasting about ten years; the other in Medina, for another ten years, from 622 to his death in 632. Following Weil and Nöldeke, Orientalists divide the Mecca preaching into three periods. I think it useful, keeping to the chronological order of Blachère, to give a summary of what Blachère says on each period and the sura numbers according to his classification.

I. Preaching in Mecca: 92 suras, A.D. 612–622
   1. First Mecca period: Nos. 1–48, A.D. 612–616
a) The first series (nos. 1–8) is on the essential theme of purifi-

cation, a call to charity, and perseverance. With the exception of nos. 1–2, the texts are isolated units and very short.

No. 1: Sura 96, vv. 1–5 No. 5: Sura 94
No. 2: Sura 74, vv. 1–7 No. 6: Sura 103
No. 3: Sura 106   No. 7: Sura 91
No. 4: Sura 93   No. 8: Sura 107

b) The second series (nos. 9–31) is richer and more varied. The argument of Athenagoras is used for the resurrection, and the eschatological element predominates. Blachère observes that the theme of the resurrection has already been evoked, and will continue to be, while the unicity of God is not even hinted at. There is instead a kind of obsession with the end of the world and judgment (Heaven and Hell). The Orientalists have pointed out that, in this period, paganism is not directly attacked. Arguments of persuasion are employed, and there is no invective against the idolators of Mecca. Allah is presented as their supreme god, man's benefactor.

No. 9: Sura 86   No. 21: Sura 88
No. 10: Sura 95   No. 22: Sura 52
No. 11: Sura 99   No. 23: Sura 56
No. 12: Sura 101   No. 24: Sura 69
No. 13: Sura 100   No. 25: Sura 77
No. 14: Sura 92   No. 26: Sura 78
No. 15: Sura 82   No. 27: Sura 75
No. 16: Sura 87   No. 28: Sura 55
No. 17: Sura 80   No. 29: Sura 97
No. 18: Sura 87   No. 30: Sura 53
No. 19: Sura 84   No. 31: Sura 102
No. 20: Sura 79

c) The third series (nos. 32–43) contains the themes of the preceding suras, but there seems to be a new element, revealing a slightly changed situation in the apostolate of Mohammed. Some passages are "answers," more or less directed against opponents. The Orientalists think that the stage where a conciliation with Arab paganism was possible has passed and the conflict with hostile paganism has begun. A new theme, which might be joined to this, is contained in a very brief reference to an earthly punishment such as happened in the past to those who refused to listen to the prophets. The argument is formulated by invoking the omnipotence of God, whose divine help sustains his messengers, and a threat to what is most dear to the impious: their earthly goods.

No. 32: Sura 96	No. 38: Sura 108
No. 33: Sura 70	No. 39: Sura 104
No. 34: Sura 73	No. 40: Sura 90
No. 35: Sura 83	No. 41: Sura 105
No. 36: Sura 74	No. 42: Sura 89
No. 37: Sura 111	No. 43: Sura 85

d) The fourth series (nos. 44–48) is suras that stand out sharply in their content from all the others. They seem to be professions of faith, very short texts in the form of a creed, and prayers of entreaty.

No. 44: Sura 112	No. 47: Sura 113
No. 45: Sura 109	No. 48: Sura 114
No. 46: Sura 1	

2. Second Mecca period: Nos. 49–70, A.D. 616–619

Blachère remarks that he sometimes differs from the classification of Nöldeke and Schwally for this period. Its characteristics are an increase of opposition to Mohammed's preaching, the dogma of the oneness of God as the essential theme, biblical tales that portray the prophet who preaches in the desert, and the divine vengeance that falls upon those who do not follow the call of God. Many of these suras have the threefold structure of homilies, and the Orientalists note a change of style in them.

No. 49: Sura 51	No. 60: Sura 19
No. 50: Sura 54	No. 61: Sura 38
No. 51: Sura 68	No. 62: Sura 36
No. 52: Sura 37	No. 63: Sura 43
No. 53: Sura 71	No. 64: Sura 72
No. 54: Cf. no. 43, *bis*	No. 65: Sura 67
No. 55: Sura 44	No. 66: Sura 23
No. 56: Sura 50	No. 67: Sura 21
No. 57: Sura 20	No. 68: Sura 25
No. 58: Sura 26	No. 69: Sura 27
No. 59: Sura 15	No. 70: Sura 18

3. Third Mecca period: Nos. 71–92, A.D. 619–622

The classification here follows Nöldeke. Blachère says that the suras of this period continue those of the second period and prepare for those of the later preaching of the Hegira in Medina. The homiletic form is kept. The Orientalists think that this form was given them after the "recitation of the sura." The foregoing themes on the oneness of God and his providence are taken up again, but descriptions of the future life become rarer and sketchy. The narrative section, regarding the stories of earlier prophets, is more developed.

No. 71: Sura 32	No. 82: Sura 39
No. 72: Sura 41	No. 83: Sura 29
No. 73: Sura 45	No. 84: Sura 31
No. 74: Sura 17	No. 85: Sura 42
No. 75: Sura 16	No. 86: Sura 10
No. 76: Sura 30	No. 87: Sura 34
No. 77: Sura 11	No. 88: Sura 35
No. 78: Sura 14	No. 89: Sura 7
No. 79: Sura 12	No. 90: Sura 46
No. 80: Sura 40	No. 91: Sura 6
No. 81: Sura 28	No. 92: Sura 13

II. Preaching in Medina: 24 suras, A.D. 622–632

For many Orientalists these suras reveal a change of spirit and personality in Mohammed — a thesis which I do not accept. At any rate, we meet themes that are common to the last Mecca period: reaffirmation of God's oneness, condemnation of polytheism, formulation of the moral duties of the believers, evoking once more the histories of the prophets who preached in the desert, and recall the last judgment and rewards for good works. Other themes, dictated by circumstances, were added to these.

Blachère writes: "The suras of Medina are nothing but the annals of Mohammed's apostolate between the years 622 and 632. Likewise the texts concerning juridical or cult matters form the embryo of a code but are not a code."[8] The characteristic traits of these suras, as reported by Blachère, are varying length and the formation of most of them by texts that were superimposed or joined together by an editor. The editor put together texts concerning particular questions, such as marriage, divorce, contracts, and the holy war. And there are many texts of juridical origin. There is a special style, and, regarding the vocabulary, one notes the influence of the Jewish environment.

No.	93:	Sura 2	No. 105:	Sura 33
No.	94:	Sura 98	No. 106:	Sura 63
No.	95:	Sura 64	No. 107:	Sura 24
No.	96:	Sura 62	No. 108:	Sura 58
No.	97:	Sura 8	No. 109:	Sura 22
No.	98:	Sura 47	No. 110:	Sura 48
No.	99:	Sura 3	No. 111:	Sura 66
No.	100:	Sura 61	No. 112:	Sura 60
No.	101:	Sura 57	No. 113:	Sura 110
No.	102:	Sura 4	No. 114:	Sura 49
No.	103:	Sura 65	No. 115:	Sura 9
No.	104:	Sura 59	No. 116:	Sura 5

Notwithstanding all this interesting critical study which the science of Orientalism has accomplished to better penetrate the Koran, we must not forget that the Koran is really a whole and, as Fr. Moubarac notes, a living unit. In this regard, it seems to me extremely useful to keep in mind the reservations he makes in appendix V of his study on Abraham, "Notes sur l'ordre Chronologique des Sourates."[9]

Supposed Sources of the Koran

Fr. Abd-el-Jalil writes:

> Islam contains elements relating it to Judaism and to Christianity. Other elements are considered a rehash of Arab religious traditions purged of their pagan meaning, or, better, an adaptation of certain doctrines that permeated the atmosphere of the Orient surrounding Arabia, such as Neo-platonism, Zoroastrianism, and Gnosticism. This indicates to the non-Muslim historian that Islam and the Koran itself are of an eclectic nature and have absorbed a large number of elements taken from different places. Nothing could wound Muslim feelings more. For the Muslim author, this variety of elements must be placed under the authority of the revelation itself.[10]

But right from the beginning of Islam, and in the Koran itself, we find the accusation that Mohammed took the themes of his preaching from Jews or Christians:

> The unbelievers say, "This is naught but a calumny he has forged, and other folk have helped him to it." So they have committed wrong and falsehood.

> They say, "Fairy tales of the ancients that he has had written down, so that they are recited to him at the dawn and in the evening."
> [no. 68, sura 25:5/4–6/5; cf. no. 75, sura 16:105/103]

Michael the Syrian maintained that Mohammed took all his teachings from the Jews; St. John Damascene said that Mohammed founded his religion after conversations with an Arian monk. Byzantine tradition generally makes the "Arab prophet" a disciple of each and every Christian heresy. In their turn the modern Orientalists, after analyzing the internal evidence to establish the chronology of the texts, have not failed to try their hand at the identification of the sources on which the text of the Koran depends.

The first work of this type we owe to Rabbi Abraham Geiger (1810–1874), whose purpose was to trace the Jewish sources in the Koran, both biblical and rabbinical. He came to the conclusion that the Koran depends almost exclusively upon Jewish sources that were passed on orally. We may note here that the majority of Jewish Orientalists emphasize this dependence upon Jewish sources, following the line of Geiger, Goldhizer, Hirschfeld, Horovitz, Schapiro, Katsh, Finkel, and Sidersky. On the other hand, Christian Orientalists tend to place the emphasis on Christian influences — Ahrens, Tor Andrae, Bell, Tisdal, Nau, and others.

The Koran seems to have but one biblical text, a citation (if it really is a citation) of Psalms 36:29: *"Justi autem haereditabunt terram"* — Koran No. 67, sura 21:105:

For We have written in the Psalms, after the Remembrance, "The earth shall be the inheritance of My righteous servants."

Biblical accounts, whether from the Old or the New Testament, rather than issuing directly from the sacred text or from apocryphal writings or rabbinical literature, were transmitted in an elaborated state — we can say pre-koranic — in an environment which was Jewish, Christian, and pagan. Ahrens, who maintains that most of the influence on the Koran was Christian, claims to have discovered, especially in the Mecca suras, many eschatological ideas and even formulas of edifying sermons in constant use in the Syrian Church. The form of proper names, for example, in most cases corresponds to the Aramaic or Syriac form used by the Jacobite or the Nestorian churches. According to Ahrens again, there is an abundance of biblical allusions. There are more than thirty texts which recall St. Matthew's Gospel, and sixty drawn from the other books of the New Testament — not counting a wide collection of images and expressions which, though not in direct dependence upon biblical texts, reflect a Christian and monastic tone: so many evangelical seeds, as it were, sown throughout the Koran.[11]

In my opinion, the conclusions drawn by Fr. Moubarac relating to the Koran's texts about Abraham, the biblical texts, and rabbinic literature can be extended to all the other accounts.

1. As far as Jewish sources are concerned, there is a fundamental difference between the accounts in the Koran and the later narratives of the Arab chroniclers. The briefer the allusion in the Koran, the more prolix are the chroniclers who are evidently dependent upon rabbinic sources and Christian apocrypha.

2. There is a fundamental difference between koranic and biblical or apocryphal narratives. To take the apocrypha first: the Koran is ignorant of a large number of elements, though even a small part would have been very useful to its purposes. Those which it makes use of are presented in a new garb and with reserve, brevity, and discernment; in other words, in a completely original manner. As for its use of the Bible, it must be said that the Koran ignores many narratives. Those that it uses show a rather accentuated "parallelism." Still, many koranic data, though undoubtedly similar to biblical data, cannot be reduced to them either by reason of terminology or content.

A particularly important and instructive fact is that the Koran, thanks to apocryphal data which have been completely reworked, can bring about a complete reversal of the biblical presentation. Further, the Koran contains data that can be considered completely original and peculiar to it, whether giving them a deeper significance or using them for its own ends.[12]

The question of the sources of the Koran, as it has been treated for more than a hundred years, was resolved by presenting Mohammed as a very clever "alchemist," a man who was able to select part of an idea from Judaism, another from Christianity, still another from Gnosticism, etc. — as much as was needed to mix with Arabism and thus present Islam to us. What a genius of an alchemist must this Arab of the desert have been to concoct all these ingredients!

The points of contact through similarity of terminology, vocabulary, and themes are not always decisive arguments in establishing a direct dependence. One has only to recall the case of the Dead Sea Scrolls, the manuscripts of Qumran, where a scholar too hastily proclaimed that the New Testament, because there is an affinity of expression and vocabulary, depended upon them.

We have lost confidence in that literal criticism which, at the beginning of the century, applied a similar procedure to the Bible and hence denied its originality (e.g., one idea comes from Babylon, another from Egypt or the Sumerians, and still another from Greek mythology). We are now in a much better position to appreciate the value of oral tradition with reference to the Bible. It seems to me that, analogously, we have to take into account a certain influence of oral tradition on the Koran. We have to reckon with various environments: Jewish, Christian, and especially the pre-Islamic Arab. It is possible that the biblical themes that are the common fund of ancient Semitic civilization spread throughout the pagan Arab cultures and were committed to memory. In this way they could have been preserved by the Arabs.

With reference to this, I call attention to another study by Moubarac. It was prepared by him as a possible line of approach, but it gives clear conclusions concerning a source of Arab tradition — or concerning a Semitic tradition handed on through Arab tradition — which reappeared as the source of the Arab soul of the Koran.[13]

Gnosticism in the Koran?

Edouard Sayous in 1880 defended a thesis at the Faculty of Protestant Theology of Montauban, France, on the origin of the ideas in the Koran concerning Jesus Christ and Christianity.[14] He claimed — and I believe he was the first to do so — that his study demonstrated the major influence upon the birth of Islam of "three derivatives of Essenism: Nazareism, Elkaesaism, and Hanifism." From Nazareism Mohammed is supposed to have taken the details for the life of Jesus. From Elkaesaism, whose doctrines would be found in the pseudo-Clementine letters, Mohammed took his teaching concerning his own person, the Scriptures, and the Koran (cf. pp. 23–24, 31). The theme was taken up again by Tor Andrae. Gabrieli, who translated this Tor Andrae work into Italian, calls the development of these ideas "the most novel and most profound pages of the book" (p. vii). However, I consider them the most confusing pages. Instead of clarifying the problem, they complicate it unnecessarily.

According to Tor Andrae, "the Arabian prophet cannot have received his doctrine of revelation from Judaism nor from Orthodox Christian Churches" (p. 98). And in the following pages an effort is made to show what the Koran owes to Ebionism, to the pseudo Clementine, to Mani, etc. Nevertheless, Tor Andrae says: "He can hardly have come into personal contact with the adherents of these Gnostic sects. Of their doctrinal systems he knew little or nothing. He merely took the ideas which had immediate relevance for the religious position in which he found himself. Mohammed's conception of revelation thus betrays a relationship to the Ebionite-Manichean doctrine which cannot be accidental" (pp. 106–107). And besides, for the rest, definite traces of Manichean teaching can be found only in a single particular, namely, Mohammed's peculiar notion concerning the death of Jesus. Mohammed does not believe, with the usual Gnostic Docetism, that Jesus himself suffered in a false body, but obviously, like Mani, and before him Basilides, that another person took his place and was crucified by the Jews.[15]

Likewise, Bell in his *Introduction to the Koran*[16] accepts this thesis, though with some reserve. Yet he too adds the probable influence of the Mondaean, identified as the Sab'îm in the Koran and also called Christians of St. John the Baptist. Blachère too, in his biography of Mohammed, *Le problème de Mahomet*,[17] alludes to these theses, recognizing the authority of Tor Andrae (pp. 22, 62–63), but he thinks, as Bell does, that caution is required and considers that, rather than in distant Elkesaism, the origin must be sought in Manicheism.

The very interesting story of George Widengren, *Mohammed,*

the Apostle of God and His Ascension,[18] proposes looking for all the sources of the Koran in the literature of the "true prophet" (4 Ezra), according to Syrian Gnosticism and Manicheism. He attributes the opposition between light and darkness, good and evil, to Manichean influences.

Since this thesis of Gnostic, Manichean, or Ebionite influences is more and more accepted as a scientific fact, I feel it necessary to demonstrate that such a theory is absolutely unfounded. First of all, as regards Ebionitism, a Judeo-Christian heresy, we can accept as reliable the presentation of Hans Joachim Schoeps, who thinks Judeo-Christianity and Ebionitism are synonymous.[19] In his study, this opinion is based not only on such fathers of the Church as St. Irenaeus, St. Epiphanius, and St. Jerome but also on rabbinic and Ebionite literature, though it is fragmentary. These are the Gospel of the Nazarenes, the gospels of the Ebionites and the Hebrews (this last being a commentary on the Gospel of St. Matthew by Symmachus), and a Judeo-Christian work of the second century which he thinks was used later in the composition of the pseudo Clementine. The Ebionites differentiated themselves from the Jews by the importance they gave to Jesus. Nevertheless, they rejected the miraculous birth of Jesus, whereas the Koran accepts the gospel datum of his miraculous birth. For the Ebionites, Jesus, if he was not merely an ordinary man, was not the Son of God but a new prophet, who takes his place after Adam and Moses and wanted only to reform Judaism. His death did not have redemptive value. The Ebionites thought that the Mosaic law had been purified of the "diabolical elements" by which bloody sacrifices had corrupted it. Jesus' work was the purification of the law. Under the influence of the Essenes and the Rechabites, the Ebionites inherited an aversion for the sacrifices and the temple itself. Notwithstanding his analysis of Ebionite thought and its striking difference from the Koran, Schoeps continues to talk about Ebionite influences on Islam. But it seems to me that none of the fundamental characteristics of Ebionitism, such as respect for the observance of the sabbath and circumcision, can be found in the Koran.

1. Though the Muslims retain the Abrahamitic esteem for circumcision, the Koran does not even hint at a command to circumcise.
2. Ebionitism, moreover, according to the testimony of St. Irenaeus, was extremely repugnant to Paul. But there is no anti-Paulinism in the Koran. Rather, there are definite allusions to "Paulinism" — something which deserves further study.[20]

Let us take a close look at the relationship between the pseudo Clementine and the Koran. There can be no doubt whatsoever concerning the difference of mentality and spirit. It never entered Mohammed's mind to preach the "gnosis," nor did he ever declare that he or the prophets before him had knowledge of the whole of the past, the present, and the future. Not a single expression in the Koran can be tied in with the doctrine of the "essential knowledge." The "true prophet" of the pseudo Clementine, besides being all knowing, is sinless and merciful (i.e., he pardons the sins of others). Now if the Koran, in true Semitic style, presents the elements of creation in pairs, this dualism has nothing to do with Gnostic dualism which is found in the rules for pairing in the pseudo Clementine. Here the good element goes before the bad, as heaven–earth, day–night, light–darkness, sun–moon, life–death, etc. In the Koran, as in the Bible, this pairing is due to parallelism and Semitic logic, whereas in the pseudo Clementine it is a metaphysico-moral dualism. We meet this dualism again in the classification of the prophets (the first of whom is Adam) of this world, and therefore evil men: Cain, Aaron, John the Baptist, and Simon Magus. In contrast stand the prophets of the world to come (good men): Abel, Deucalion, Moses, Jesus, and St. Peter. How can anyone see in this classification the origin of the koranic list of prophets, as Tor Andrae (pp. 101–102) does? In the Koran we find no special role assigned to the apostle Peter, simply because he (and all the other apostles of Jesus) is not even mentioned!

These remarks, I think, also hold good for whatever Manichean influence there could be. In my opinion, there is not a single element that would justify seeing koranic ideas as dependent on Manicheism.[21]

I do not think one has to go very far to find the sources of the Koran. What must be done is to place it in the framework of the culture of Arabia in the seventh and eighth centuries.

The Koran Is a Semitic and an Arabic Book

In the past, the study of the Koran has roused but little interest in the West, except for an Orientalist here and there and some missionaries. However, it must be admitted that the manner of its presentation discourages a reader who has not had some preparation for it. It has the appearance of a conglomeration of stories, commands, exhortations, repetitions, incoherent passages, disconnected parts, etc. Western Orientalists are rather severe on it because of these defects. But if we wish to penetrate the secret of the religious sense of the Koran, we must have preparation. Before discussing the problem of the superhuman quality of this book, we must study the book as it is given to us.

The Koran is a book which made its appearance in a Semitic-Oriental environment. Muslim exegesis has studied the Koran for centuries solely in its aspect of a "divine" production, and has neglected the human aspect. I think it is the duty of Christian students to help the Muslim place the texts of the Koran back in the living environment in which the texts were born. Now that criticism has tried to establish the chronological order of the suras, and to get back to the sources, we have to apply to the Koran the principles of literary criticism which are employed at present in biblical study. The Semitic mentality in general must first be studied, followed by special study of the Arab mind, with special attention to the analysis of thought structures. Instead of pursuing the analytic and divisive literary criticism so predominant among the Orientalists of the last century and the beginning of this one, which led to the fragmentizing of texts (Bell's translation of the Koran is a good example of this), we must make a new start by turning to linguistic semantics.

It has been brought sharply into relief by Boman, for instance, that Semitic thought (Hebrew, Arabic, Syriac) is dynamic, contrary to Greek thought, which is static. Whereas the Greek mentality appears as harmonious and tends to harmonize, thereby having the need to systematize ideas, the language of the Semite shows him as dynamic, vigorous, passionate, explosive, imaginative; hence there is emphasis upon exaggeration. A Greek would be tempted to judge all this as immoderate and discordant; his esthetic sense would call it bad taste. This is the meaning of the statement that the temperament and the spirit of a person or a people show up in language.

Analysis of Semitic languages reveals the psychology of the Semite. Thus, to take an example, the verbs, in their fundamental meaning, express a movement, an activity. The verbs which express a state of rest, such as *stand, sit, lie,* may also express motion, and are often used in a parallelism with a verb of rest. For the Semite, the two concepts of rest and motion are not opposite concepts, as with us, but relative concepts which together are able to form the "unifying coupling of concepts." Arab grammarians give this the name *addad.* For example, *death* and *life* are not opposed ideas but are related and in continuation, because death is only a weak form of life!

For the Semite, only those beings which stand in profound relationship to something active and moving are real beings, because only motion is real, whereas, with us, verbs designating quality and property, etc., express "being." In a Semitic language these same verbs primarily express "becoming," because the condition or state is not fixed but is always fluid. The distinction between "being" and "becoming," which is so important in Greek thought, appears irrelevant to the Semitic mind, which always thinks dynamically. That is why the Semites have no need for the copulative verb *to be*. The principal meaning of the verb *kana* is "to become," "to be," and "to effect."

So we come to realize that the world, a reality, is looked upon by the Semitic mind as dynamic. Things do not seem to them as they do to us, fixed or motionless, but in motion and changeable; thus even stones and rocks are changeable. Only God is immobile, and the apparent immobility of the earth is an illusion.

In Greek thought, the antithesis between being and nothingness or non-being is perfectly grasped, but, for the Semite, non-being or nothingness has a certain existence. For the Hebrews, the word refers to all realities: word, deed, concrete objects. When they want to express non-being or nothingness, they say a non-word: *lo-dabbar*.[22]

In all the ancient Orient: Assyria, Babylonia, Egypt, and among Israelites as well as Arabs, the "word" was not primarily the expression of thought but a powerful and dynamic *force*. In ancient times the Assyrians and Babylonians conceived of the divine word as a physico-cosmic power. In all of the Semitic world, the *divine word* has tremendous power. (Exegetes of the Koran should have taken this into account when considering the expression applied to Jesus by the Koran: *Kalimât Allah*, "Word of God.")

Another characteristic of the Semitic mentality is the "collective name." Concepts are not abstractions, drawn from singular concrete things, but represent a real totality, which includes individual beings. And because these collective names are not abstractions but terms denoting the totality, the class, the singular individual is identified with the group (family, tribe, nation), and the group includes the past, the present, and the future as one, single person.

When *we* want to describe something, we use the actual images of what we see; we try to communicate the photographic appearance of things or persons as they appear to us. The Semite is not interested in appearances. His interest is in the practical use of things, which always remains on the level of tools and utensils for divine and human activity.

This difference in patterns of thought between Semite and Greek is also seen in the evaluation of sense perception as related to the ideal of beauty. It is significant to reflect on the images of feminine beauty in the Song of Songs, where the language tends to express qualities which are beyond merely external forms, namely, those spiritual qualities which are hidden in the material objects. The beautiful and the good are identified in everything that is living and they produce a sensible response which has a rhythm; but, more than this, they manifest a power and authority. We can see, then, how the sensations of light, color, song, sound, perfume, and taste are means by which to approach beauty. This is quite different from the Greek concept of beauty as the harmony of forces or form. So we should not be surprised at the anthropomorphism that is found in the Bible, as well as in the Koran, because it expresses something beyond the image — as in the statement that God loves to smell the odor of sacrifice! The sense images of the Semite, particularly the visual ones, do not represent only the static appearance of beings but qualities, because every material object has a dominant quality which is its inner meaning.

This mentality gives rise to the vision and the "symbolic" meaning of objects and all reality. The religious sense of the Orient especially felt the need of expression in figurative-symbolic language. Thus material things have the faculty of evoking either naturally or conventionally nonmaterial realities. Everything else is "sign." Every sign enables man to discover something beyond it, and so has some worth. Hence the importance of the signs (ayyât) in koranic theology. God speaks through signs. Yet not every sign is a symbol, even though every symbol is an "opaque" sign; and it is just this opacity which gives a sign the power to evoke the profound meaning of the symbol.

Another great difference between the intellectual structures of the Greek and the Semite worlds is their concepts of space and time. We, with the Greeks, give a plastic, spatial expression to time. We see it as a straight line. We are at a certain point on this line (the present), looking backward and forward to the past and the future. We reflect this type of thinking in our verbs, which have present, past, and future tenses. Time among Greeks and Indo-Germanic peoples is the measure of one movement following another and can be accurately measured through the movements of the stars and, especially, the sun. The Semite measures time and seasons by the *variable* movements of the moon.

The Semite talks of the functions of the heavenly bodies in their relation to man (the sun lights up the day and the moon the night) while the Greek marks the position of sun and stars in reference to the celestial movements. The Semite differentiates day and night, not only by light and darkness but also by the qualities of good and evil which he associates with them. Rather than thinking of the linear quality of time, the Semite arrives at a rhythm given by the movements of his body (pulsation, respiration, walking and standing still, sleeping and staying awake), without reference to spatial movements outside himself. There is the alternating rhythm of light and darkness, the phases of the moon, cold and heat, the circular movement of the sun's rising and setting. That is why the great reality for the Semite is rhythm (to understand their psychology, you have to understand the importance of the dance and syncopated music). Time goes with a rhythm both weak and strong. The short, or weak, rhythm of the day fades into the longer rhythm of the week, the rhythm of the week into that of the year.

Duration in Semitic thinking corresponds to recurrence (the return of something). Time is determined by what it contains, and so is experienced "qualitatively." History is seen rhythmically. It is marked by mighty events (the intervention of God), by victories, and by weak events, such as defeats. One must keep in mind that what the Semite means to express by a verb is not so much the determination of *when* an action took place (in the present, past, or future) but a qualification of the action, deed, or event (perfect tense: the action is done; imperfect tense: the action is not finished, still undone, or is still being done). But this qualification of completed or uncompleted action has nothing at all to do with our "spatialized" concept of time. We look at actions objectively, impersonally, and spatially. Semites always think from the viewpoint of the one who is talking, and hence subjectively — personally and temporally — because, from the point of view of the speaker, there are but two kinds of actions and facts: those that are completed and those that are not.

We have to link the Arab mentality to this general psychological mentality of the Semite. Arabic is a Semitic language and therefore has a dualistic, ambivalent, and rhythmic structure, composed of phonetic and semantic contrasts. Semitic dialectic has two terms, as opposed to Greek dialectic, which has three. Hence Arab reasoning does not proceed, like the Greek syllogism, by an appeal to universal ideas. It affirms the concrete, the particular, whose evidence is the authority who asserts it. This Arab type of language and this Arab dialectic are found in the Koran. Perhaps no one, up to the present, has brought out the characteristics of the Arabic languages as well as Professor Louis Massignon, who wrote:

> The Arabic language is magnificently instinctive and capricious. Its grammatical structure carries us back to the farthest horizons of the Semitic past. It coagulates and condenses to a metallic hardness, and sometimes to a crystalline transparency, the idea it wishes to express. The idea blooms from the whole of the sentence, like a spark, elliptical and gnomic, discontinuous and abrupt.[23]

Even the handwriting of the language brings out this density, because the written word gives us only the "body." The "soul," the vowels, which give life to the consonants, are not written. The idea comes to us in "condensed" fashion, while in our languages it is explicit.

Keeping in mind all these characteristics that are peculiar to the Semitic mentality and the Arabic language, we must confront the study of the Koran, an Arabic and a Semitic book, to find in it those ways of thinking, feeling, and expressing oneself that are common to the Semites and the Arabs. The style of the Koran is

tied to a collective form of expression called "desert civilization."
This style was obviously current before Mohammed's time, who,
despite his profound originality, had no other style in which to
express himself. This inheritance of thought and tradition came
to him from the common soul of the ethnic group to which he
belonged.

Symbolism, Imagery, and Parables in the Koran

I have already called attention to the importance of symbolism
for the Semitic mentality. Since the Koran also belongs among
the products of Semitic literature, we can conclude, a priori,
that there are many symbols in this book — many more, perhaps,
than have been suspected — which originated in the effort to
express aspects of reality surpassing the ordinary limits of abstract
expression. The expression of an idea is limited but the horizon
of thought is endless. The symbol comes to the aid of expression
where the word is lacking. A common manner of expression, especially of religious realities, must be acknowledged in the Semitic
languages, and this manner is found especially in their use of
symbolic language. It is for this reason that I am convinced that
we have to interpret the symbolism of the Koran in the light of
biblical symbolism.

In the Koran, nature and its phenomena are constantly alluded
to as "signs," as a reality which conceals a higher reality. It is
through these signs that the soul discovers God (the cosmic
revelation to which the Koran continually refers). The world
that is perceptible to the senses is a sacrament of the Godhead:
everything is a shadow of the heavenly reality. The kingdom of
nature is a representation of the kingdom of God.

Thus if natural phenomena such as rain, the fertility of the

soil, and the great elements of the cosmos: stars, moon, sun, etc.,
are "signs," they are symbols as well. Fire is the symbol of the
Spirit of God, which "purifies" and "proves" men. It is the
symbol of the divine justice, which, in Hell, eternally consumes
what cannot be purified. Water symbolizes the life principle; it
is a theme constantly evoked by the Koran (cf. no. 17, sura 80:25;
no. 56, sura 60:9; no. 57, sura 20:55/53; no. 62, sura 36:33).
Associated with water is the symbolism of clouds, which at times
express the presence of God, or his grace, etc. (cf. no. 88, sura
35:10/9–11/10; no. 89, sura 7:55/57–56/58; etc.). Mountains
are sometimes symbols of pride, the dwelling place of idolatry; at
other times they are symbols of safety, of God's protection. Mount
Sion, very often mentioned in the Koran, means the Mosaic covenant, or the Mosaic law, etc. The stars are symbols of the ranks
of angels (cf. no. 52, sura 37:6; no. 59, sura 15:16, etc.; no. 91,
sura 6:97). The stars serve as guides to men. Helping them find
their way on a journey, they are symbols of the angels, who guide
men.

Very few animals are named in the Koran and, where they are
named we can again ascertain a symbolism (cf. no. 89, sura
7:175–176). Semites generally considered the dog an unclean
animal (cf. the meaning of the unclean person in Dt 23:18).
Dogs, on the lips of the average Hebrew, meant the non-Hebrew
(cf. Mt 7:6, 15:27, Rv 22:15, etc.). The Koran (no. 70, sura
18:21/22), speaking of the seven sleepers, refers to "their dog."
Some of the Shi'ites (the Muslim sect which upholds the rights
of 'Ali) look upon this dog as the symbol of 'Ali; others of the
sect consider it the symbol of Salman the Persian, a friend and
confidant of Mohammed. It could also be interpreted as someone
who is not a Christian.[24]

Thus the texts that say "God made some of them apes and
swine, and worshippers of idols" (no. 116, sura 5:65/60; cf. no.
89, sura 7:166; no. 93, sura 2:259/257) are not to be understood
literally as Muslim exegesis usually understands them but meta-
phorically, because of the peculiar symbolic meaning these animals (apes and pigs) have in the Semitic Orient. The bee is

mentioned in the sura called "The Bee," though just a few verses speak of the bee's activities (no. 75, sura 16:70/68–71/69). Here, too, we have to remember that the bee was the symbol of industry and foresight. Thus the Septuagint version of Prv. 6:6, after giving the example of the ant, adds as parallel the example of the bee: "Or go to the bee and learn how industrious he is, how earnestly he does his work. Princes and vassals use his products for their health's sake. It is coveted and honored by all. It is weak, but because it honors wisdom, it obtains honor."

The Koran lists among God's benefactions, along with honey, which is the symbol of sweetness, of the Word of God, and of Wisdom of God (Ps 119 (118): 103, Prv 24:13–14, 25:16, etc.), milk as well (no. 75, sura 16:68/66). The bird is the symbol of the soul brought back to life. Thus God is glorified in the heavens and on earth by birds which spread their wings: a symbolic picture of souls or angels (no. 107, sura 24:41). Jesus, who is the principle of the resurrection, creates a bird from mud (no. 99, sura 3:43/49; cf. no. 93, sura 2:262/260; no. 65, sura 67: 18–19) — a text which has no connection with its setting unless one gives it the symbolic meaning of the resurrection. Likewise for no. 75, sura 16:81/79; no. 79, sura 12:36, 41; and no. 91, sura 6:38, which can scarcely be understood unless they are given the symbolic interpretation of risen souls. In Paradise the martyrs are symbolized by flying birds.

When it comes to trees, we have the olive tree, which is often associated with the fig tree and also with Mount Sinai (cf. no. 10, sura 95:1–2; no. 66, sura 23:2–21, etc.). The olive and olive oil are messianic symbols. The fig is the symbol of the people of Israel. Likewise, the palm and the date tree go together, as do the vine and the grape, in frequently recurring passages (cf. no. 17, sura 80:27–32; no. 84, sura 31:9/10; no. 88, sura 35: 25/27; no. 91, sura 6:99, 142/141; no. 92, sura 13:4; etc.). In biblical language, the palm is the symbol of the just man. The Koran, with its Arab background, looks upon the palm as the good tree, par excellence. Its fruit is sweetness and it has medicinal powers; it is the symbol of the "good word" (cf. no. 78, sura 14:

29/30); it is even the symbol of the Arab race.[25] I believe a symbolic interpretation should be given the fruits of gardens (symbolizing the Garden of Paradise), which are the grape, the olive, dates, and pomegranates (cf. no. 28, sura 55:68; no. 91, sura 6:99, 142/141).

Rereading the Koran and finding a deeper meaning through its biblical and Semitic symbols lead us into a new spiritual dimension which perhaps has not dawned upon Muslims to this very day who have been chained to the letter, which kills (always excepting the exegesis of the Sufis and the Shi'ites).

The same may be said of the symbolism of colors. The Koran has a preference for green, an obvious psychological preference of anyone who lives in a desert. It is the sign of life (oases, vegetation, water.)[26] In Heaven the pure are clothed with green (no. 34 *bis,* sura 76:21), while in Revelation they are clothed in white.

Because it is a Semitic book, the Koran is rich with powerful and living imagery. I confine myself to just a few instances. The activities of the infidel are like mirages on the plain: the thirsty traveler takes them for water (the most necessary item for a trip across a desert), but when he arrives at the spot he finds nothing (no. 107, sura 24:39).

The earth's trees become writing pens, and the sea, multiplied sevenfold, becomes the ink which writes the word of God; but all of this is insufficient to exhaust the word of God (no. 70, sura 109; no. 84, sura 31:26/27).[27]

Long ago, Muslim commentators called attention to the great number of *mathal* (proverbs, parables, examples) in the Koran, such as:

And that those in whose hearts there is sickness, and the unbelievers, may say, "What did God intend by this as a similitude?" [No. 36, sura 74:33/31]

This text brings out the allegorical meaning of the Koran and the "temptation to take everything literally."[28]

Some of the narratives are in parable style and greatly resemble the parables in the Bible. Examples are the parable of the masters of the garden (no. 70, sura 18:31/32–42/44; cf. no. 51, sura 68:17–32), the citizens of the city (no. 62, sura 36: 12/13–30), the two men, one of whom walked with his face to the earth and the other with head erect (no. 65, sura 67:22), the good word (the Word of God) and the bad word, which resemble the good tree and the bad tree (no. 78, sura 14:29/24–32/27), and the spider (no. 83, sura 29:40/41), symbol of frailty and uselessness, which is also found in the Bible (cf. Jb 8:13–15, 27:18, Is 59:5–6, etc.).

The distinction between parable and allegory is not always clear. And we also find in the Koran certain stereotyped forms long in use in the Bible and rabbinic literature: God is represented as the king or the master; the faithful are servants, or the vineyard or the flock; darkness and fire represent eschatological punishments; etc. The unfaithful are compared to cattle, which hear you shout at them but do not understand; they are deaf, dumb, and blind (no. 93, sura 2:166/171). It is particularly sura 2 that has an abundance of parables and allegories (vv. 16/17, 18/19, 24/26, 261/259, 263/261, 266/264, 267/265, 268/266). The Jews are labeled harder than stones (no. 93, sura 2:69/74) and compared to the ass carrying a load of books it cannot read (no. 96, sura 62:5).

There also can be found in the Koran some examples of "numerical proverbs," which, as in the Bible, are sometimes maxims, sometimes enigmas or similitudes (cf. no. 70, sura 18:21/22: "They will say 'Three; and their dog was the fourth of them.' They will say 'Five; and their dog was the sixth of them.' . . . They will say 'Seven; and their dog was the eighth of them.' ") The thousand years as one day (cf. Ps 89:4; 2 Pt 3:8) becomes a proverbial phrase in a sura (no. 72, sura 32:4/5), losing the meaning of its biblical context.

Semitic Parallelism in the Koran

Semitic parallelism, often found in the Bible, is a Semitic stylistic method, consisting of the statement of the same thought in two or more balanced and synthetic phrases. It is found in the Koran as the expression of a mentality that makes its point with two terms (Semites do this) rather than with three (as do the Greeks). We find parallelism of words and ideas — of persons, scenery, and pictures. A thought that has already been expressed is repeated in equivalent terms, sometimes with a heightening of effect that is truly beautiful. For example:

> Behold, the sinners were laughing at the believers, when they passed them by winking at one another, and when they returned to their people they returned blithely, and when they saw them they said, "Lo, these men are astray!" [No. 35, sura 83:29–32]

The crescendo of this scene is obvious: first the smile, then the wink of the eye to catch attention, then ridicule, and finally the sinners launch a sentence of condemnation against the just ones!

One frequently finds what has been called "antithetic parallelism" or "parallelism of opposition," both in the idea and in the picture. An example is the idea of the sun and day in opposition to the moon and the night, heaven and life opposed to earth and death:

> It is God who created the heavens and the earth . . . and He subjected to you the sun and the moon constant upon their courses, and he subjected to you the night and day. [No. 78, sura 14:37/32–37/33]

> Equal it is for them, whether thou askest forgiveness for them or thou askest not forgiveness for them; God will never forgive them. God guides not the people of the ungodly. [no. 106, sura 63:6]

A parallelism of scene or picture is found in the manner in

which the judgment is presented, as when the behavior of the misbelieving is set against the behavior of the God fearing (no. 82, sura 39:33/32–42/41). Likewise, the annunciation to Zachary and the birth of John the Baptist are scenes that parallel the annunciation to Mary and the birth of Jesus (cf. no. 60, sura 19: 1–15—16–34/33; no. 99, sura 3:33/38–36/41—37/42–43/48).

"Progressive parallelism," which resembles numerical proverbs, presents an augmenting enumeration (cf. no. 70, sura 18:21/22):

> Three men conspire not secretly together, but He [God] is the fourth of them, neither five men, but He is the sixth of them, neither fewer than that, neither more, but He is with them, wherever they may be. [no. 108, sura 58:8/7]

Parallelism, a kind of interior rhyme of meaning, lends harmony of verse and phrase, which is the identifying characteristic of the Semitic style. A detailed study of the whole of Koranic parallelism, including the various metaphors, proverbs, and parables, demonstrates, without a shadow of doubt, the Semitic character of the book's style. It expresses itself in the mentality of the environment that produced it.

Literary Forms in the Koran

The discovery of South Arabian inscriptions and study of the Hebrew and Christian communities of Arabia prior to and during Mohammed's lifetime make it quite clear that the Koran has been "conditioned by Mohammed's surroundings." [29] "Muslims believe in the strict inspiration of the Koran, the Word of God," writes Fr. Moubarac, "but this does not necessarily prevent research into the Koran's 'sources.' " [30] Nor, it seems to me, does it forbid the study of the literary forms in it, just as the Bible is studied.

Such study is urgently needed. First of all, the literal sense of the texts must be established. We must find out, first, what the author wished to convey. Next we have to uncover and make precise the proper character of each text by applying the same principles used by modern biblical criticism in order to highlight its human and specific aspects. We have to bring out the historic dimensions of the "koranic revelation," for it is part and parcel, as is biblical revelation, of a given environment — in this case Arabia of the seventh century. This has to be tied in with the psychology of both the proclaimer and the recipients of the message.

It must be remembered that the Koran was not something Mohammed sat down and wrote from the first to the last page; it cannot be called "a book written by Mohammed." As is well known, it was put into writing only after Mohammed's death.[31] He was not some sort of scribe who returned to his home to polish phrases that he had acquired here and there. His mission was to "proclaim," to announce, whatever an inner voice made known to him. These occasional announcements of his were spoken, sometimes before a small group of friends, at other times in front of a public composed of different kinds of people, some of them Jews and pagans, and different social levels. Some of the communications were for him alone, and came to him during periods of ecstasy.

Hence the style is affected by the main didactic and pedagogic aim he had in mind, rather than by an exclusively esthetic aim. The fact that Mohammed preached, and did not write, must be kept clearly in view if we wish to fix the amount of personal contribution he made in relation to what was announced. Hence — more than the idea of "sacred writer," as in the Bible — we must keep in mind the concept of "prophetic" inspiration, of oracles, when we study the phenomenon of Mohammed's inspiration. Both types of inspiration have much in common, but they must be kept distinct. This distinction will help to clarify the Muslim concept of "literal inspiration."

The fact that Mohammed merely announced, that is, preached a doctrine which others carefully memorized and later committed to writing, explains the varied and fragmentary character of the suras' relationship to one another, as well as the composition of the individual suras. The guidelines used by the people who put together the written material were certainly different from the rules followed by modern criticism to discover the "literary form" of a work. Such a study in depth has not yet been done by modern scholarship. The various texts must be sorted out and classified, such as

1. Oracles: divine sayings that the prophet contented himself with simply repeating
2. Apocalyptic visions (the "Kahin" form)
3. Psalms, hymns, prayers
4. Historic and legendary stories
5. Legislative texts (cult and civil laws)
6. Archival material (proclamations of war and treaties)

It is not my intention in this work to make a real or thorough study of the literary forms of the Koran but to present an essay which may stimulate others to further research.

ORACLES

I have said that the Koran does not appear in the form of something produced by a hagiographer but "as a supernatural dictation, received by the inspired 'prophet.' He is a simple messenger entrusted with the mission of this deposit."[32] That is why the "prophet" limits himself to passing on a "divine oracle" which has sounded within his spirit. At times this divine word, which the "prophet" passes on in a purely passive manner, clothed in terminology found already in his mind, may go far beyond the people it is immediately addressed to, and have within it a "fullness of meaning" (*sensors plenius*) surpassing what the "prophet" and his companions may make of it. His task is simply to pass on, and not necessarily to understand, a vision or a word, the complete and deeper significance of which may remain concealed. This character of a messenger, who is merely the transmitter of a word which remains hazy to him, could result in a distorted interpretation.

In most koranic texts the speaker is God. At times he speaks directly to Mohammed; at other times he speaks directly to Mohammed's audience through the ministry of the prophet. It must be accepted as a general principle that it is God who is speaking in every text in which the first person plural is used. There are some very rare texts in which a different subject appears. One interesting fact should be emphasized: God rarely speaks in the first person plural in the Bible (cf. Gn 1:26). This is true of the New Testament even after the revelation of the trinitarian mystery. In most texts of the Koran, however, which report discourses of God, God speaks in the first person plural (except in a few cases, such as no. 34, sura 73:11; no. 36, sura 74:11; no. 49, sura 51:56; etc.). Coming, as it did, after the revelation of the mystery of the Trinity, the koranic "revelation" used this *We* as a step toward the three divine Persons, rather than merely as a majestic plural. Where the first person singular appears in the texts, we must recognize, most of the time, not the direct word of God but the voice of the angel (Gabriel) who brings the "revelation" to Mohammed (cf. no. 58, sura 26:193; no. 30, sura 53:5; no. 85, sura 42:50–52). Consequently, every text must be analyzed to see whether the speaker is God, the angel, or Mohammed.

In the order of time, the first sura in which the *We* appears is 94 (no. 5), where God's special action upon Mohammed is shown. In certain places where there is a personal conversation especially affecting Mohammed, the singular and plural are used on the same occasion (cf. no. 34, sura 73:11, whereas in vv. 5, 12, 15, etc., we find *We* [no. 51, sura 68:44–45]). Nevertheless, in the vast majority of instances where God speaks and where the message is for Mohammed's hearers, we find the first person plural. At times there are threats, accompanied by references to prior events, mostly biblical stories; sometimes there are exhortations, promises, directives for worship, or moral instructions.

We often encounter introductory formulas: "Hast thou received the story of Moses?" (no. 20, sura 79:15; cf. no. 57, sura

20:8/9); "And recite to them the tiding of Abraham" (no. 58, sura 26:69); "The mention of thy Lord's mercy" (no. 60, sura 19:1); etc. These formulas, which are most often found in connection with the biblical stories, directed, in my opinion, principally to the Jews (first in Mecca and later in Medina), are a sort of appeal to the "sons of Israel" as a meditation upon their past history and can be looked on as that type of historical retrospection similar to examples in Ezekiel or Deutero-Isaiah (cf. the "Remember!" of chaps. 40–45 in Is).

The use of *We* by God in the Koran cannot be of rabbinic origin. We have only to keep in mind the Jewish-Christian controversies in which the Christians used texts of the Old Testament to prove the existence of the Trinity and the divinity of Jesus (Gn 1:25, Dt 4:32, etc.). For them, the texts could mean an "internal plurality of divine Persons in the one God." The rabbis explained the texts by saying that God had the habit of consulting the Torah, or his heavenly court which is his family.[33]

It seems to me that the constant use of *We* in the Koran has to be a "preparation" leading to the knowledge of the mystery of the Trinity, a hint at the Christian mystery, such as is found in passages of the Old Testament.

APOCALYPTIC VISIONS (THE "KAHIN" FORM)

It has been pointed out that, in the suras of the first period of Mohammed's preaching in Mecca, what is called the "apocalyptic style" predominates. Fr. Moubarac correctly observes that the Koran uses the reverse process of what we find in the Bible. In the Bible the apocalyptic form appears as a development of the "prophecy," while in the Koran the apocalyptic, eschatological announcement precedes the prophetic one. Prophecy in the Koran is essentially "the annunciation of an event which is supposed to lead hearts back to the fear of a unique God, Lord of the World."[34]

Apocalyptic form, or style, as has been remarked, is poetic and emphatic; it prefers generalization. Most of the time it proceeds in a mysterious, obscure, imaginative, and evocative fashion. All the Orientalists have emphasized that the Mecca suras are full of warmth and poetry. They have placed these compositions alongside those of the soothsayers and poets before Islam, whose works they have labeled the "Kahin form."[35]

In these works, they maintain, they find "deprecatory oaths of a magic type."[36] Instead of looking upon these texts in the usual way as oaths, I feel that we must see them as passages which call to mind apocalyptic visions seen by Mohammed which he, at times, recalls in very simple terms. They are symbolic visions which suggest ideas coming from an inner inspiration. These intimate images in his mind's eye are meant to cast into relief, as in sculpture, the main idea that was furnished him, or which he inwardly perceived as the cry of an angel or the very voice of God. In these texts the imagination is quick, exuberant, and light. The pictures pile up on one another, without apparent regard for their coherence, like pictures on a strip of film, which at the end finally express the leading idea. The apocalyptic nature of the visions allows us to see the whole picture as Mohammed saw it. All the predominantly visual images, as well as the acoustic ones, are in harmony, and it is especially the auditory images in the form of solemn declarations that are the most important. Tor Andrae speaks of this visual psychology. He thinks that Mohammed naturally tended to stress the auditory image, and my own analysis of the "apocalyptic" texts bears this out.[37]

> By the white forenoon
> and the brooding night!

> *Thy Lord has neither forsaken thee nor hates thee*
> and the last shall be better for thee than the First
> Thy Lord shall give thee, and thou shalt be satisfied.
>
> [no. 4, sura 93:1–5]

In the above passage we find the elements of Mohammed's vision. There is a picture of the light of high morning — light being the symbol of earthly life. These two symbolic pictures,

very simply evoked, are used to fix the central thought: Thy Lord
has not forsaken thee. The verses that follow (5–11) are a kind
of proof that God has not abandoned him. Since there is no *We*
in this sura, it seems that the interior voice that speaks to Mohammed is not God's but the angel's.

In my opinion, all the introductions where the conjunction *waw*
is met (and considered as deprecative: the Kahin form) should
be interpreted in the same manner, though I think that the copulative *waw* can be retained in its grammatical sense of joining
words that are merely evocative.

With this in view, the introductions of certain suras deserve
special attention (no. 25, sura 77:1–7; no. 49, sura 51:1–6; no.
52, sura 37:1–3), in which it seems that we are dealing with
apocalyptic visions of ranks of angels in a judgment scene:

[By] the [angels] sent in ordered ranks
Who rush on rapidly
Scattering all about [the commands of God]
Separating by the separation [the good from the bad]
who communicate the admonition
excusing or warning
IN TRUTH, THAT WHICH HAS BEEN THREATENED YOU
SHALL SURELY BEFALL YOU.

[no. 25, sura 77:1–7]

The text which follows is a scene of the general judgment, announced by the destruction of the cosmos (vv. 8–14):

[By] the [angels] scattering everywhere
[God's commands]
carrying a burden,
those who run rapidly
who distribute in accordance with the
Divine Command
THAT WHICH IS BEING THREATENED IS TRUE AND
WITHOUT ANY DOUBT THE JUDGMENT SHALL COME!

[no. 49, sura 51:1–6]

This scene of angels' broadcasting the word, or the commands of God, occurs frequently in the Koran. The word is looked upon as a burden since it concerns the warning of divine punishment and final judgment (cf. Is 10:27, Mt 11:29):

[By] those who form ordered ranks [the angels]
Those who violently repel
Those who communicate the admonition
TRULY YOUR GOD IS ONE
[no. 52, sura 37:1–4]

Muslim commentators usually consider feminine participles (al-Dâriyati, al-mursalât) as referring to a subject not explicitly mentioned. An example would be the winds which scatter the clouds. But other commentators favor the angels as the nonexpressed subject, because the word for spirit and also for wind (rûh) is feminine in Arabic. (The plural of the word for angels, al-Mala'-ikat, is also feminine.) The pagan Arabs thought of the angels as beings of female sex, as the Koran informs us (no. 30, sura 53:28/27; no. 52, sura 37:150; no. 63, sura 43:18/19; no. 74, sura 17:42/40; no. 75, sura 16:59/57–64; etc.).

This apocalyptic style is repeated in the descriptions of the end of the world and the general judgment. Images familiar to Hebrew and Christian apocalyptic literature occur: the earth which rejects the dead (no. 11, sura 99:2; cf. Is 26:19, Hos 13:14), the heavens which melt, the planets which disappear, the seas which burst their bounds (no. 15, sura 82:1–4; no. 18, sura 81:1–4; no. 19, sura 84:1–6; no. 23, sura 56:1–7; cf. Rv 6:12, 8:8), etc.

PSALMS, HYMNS, PRAYERS

From the most remote antiquity, the "psalmodic" form has been part of the religious literature of the Orient. Thus there is nothing surprising about the appearance of "brief flashes of psalms" even in the Koran. But we must know how to recognize them. These compositions are the fruit of a vivid experiencing of God — the confession of an impassioned soul which perceives all the majesty and grandeur of the mystery of God. They are expressions of joy and marvel before the power, magnificence, and goodness of the God who created this wonderful universe, who, with his wisdom, keeps order within it, that where every being and created phenomenon is a voice, a sign, that proclaims the presence and the greatness of God.

One text of the Koran, considered to be of the Medina period by the Orientalists, though it comes just after a primitive text of the Mecca period, seems to be a "ritual instruction" by the angel on how to recite certain texts in psalm fashion:

> Thy Lord knows that thou keepest vigil nearly two-thirds of the night, or a half of it, or a third of it, and a party of those with thee; and God determines the night and the day. He knows that you will not number it, and He has turned towards you. Therefore recite of the Koran as much as is feasible. [no. 34, sura 73:20]

From the beginning, the first followers of Mohammed met together to recite these psalms during the night as "invocations of the Name of the Lord and a total consecration to Him" (cf. no. 34, sura 73:6–8).

I believe that we can classify as "brief invitatory psalms" other passages which call to prayer:

> Magnify the Name of thy Lord the Most High who created and shaped, who determined and guided, who brought forth the pasturage then made it a blackening wrack. [No. 16, sura 87: 1–5]

> Recite: In the Name of thy Lord who created, created Man of a blood-clot.

> Recite: And thy Lord is the Most generous, who taught by the Pen, taught Man that he knew not.
>
> [no. 1, sura 96:1–5]

The Sura of the Merciful One (no. 28, sura 55), which is similar to Psalm 136, may be a liturgy of thanksgiving wherein, at each statement of God's favors, the verse is repeated (and probably chanted by the whole assembly in the manner of a litany response), namely: "Which, then, of God's benefits will you deny? O which of your Lord's bounties will you and you deny?" The psalm ends with the doxology (v. 78): "Blessed be the Name of thy Lord, majestic, splendid."

There is a short psalm of thanksgiving after a military victory:

> God has bought from the believers their selves and their possessions against the gift of Paradise; they fight in the way of God; they kill, and are killed; that is a promise binding upon God in the Torah, and the Gospel, and the Koran; and who fulfills his covenant truer than God? So rejoice in the bargain you have made with him; that is the mighty triumph. [no. 115, sura 9:112/111; cf. no. 113, sura 110:1–3]

There is a psalm of "malediction" after the success of the Hudaybiya treaty:

> It is He who sent down the Shechina [Presence] into the hearts of the unbelievers, that they might add faith to their faith — to God belong the hosts of the heavens and the earth; God is All-knowing, All-wise — and that He may admit the believers, men and women alike, into gardens underneath which rivers flow, therein to dwell forever, and acquit them of their evil deeds; that is in God's sight a mighty triumph; and that He may chastize the hypocrites, men and women alike, and the idolators, men and women alike, and those who think evil thoughts of God; against them shall be the evil turn of fortune. God is wroth with them, and has cursed them, and has prepared for them Gehenna —
> an evil homecoming!
> To God belong the hosts of the heavens and the earth.
>
> [no. 110, sura 48:4–7]

There are "cosmic" psalms, in which is chanted the "royalty" of God:

> All that is in the heavens and the earth magnifies God. His is the Kingdom, and His is the praise, and He is powerful over everything.

It is He who created you. One of you is an unbeliever; and God sees the things you do. He created the heavens and the earth with the truth, and He shaped you, and shaped you well; and unto Him is the homecoming. He knows whatever is in the heavens and the earth, and He knows what you conceal and what you publish. God knows the thoughts within the breasts.

[no. 95, sura 64: 1–4]

All that is in the heavens and the earth magnifies God, the King, the All-holy, the All-mighty, the All-wise.

It is He who has raised up from among the common people a Messenger from among them, to recite His signs to them and to purify them, and to teach them the Book and the Wisdom, and others of them who have not yet joined them. And He is the All-mighty, the All-wise.

That is the bounty of God; He gives it to whom He will, and God is of bounty abounding.

[no. 96, sura 62: 1–4]

These psalms are prayers of adoration and profession of faith. The imperative mood, *Qul* Say is considered a command of God himself. Yet it may be interpreted as the direction given by a rubric, granted that the texts were meant for the purposes of worship.

> Say: "He is God, One, God, the Everlasting Refuge,
>   who has not begotten, and has not been
>   begotten, and equal to Him is not anyone."
>
> [no. 44, sura 112: 14]

This text is always taken as anti-trinitarian, both by Muslim theology and Christian polemics. But, as Massignon declares, it is an affirmation of the unity of the divine essence (*tawhîd*) rather than a statement of the unique personality of God.[38] It can be taken as the Arab affirmation of the divine essence that is common to the three Persons, as the Fourth Lateran Council defined: *"Illa Res non generans neque genita"* (that reality does not beget, nor is it begotten").[39] Hence it is not actually a refutation of the Christian dogma concerning the Trinity, which does not seem to be the subject of attention either here or in any other section of the Koran.

The famous Verse of the Throne, often recited with great devotion, is a psalm-type confession of faith:

> God
> there is no god but He, the Living,
> the Everlasting. Slumber seizes Him
> not, neither sleep; to Him belongs all
> that is in the heavens and the earth.
>
> Who is there that shall intercede with
> Him save by His leave? He knows what
> lies before them and what is after them,
> and they comprehend not anything of His
> knowledge save such as He wills.
>
> His Throne comprises the heavens and earth;
> the preserving of them oppresses Him not;
> He is the All-high, the All-glorious.
>
> [no. 93, sura 2:256/255]

Prayers of abandonment to God, refuge of the believers, are also introduced by the imperative *Say:*

> Say: "I take refuge with the Lord of men,
>   the King of men,
>   the God of men,
>   from the evil of the slinking whisperer
>   who whispers in the breasts of men
>   of jinn and men."
>
> [no. 48, sura 114]
>
> Say: "I take refuge with the Lord of the Daybreak
>   from the evil of what He has created,
>   from the evil of darkness when it gathers,
>   from the evil of the women who blow on knots,
>   from the evil of an envier when he envies."
>
> [no. 47, sura 113:1–5]

In the Name of God, the Merciful, the Compassionate

Praise belongs to God, the Lord of all Being,
the All-merciful, the All-compassionate,
The Master of the Day of Doom.

Thee only we serve; to Thee alone we pray for succor.
Guide us in the straight path,
the path of those whom Thou hast blessed,
not of those against whom Thou art wrathful,
nor of those who are astray.

[no. 46, sura 1]

"A humble and solemn faith — but not a sad one," observes Fr. Abd-el-Jalil.[40] It can also be called a generation of spiritual joy in more interior souls, but this joy is rather serenity and obedient abandon than jubilant rejoicing. It is a faith without "beatitude." This is the characterizing note that sets these prayers off sharply from the psalms and, in general, the Old Testament. Still, they *remind* one of the Old Testament, and are connected with it by the sense of the majesty and omnipotence of God, as well as by the consciousness of the sinfulness and dependence of man.

HISTORICAL AND LEGENDARY NARRATIVES

Almost all of the historico-legendary accounts, the majority of which have to do with biblical personalities, are presented within discourses which repeatedly appeal to the preaching of Israel's prophets. In the second and third Mecca periods particularly, the Koran gives examples of an oratorical-homilectic form, divided into three well-balanced parts. This form has been compared to the Christian homiletics of the Syrian churches.[41]

The Koran calls upon mankind to focus its attention upon the "cosmic revelation," that is, to rediscover God through his providence, which shows itself in the creation all around us. All the elements of the world are in God's service: they are for his glory; but at the same time they are at man's service, to prove to him the munificence and favor of God.

It is He who makes the rain come down

After they have despaired,
and so spreads round his mercy.

[no. 70, sura 18:15/16]

Water is the source of life and an image of the grace of resurrection. The desert, turning green after the dry season, symbolizes
resurrection after death. This language is symbolic in itself, but
it also recalls biblical symbolism wherein rain is an image of the
word of God (cf. Hos 6:3). Just as water vivifies, so does the
word of God, announced by the prophets (cf. no. 63, sura 43:
10/11; no. 88, sura 35:10/9; no. 89, sura 7:55/57; etc.).

The sea is a sign of divine mercy and, simultaneously, of God's
tremendous justice, which reveals to man his own impotence and
wretchedness in the face of nature, which is capable of becoming
the instrument of God's anger:

Your Lord it is who drives for you the ships on the sea that
you may seek His bounty; surely He is All-compassionate
towards you. [no. 74, sura 17:68/66]

Hast thou not seen how that the ships run upon the sea by the
blessing of God, that He may show you some of His signs?
Surely in that are signs for every man enduring, thankful.

And when the waves cover them like shadows they call upon
God, making their religion sincerely His; but when He has
delivered them to the land, some of them are lukewarm. And
none denies Our signs, except every ungrateful traitor.

[no. 84, sura 31:30/31–31/32]

When they embark in the ships, they call on God, making their
religion sincerely His; but when He has delivered them to the
land, they associate others with Him. [no. 83, sura 29:65; cf.
Ps 107]

The cycles of night and day, of months and yearly seasons, are
a sign which reveals, in a mysterious manner, the wise ordering
God has impressed upon nature for man's sake:

Say: "What think you? If God should make

the night unceasing over you, until
the Day of Resurrection, what god other
than God shall bring you illumination?
Will you not hear?"

Say: "What think you? If God should make
the day unceasing over you, until
the Day of Resurrection, what god other
than God shall bring you night to repose in?
Will you not see? Of His mercy He has appointed
for you night and day, for you to repose in and
seek after His bounty,
that haply you will be thankful."

[no. 81, sura 28:71–73]

It is by means of this "cosmic revelation" that man is to discover that all reality exists in God and through God, from whom everything comes through creation and to whom everything must return. By means of this teaching of the Koran, man discovers the "sacred" and the sense of God by reflecting upon the cosmic phenomena. Thus begins that colloquium of gratitude which man must make with God, who now begins to uncover for him some facets of the mystery of God. It is an education which God gives man, to give him the feeling of invisible realities, to allow him to perceive the greatness of the creator and the misery of the creature. More than anything else, it unveils the presence of God, working in the universe. Thus it prepares man to recognize the intervention of God in human history by means of "personal revelation," through which God enters into personal communication with men through the use of his "sent" ones.

In some manner, this personal revelation begins by the action of God in the consciousness of each individual man, provided he adverts to it:

In the earth are signs for those having sure faith; and in yourselves; what, do you not see? [no. 49, sura 51:20–21]

The Koran appeals to this "testimony of the heart" (cf. no. 56, sura 50:36). Here the "revelation" imprints itself by an interior process, either by directly and mysteriously taking possession or by means of the word of God transmitted through angels.[42] Man receives the divine message, not as the result of a rational chain of dialectical arguments of philosophical truth through a logical process but, rather, the divine message is communicated to man — according to the Koran — through testimonies which he must listen to, coming from the reading of a sacred text or the sacred text written in nature, in history, and holy books (cf. no. 85, sura 42:50–51).

This is why I cannot talk in terms of a "natural religion" when treating of the Koran. The religious spirit of the Koran always supposes revelation in the line of descent from the historical and supernatural revelation of the God of Abraham. If man does not come to realize the greatness and presence of God by looking at the world with all its dynamic forces, nor through the "witness" of his conscience, God then, in his mercy toward man, intervenes by sending his "messengers." These are principally witnesses to the oneness of God. It is their task to remind mankind continually that he must observe the "primitive pact" by which all men (included in the seed of Adam, according to the Koran) are under obligation to acknowledge God, renounce every idolatry, and render him sincere worship (no. 89, sura 7:171–172 — a text of rare force and depth, in which is contained the whole meaning of human history and destiny).[43]

When Mohammed first began to preach, he functioned as a *Nadhir* or herald of the future life and of judgment to the Jews and pagan Arabs of Mecca. The content of his preaching referred back to the biblical revelation and had an essentially eschatological tone. He first appears as an "admonisher." He recalls past deeds, when God intervened with threats and punishments to bring men back to the observance of the First Commandment. Many of these stories belong to the "legends of the ancients" (cf. no. 51, sura 68:15; no. 35, sura 83:13; etc.). Their roots are in Arabian traditions.[44] Fr. Moubarac has made some interesting studies (in various publications) of the message of the messengers and the biblical prophet (*nabi*) mentioned in the Koran.[45] A general view of all the personalities in the Koran is presented in a beautiful volume of Fr. Moubarac, *L'Islam*.[46]

There are, obviously, elements of legend in these "historical" accounts, and they have to be weighed accordingly. But *legend,* as Fr. Lagrange observed while speaking of the legends in the Bible, is not a synonym for *falsehood;* it is truth as expressed by the popular imagination. The preoccupation of the historico-legendary tales in the Koran is not to give dates, chronologies, or biographies but to render witness to the faith. So it is "beyond the letter" that one must look for the true principle and spiritual senses which are the reason for a story's being told. We must also take into account that the stories are full of "reflections," or that they invite the hearers to make reflections at the conclusion, and that still others have an apologetic purpose.

Geography seems absent from the Koran; and the historical tales are related without any precise localization. There are very few allusions to Mecca, to Abyssinia, to the Holy Land and Jerusalem — in contrast to the Bible, which teems with names of places and villages within Palestine and often mentions the neighboring countries: Egypt, Syria, Babylonia. At the end of the narratives, typical formulas are often found which have been called "Semitic inclusions." They consist of the repetition at the end of a story of a statement or word which recalls its beginning, so as to give a sort of unity to the whole (cf. no. 58, sura 26:7/8, 67–68, 103–104, 121–122, 139–140, 158–159, 174–175, 190–191, etc.). If, at present we are willing to face the results of biblical criticism regarding the literary historical forms of the Semitic Orient, we can no longer talk of the Koran's narratives as having historical error in them, as Christian apologetics has done for centuries.[47]

It must be kept in mind that, in the Koran, history is narrated according to the spirit of "popular narrations." At the same time, however, as opposed to "midrashic" presentation, the Koran tends to emphasize the direct action of God much more than is done in the same stories in the Bible. I suggest that this shows that Mo-hammed's preaching of biblical material was aimed at the Jews, whose tendency is to present the absolute sufficiency of man, who does not need God for his "justification" but controls his own destiny. Attention must be paid, likewise, to the possibility that biblical stories, spread among the Arabs, took on some of the folklore of the desert and the lyricism of the Arab soul. To this may be added that Oriental phenomenon called "amplification," that is, the tendency to inflate the facts to give them more importance than they would apparently have had in reality.

LEGISLATIVE TEXTS (CULT LAWS, CIVIL LAWS)

Analysis of the several "literary forms" in the Koran assuredly helps us determine and make precise the ideas expressed in it. It also helps us have a better acquaintance with the social conditions, the psychology of one or more communities, and even the historical development of the message. The Orientalists have recognized, in the suras of the period in Medina, a more developed "juridical sense." It is certain that the Islamic "community" took form in Medina, and hence a body of juridical decisions regulating the life of the new community would begin to develop. Mohammed, the Semite, had a total vision of life. For him there were no such things as departments labeled "civil" and others "religious." Besides, manifestations of life for a Semite are essentially communal, and so they have a social and at the same time political worth. It is easy to understand, then, placing ourselves within this mentality, why the most "civil," the most purely temporal directions of the laws and usages referred to in the Koran, are all by God's authority. In reality, every aspect of life and every human activity is under God.

The study of the Koran's legislative texts is all the more interesting because, up to Mohammed's time, a written law does not seem to have existed in Arabia. Guidi writes: "The judge (*sayyid–shaikh*) was not able to consult a written law because there was none. All he could do was apply ancient norms and customs to a case. The customs of the ancients were the essential source of rule and law in every department of life."[48] To have given the

Arab people a written law, therefore, was a great step forward, and this written law was destined primarily for the Arabs.

The fact that the legislative texts are gathered together in the latter suras of the Medina period — except those in the suras of the last period at Mecca — does not mean, it would seem, that this legislation was given in this final period. We have to take into account the practical dispositions made by the redactors and collectors of the texts if we are to understand the position of these texts in the suras today.

The interpretation of the laws, their characteristics and their classification, should take into account the circumstances in which they originated, which is something that Muslim exegesis has not always respected. The geographical conditions of the desert were certainly of direct or indirect influence. Note, for example, that in the Bible the camel is an impure animal (Lv 11:4, Dt 14:7). Arab tradition, which preceded Islam, and the necessity of the camel for desert life, however, certainly modified the Arab-Semite mentality in regard to the camel. It was a sacred animal for them, and in the Koran it remains an animal especially given by God to the Arabs (no. 75, sura 16:5–7). The nature of the territory is also an important factor in determining which animals and plants are edible or forbidden, and the change of the seasons influenced the choice of sacred months, etc. These observations must be kept in mind when we make a comparative study of Koranic laws and the laws of the other Semitic people. We must also be aware of economic conditions that played a part in the formulation of practical laws concerning lending, usury, commerce, and the integration of the tribe and family into the community. We must consider the historical conditioning of contacts with other communities, especially the Hebrew and the Christian; the psychological character of the Semite-Arab, in whom an immediate and practical spirit predominates; the predominance of the social over the individual; and, especially, the religious character of every human activity, all of which is destined for the "return to God."

This legislation is scattered here and there, and has a fragmentary, practical, and occasional character.

CULT LAWS

Muslim faith is, above all, a response to God's election. He asks a total submission in obedience (cf. no. 75, sura 16:121/120–123/122). Against the temptation to legalism — to a religion satisfied with the purely external carrying out of acts (a legalism with which Christian authors have often reproached Islam) — is a beautiful text in the Koran which is considered the foundation of inward religious spirit:

> It is not piety, that you turn your faces
>   to the East and to the West.
>   True piety is this:
> to believe in God, and the Last Day,
> the angels, the Book, and the Prophets,
> to give of one's substance, however cherished,
>   to kinsmen and orphans,
> the needy, the traveller, beggars,
>   and to ransom the slave,
> to perform the prayer, to pay the alms.
> And they who fulfill their covenant,
>   and endure with fortitude
>   misfortune, hardship and peril,
> these are they who are true in their faith,
>   these are the truly godfearing.
>
>   [no. 93, sura 2:172/177]

In its legal-canonical division (*Fîqh*), Muslim theology has minutely regulated every facet of human life by divine norms. Like the Old Testament, it does not know any clear distinction between moral, juridical, and political rules, nor of private and public law, since all regulation of human conduct springs from the same sacred source.[49] The outward aspect of acts has called attention to what are called the "five pillars" of Islam: (1) the *Shahâda,* the profession of faith; (2) the *Salât,* ritual prayer; (3) the *Zakât,* legal almsgiving; (4) the fast (*Saum*) during the month of Ramadan; and (5) the *Hâjj* or pilgrimage.

But it must be remembered that the religious and moral training of the Muslim soul is accomplished essentially through reading and meditating upon the Koran — "that Arabian edition of the Bible reserved to the carnal descendants of Abraham through the line of Ishmael (Massignon)." So we encounter a number of koranic texts which, though they apparently do not have any legislative character, contain the Torah, or commandments of God, presented through a description of the "pure ones." The "pure ones" are those who have observed the "divine precepts" during their lives, whereas the "wicked," or sinners, are those who during their lives violated the commands of God. (cf. no. 33, sura 70:22–35, where we are given the portrait of the "just man," and no. 23, sura 56:27/28; no. 34 *bis,* sura 76:5–22. No. 35, sura 85, is entirely occupied with putting men on their guard and reminding violators of God's law.)

Next to this can be placed the portrait of the generous, the charitable man, who is "the just one" (no. 40, sura 90:12–18), and that of the egotist, who thinks only of himself (no. 42, sura 89:18/17–21/20). It must also be stressed that there is a constant preoccupation in the Koran with the orphan and the poor. Mohammed himself had bitter experiences in this regard (no. 4, sura 93:6–8).

CIVIL LAWS

Legal directives concerning personal status contain laws on marriage, divorce, inheritance, etc. Though Orientalists have accused Mohammed of playing politics in Medina, the Koran makes not the slightest reference to the political constitution of the state; a theocratic constitution is presupposed. Mohammed remains the man sent by God to teach his people, and they are to obey him:

> O believers, obey God, and obey the Messenger and those in authority among you. If you should quarrel on anything, refer it to God and the Messenger, if you believe in God and the Last Day. [No. 102, sura 4:62/59]

The above sura is characteristic of the entire legislative section. It contains a series of juridical texts on the administration of orphans' goods, on the "condition" of female orphans, on inheritances, fornication, directives concerning marriage, social relations, the state of purity before prayer, etc. These texts seem to have been given by Mohammed in his capacity as head of the community, and the word of God, with the *We,* is inserted as a divine confirmation (no. 102, sura 4:35/31, 37/33, 41/37–48/38, 45/41).

A detailed analytic study would be needed to show the difference in gravity between the commands given directly by God (*We*), by the angel, and by the prophet. For example, study must be made of the style in which the orders are expressed: whether they are direct commands, using the imperative, or specific cases introduced by certain formulas, such as "The believers will ask you." Also to be determined is the special significance of the formula "Here are the bounds of God!" (cf. no. 93, sura 2:183/187, 229 [it occurs in this verse four times]–230; no. 102, sura 4:17/13; no. 108, sura 58:5/4; no. 115, sura 9:98/97, 113/112). This particularly solemn formula is used after directions (usually prohibitions). Above all, we need to clarify the difference between legislative directions occasioned by some happening and those which concern the moral aspects of the actions in their relation to divine law. The theory called the Abrogator and the Abrogated (*An-Nasikh wa 'l-mansukh*), developed by Muslim theologians for the arbitrary action of God, whereby at his good pleasure he changes his own directives, should also be investigated in greater depth (cf. no. 75, sura 103/101; no. 93, sura 2:100/106).

We must also keep in mind that this insistence upon the "contingency" of the legislative order is clearer when it is seen in the historic context of a polemical position against the immutability of the law claimed by rabbinic Judaism. Another point is that koranic legislation is expressed by relationship to Hebrew legislation, either in opposition to it or going beyond it. There is no evidence of any statement in the Koran that makes direct allusion to Christian laws.

It is interesting to note that when the Koran disputes with the Jews, it ignores the difference the latter had introduced into the commandments God had made especially for the sons of Israel (the 613 commandments of the Law of Sinai) and the Seven Commandments (six of them given primitively to Adam, the seventh added after the flood) that were given to the gentiles (the sons of Noah), commandments that the rabbis called the Commandments of the Sons of Noah (*Mizwot Bene-Noah*).[50]

ARCHIVAL DOCUMENTS
(PROCLAMATIONS OF WAR AND TREATIES)

Because of the Muslims' special manner of conceiving the Koran, it will not be easy to persuade them that it contains documents which are purely human, and which we may call archival. For example, in sura 9 (no. 115) we note the absence of the introductory formula: "In the name of God, the Merciful, the Compassionate," for which a number of explanations have been offered. I suggest that the reason is precisely because most of the contents are "profane" documents, that is, treaties, military proclamations, and so forth. The first one is probably a treaty that introduces a truce:

> An acquittal, from God and His Messenger, unto the idolaters with whom you made covenant: "Journey freely in the land for four months; and know that you cannot frustrate the will of God, and that God degrades the unbelievers." [vv. 1–2]

A second document immediately follows:

> A proclamation, from God and His Messenger, unto mankind on the day of the Greater Pilgrimage: "God is quit, and His Messenger, of the idolaters. So if you repent, that will be better for you; but if you turn your backs, know that you cannot frustrate the will of God. And give thou good tidings to the unbelievers of a painful chastisement." [v. 3]

This seems to be a proclamation of Mohammed in which he denounces the accord of Hodaibiyya, after the taking of Mecca in 630. Some authors maintain that it is the definitive condemnation of polytheism and a declaration of war against paganism, from now on considered beyond the pale.

Verse 4 could be a clarification by Mohammed of the different orders he had given or, as some think, the consequence of the proclamation just preceding:

> excepting those of the idolaters with whom you made covenant, then they failed you naught neither lent support to any man against you. With them fulfill your covenant till their term; surely God loves the godfearing.

Some of the directives in this sura must be considered military orders for battle. As such, then, these military orders cannot have a permanent character and are valid only for a given situation. Their weight is strictly limited and relative. Hence they cannot become "permanent rules" or divine laws, as Muslim tradition has looked upon them:

> Then, when the sacred months are drawn away, slay the idolaters wherever you find them, and take them, and confine them, and lie in wait for them at every place of ambush. But if they repent, and perform the prayer, and pay the alms, then let them go their own way; God is All-forgiving, All-compassionate. [v. 5]

In verse 30 we find another military order, again relating to an actual situation, and not a revealed principle, as Muslims think:

> Fight those who believe not in God and the Last Day and do not forbid what God and His Messenger have forbidden — such men as practice not the religion of truth, being of those who have been given the Book — until they pay the tribute out of hand and have been humbled.

Generally in these texts we do not find the *We,* which indicates that they are not to be taken as pronouncements of God. They refer to particular situations, and I do not see the necessity (as Muslim exegetes do) of regarding them as laws that rescind the previous, much milder laws, which breathed a more tolerant spirit concerning polytheists, Jews, and Christians (cf. no. 93, sura 2:130/136–131/137; no. 109, sura 31:17). More than this, it seems to me, the fact that the above text does not make a clear distinction (though I think it refers to the unbelieving Jews) between these three classes of "unbelievers" is another proof that it is a military order of Mohammed and, hence, would be concerned with all his enemies, in general, at a given moment.

Static and Dynamic Exegesis and Muslim-Christian Dialogue

The study of the literary forms in the Koran has not yet been seriously undertaken. We would do a great favor for Muslim exegetes if we could persuade them to begin this endeavor themselves, using the principles of modern criticism which have been so successful. Such a study of literary forms will do much to free them from a number of temptations to which they have invariably succumbed during the course of centuries.

The first temptation has been to yield to the tendency to see everything as strictly and literally historical. Many have lost sight of the point that facts may be remembered or reported in various ways, depending on the emphasis and purpose of the reporting. Hence different forms or ways of expression have to be recognized. *Real* truth is not always and necessarily *historical* truth. A man may express this former meaning in a simple but figurative language that is better suited to the mentality of his audience.

Succumbing to a second temptation, the Muslim exegete tends to see the "word of God" as immobile, fixed, absolute. This attitude is the result of Muslim theology, conceiving a literalist theory of inspiration that is elaborated with an Aristotelian mentality. Hence he succumbs to the temptation to rigidity and the Koran then becomes an absolute, an eternal scripture. But when the texts are analyzed, many elements are found which refer solely to specific, temporary, and passing situations. He could, nevertheless, look upon the Koran as a "dynamic" text, a living thing which lends itself beautifully — as it has to so many pious Muslim souls — to becoming a spiritual vehicle that carries one to the encounter with God. Once freed from the static view of the usual exegesis, many points of dynamic orientation can be found which spur souls along the way of a spiritual journey. It is then discovered that the Koran has a Semitic dialectic of thought and prayer, a deep aspiration toward the mystery of God, to which one must open oneself as a response to his loving call.

Once the Koran was taken as "absolute," Islam became isolated. That is why any research into possible influences upon the formation of the Koran is excluded. The theory that makes the Koran the book "fallen from heaven" prevents the Muslim from discovering, through scientific literary criticism, all the cultural, literary, religious, juridical, and social influences which have worked together to form it. To overcome this third temptation or failing, Muslim exegesis has only to look about to see how other books, which the Koran itself recognizes as of divine origin, are studied and intelligently understood through their countries of origin, the historical circumstances in which they took shape, and the like.

I am convinced that these scientific methods, developed in the study of the Bible, would result in a much more profound appreciation of the holy book of Islam from both a human and a religious point of view. This is the first and most urgent condition for entering upon effective dialogue between Muslim and Christian.[51]

PART THREE

THE MEANING OF
THE KORAN'S MESSAGE:
MOHAMMED'S PROVIDENTIAL
MISSION REINTERPRETED IN
THE LIGHT OF CHRIST

The Koran and Christianity

It is almost impossible to find points of contact between Christianity and Islam in the traditional Muslim interpretation of the Koran. Nevertheless, I shall place in relief some of the more difficult obstacles which must be overcome by the Muslim in making such contact, following the lines suggested by J. Jomier O.P.[1]

1. "For the Moslems, all the prophets sent before Mohammed had missions limited in time and space. Mohammed alone was given a universal message. According to them, the Islam of the Koran is destined to be the religion of all men until the end of the world" (p. 21).

2. "The Moslems continued to proclaim their faith in the earlier messengers of God, and in the revealed Books (Torah, Psalms, Injil). . . . But what does faith mean in practice? They suspect the correctness of the present state of those Books, and therefore limit themselves to the Koran. They do not read our Scriptures" (p. 29). "Hence, in practice, Moslems, except very few exceptions, do not read our Scriptures. They look upon the Koran as containing all the truth, even the true Judaism and true Christianity. It is enough for them. Their respect for the Torah and the Gospel is something abstract" (p. 34).

3. Regarding the person of Jesus Christ, Fr. Jomier says: "On the one hand, the Koran speaks of Jesus with great respect; several statements suggest His holiness very clearly. But on the other hand, the Koran mentions Jesus in an apologetic context

to show that He is just a mere creature" (p. 79). "Also we must not forget that the Koran states very definitely that Jesus is only a creature. It rejects clearly the mystery of the Incarnation" (p. 84).

" 'Do not say Three!' This absolute general statement is applied by the commentators to the Christian Trinity, which the Koran does not mention. The Koran refers to a Triad: Allah, Jesus and Mary, which is not the orthodox Christian doctrine.

"Moslems, who do not realize the real significance of the term Messiah, see in the word a title of honor given to Jesus. . . . The high titles which the Koran gives to Jesus, if their full implications were understood properly, might be taken as remnants of an earlier revelation. . . . But, for the time being, categorical statements prevent any advance.

"The idea that religion is completely perfected with Islam, that the Koran has everything necessary to salvation (XVI, 91/89), and the affirmation that Jesus is only a creature (XLIII, 59) are brought out by Moslems to justify their position" (p. 86).

"According to the Koran's teaching, salvation comes directly from God. . . . Islam is opposed to any idea of sacrifice, mediation; it brings forward the ever repeated objection that God does not need all this in order to forgive; . . . Islam rejects altogether all idea of redemption" (p. 87).

4. "The religious view of the history of the world in the Koran differs completely from that of orthodox Judaism and of Christianity" (p. 112). "For Islam, on the contrary, there is no progress in the revelation of the mystery of God. The prophets periodically remind men of the religion, an unchangeable natural religion. . . . Thus it is that Islam presents itself as the last historical community in the history of the world, destined now to intransigent monotheism, destined to call upon men to worship their creator" (p.114).

This interpretation, which Muslim theology has for centuries given of the Koran's message and Mohammed's mission, after the first hundred years of the Hegirah, was primarily the work of Jews and Christians who converted to Islam. Their contribution, it is easy to understand, unfortunately had a strong influence on the anti-Christian orientation which Islam adopted in its historical and doctrinal development. If this is indeed the sole interpretation the Koran may have, I do not see how dialogue between Christians and Muslims can be successfully initiated.

I believe that Pius XII's invitation, "Show that everything that is good and right in other religions finds its deepest meaning and its ultimate perfectioning in Christ," is a challenge to the studious Catholic to find other possible interpretations for the Koran. The Easter Message of Pope Paul VI (1964) also speaks clearly of the light to be found in other religions.[2]

Therefore, before we reject the Koran entirely, because the ordinary interpretation by Muslims does not permit Catholics to see any authenticity in it, why should we not see whether another interpretation, made "with the light of Christ," might not let us find what the Muslims have not succeeded in finding?

A Muslim mystic who, touched by God, gave up a life of brigandage for one of prayer and penance — Fodayl Ibn 'Eydad (died in Mecca in the year 187 of the Hegirah, A.D. 803) — taught that "he who has understood the hidden meaning of the Koran has no need of the books of the Hadîths."[3] Is it not possible that this hidden meaning of the Koran, which many mystical Muslims suspected and attempted to uncover, and which, once discovered, could bypass the traditional interpretation of the Hadîths and the Tafsîr, could be found especially in the light of Christ's revelation? I am not talking about some esoteric meaning, as suggested by Réne Guenon and Frithjof Schwon.[4] It is more and more admitted today, and among Catholics as well, that Islam is a very special case in the history of religions because of its relationship to biblical revelation. And if we admit, as Abbé Ledit said in his letter and as I myself believe, that Islam "came to challenge Israel for its judgment of the Messiah and to impel the Church to put an end to its divisions," it is proper that the Church interpret the Koran. Just as she has the "key" to interpret

the Old Testament, she also has the "key" for the correct explanation of the Koran. But now we meet a paradox: it is not easy to
get the Muslim to accept this idea but it is far more difficult, at
the present time, to get the Christian to accept it.

Islam recognizes what it calls *al-ijtihâd,* the research and personal effort of Muslim teachers. They are not looked upon as
representatives of the community, with the charge of being spokes-
men, but as prudent and serious people, as experts who, because
of their learning, have some right to be listened to. In fact, every
Muslim who is competent may exercise this right — not, however, in any unlimited critical or Rationalist sense.[5]

It is certain that the Christian interpretation of the Old Testament has given entirely new dimensions (unknown and not accepted for twenty centuries by rabbinic learning) of the "revelation of Israel." As a Christian, however, I am not obliged to receive the Koran as a holy book, because the Church has not
accepted it as a book of the biblical canon. But we have to take
serious note of the fact that, for many centuries, part of the human
race has believed that this book has a divine origin. I accept this
fact, and am inclined to believe that it may have a real foundation. My Christian faith, at least in general, allows the possibility
of private, special, and relative revelations. Suppose, then, we
hypothetically accept this Muslim datum: that the Koran is a
revealed or inspired book (we do not thereby accept the explanation of inspiration furnished by Muslim theology). If I use the
principle of *ijtihâd,* could I not try to see whether the message of
the Koran might look quite different when it is viewed in the
authentic light of Christian revelation?

If the Koran is really, as the Muslim faith believes, a revealed
book, I should be allowed to assume this as a hypothetically accepted fact. Then, proceeding from this point, I can try to place
the Koran within the complex development of revelation by means
of a "Christian reading."

How to Read the Koran in a Christian Manner

In my opinion, the fundamental error of Muslim exegesis, as well as the theories of the Koran detailed by *kalâm* (Muslim theology), is to have made the book an "absolute," analogous to rabbinic treatment of the Torah. The Muslim exegeses and theologians forgot that the expression of the word of God through human language is a historic fact and, therefore, comes into being in time and space and in the order of the contingent and the relative. If I hypothetically accept an essential datum of Muslim faith, namely, that the Koran is a book of divine origin, I do not thereby necessarily accept all the explanations of this fact as made by Muslims, because I am convinced that these explanations are not demanded by the Koran's texts.

So as to judge better the essential datum of Muslim faith, that the Koran is an inspired book, I am convinced that Catholic scholars can verify this assumption by applying all the rules of hermeneutics which Catholic exegesis uses for the Bible. The Christian is concerned with discovering a reality that is much more profound than that which appears from a simple glance at the literal sense. He knows that the Scripture is pregnant with the mystery of Christ. If we start with the hypothesis that even the Koran may be inspired, not with actual biblical inspiration but still with supernatural inspiration, the mystery of Christ may also be found in the Koran. This is not to be accomplished by looking for superficial resemblances, which may be more or less ingenious, or by stretching the imagination. We are talking about shedding the light of authentic revelation on this mysterious book and trying to "open" it with a Christian key, to discover what the Spirit may have hidden in it.

Again, we are attempting to reread the Koran by applying a Christian key or interpretation which can only be derived from the New Testament. Hence we shall have to pay close attention to every word, every phrase and expression, every idea in the Koran to uncover their literal meaning. We have to place ourselves within the living context of Mohammed's religious activity and find how he used such-and-such an idea, why he used it, and to whom he was speaking. Then we must pass to biblical territory to see what this idea means there, and especially in the New Testament and the context of Christian revelation. Then we return with this biblical meaning to reinterpret the text of the Koran, which thus becomes "renewed" and is read in a more profound dimension.

It is true that Muslims understand and interpret the text of the Koran according to "the letter." Their method is preoccupied with analyzing every detail of the text, accepting everything in an absolute sense, and not considering either the context in which the text is found or the relative and occasional circumstances in which the text was given. We have to bring out very clearly the religious — and imperfect — situation in which Mohammed worked out his mission, with a view to its orientation to the mystery of Christ.

It is not necessary to admit that Mohammed, and after him his followers, understood the complete sense of the Koran's message. It is well to remember what St. Thomas wrote about the knowledge the prophets may have had about what they were writing: "Since the mind of the prophet is a defective instrument, even true prophets did not always know everything the Spirit intended by visions and words and deeds."[6]

When Mohammed makes use of a particular word or concept, by an inspiration coming hypothetically from God, it is not claimed that he perceives the entire extension of meaning, the totality, which that expression could carry, because of the very use Judeo-Christian revelation had previously made of that word or concept. Thus we Christians are able to understand it more profoundly, in its truer and fuller meaning, than the Muslims have been able to grasp it up to the present. Here we must consider all that Catholic exegetes have emphasized about the so-called *sensus plenior* in the Koran, which Christians are able to track down in its reading and can fraternally point out to Muslims. Thus the

"Christian light" gives the true key to the interpretation of the Koran, permitting us to include, in some manner, the prophetic mission of Mohammed in the context of the history of Christian revelation.

St. Paul speaks of the "veil" which falls between the reader and the Old Testament, with the result that Jesus was not believed in (cf. 2 Cor 3:14–16). I think an analogous veil prevents the Muslim from seeing the true and authentic countenance of Christ, and this starts with the Koran itself. Only brotherly, sincere, and loving help on the part of Christians could bring Muslims to discover in their holy book the real meaning of this message, oriented toward the "good news" of the gospel. The Muslim, then, will realize that he is being given true enrichment because he is not asked to look elsewhere, except in the book that he accepts as his only criterion of truth.

To Whom Was the Message of the Koran Addressed?

Fr. Thery O.P., under the pseudonym Hanna Zakarias, wrote:

In the course of our reading of the Koran . . . there appeared a Mohammed who was not the traditional Mohammed, disguised and camouflaged by stupid legends. We think that Mohammed has absolutely nothing of the prophet about him. His story is much more human, much simpler. In middle age, this man who till then had lived as a pagan is converted to Judaism, to the pure religion of Israel. He was spurred thereto, without any doubt, by his wife, and surely, too, by a rabbi. It was a rabbi who introduced him to Moses and the revelations of Yahweh on Mount Sinai. But there is more than this. It was a rabbi who made Mohammed the apostle of Judaism. Mohammed was nothing else but a tool in the hands of the Jews for the purpose of judaizing Arabia.

At Mecca he began nothing whatsoever, whether intellectual or apostolic. There is even more: The Koran which is presented to us as the greatest miracle of Mohammed is the work of this great rabbi![7]

In more than twenty-five years of reading the Koran, I have come to quite different conclusions. *"Amor dat novos oculos."* The majority of Islamic scholars have always insisted upon Mohammed's dependence upon Jewish doctrines — a thesis that is widely recognized, and particularly by Jewish Orientalists. But Fr. Moubarac's studies, following those of Massignon, have cast doubt upon this thesis and have advanced strong arguments establishing the Koran's originality. My conclusions are diametrically opposed to those of "Hanna Zakarias" and may, at first sight, seem inconsistent as I develop what seem to be the logical consequences of my research.

Those to whom the message of the Koran was first addressed were the Jews of Mecca and, secondly, the Jews of Medina, together with the pagan Arabs. At Medina, where Mohammed had hoped to be more readily heard by the Jewish element, he was obliged to engage in even more vigorous polemics and to defend himself from a stronger opposition. Some Christians were included in the polemics, though secondarily.

1. THE JEWS OF MECCA

Lammens, and later Montgomery Watt, have brought out the character of Mecca as a city of commerce and, therefore, a financial center. Now in general, for some unknown reason, Orientalists, and especially Jewish ones, tend to attribute more importance to the Jewish colony of Medina (Yathrib) than to that of Mecca. For example, Wensinck asserts that there were few Jews in Mecca. Hirschfeld is even more categorical: "Few Christians — not a single Jew." Fr. Lammens limits himself to the admission that "Mecca — a banking city, center of great commercial speculations, could not have been unknown to the Jews." This position has led the Orientalists to regard every Mecca sura which contains clear references to the presence of Jews as suspect. Fr. Moubarac has shown to what degree this critical principle has been responsible for relocating texts of the Mecca period to that of Medina.[8]

The presence of Jews in Mecca seems to go back to very ancient times. According to a tradition reported by Diodorus of Sicily, the sanctuary at Mecca was founded by Israelites during the reign of David, particularly by descendants of Simeon. These Simeonites — the Bani-Zomenes — are, according to Diodorus, the so-called Ishmaelites, whom the Arabs called the "first Gorhum." The feast at Mecca is supposed to have been started by the Gorhum and the ceremonies that were celebrated there were based on Hebrew history. Moreover, Jews who escaped the Babylonian exile are supposed to have taken refuge in Mecca and other parts of Arabia, and these Jews were labeled "second Gorhum" by the Arabs.

The fact that Mecca had extensive commercial dealings with Abyssinia from earliest times, and that even today there is a group of Jews in Abyssinia called the Falashas, seems to me to point to the early presence of Jews in Mecca. Indeed, it is very probable that the Abyssinian Jews came originally from Arabia, rather than from Egypt. They claim to be descendants of Jews who emigrated in Solomon's time. Rudolph Leszynsky thought he detected Sadducee traditions among the Falashas of Abyssinia, as well as in the Karaite movement.[9] Goitein remarks that the controversies with Jews in the Koran show a Karaite tendency among them.[10] But the Karaite movement began only in the eighth century.

I am inclined to think that just as the Jews of Abyssinia preserved many doctrinal aspects of the Sadducees, so did the Jews of Mecca in Mohammed's day. Although, following the destruction of the Temple in A.D. 70, the Sadducees lost influence as an organized party, and the Pharisee movement came to dominate all the Jewry of the Talmud and the rabbinate, Sadducee thinking nevertheless survived here and there, and particularly in remote places where contact with the rest of the Jewish communities of the Roman Empire was rare.[11] To me, the Koran clearly indicates that the Jews of Mecca and Medina were heavily influenced by Sadduceeism. They interpret the Torah according to the letter.

They are hard and arrogant. They are smugly complacent about their prosperity and economic position. They are not concerned with the coming of the kingdom of God, nor are they awaiting the Messiah. All their efforts aim at maintaining their privileged social position. They reject the doctrines of the resurrection of the dead, personal immortality, rewards and punishments beyond the tomb, and the existence of angels and devils.

Politically, they have found a modus vivendi with their pagan neighbors, and Mohammed's activity is resented because it disturbs the good relations between Jews and pagan Arabs. They are aware of the power of Arab pagan tradition, and a change of the religious-social-political institutions was felt to be a threat to their interests.

They therefore accepted the dominance of the pagan Arab, who in turn respected their Jewish religion, allowed them freedom to worship in their way, and conceded them a certain "tribal" autonomy. Add to this that, from time immemorial, the Jews termed the Arabs *dodanim,* "cousins" (from the word *dod,* "uncle"), and *Ishmaelites,* thus recognizing them as spurious children of Abraham.[12]

Taking all this into consideration, I think we must conclude that the largest group who heard Mohammed, and to whom he addressed his message from the very start of the first Mecca period, was the Jews.

2. THE JEWS OF MEDINA

In 622 (the year of the Hegirah), when Mohammed had to quit Mecca and seek shelter in Yathrib, which was renamed Medina ("the city"), he knew that he would come into contact with a strong Jewish community. In no other part of Arabia (except the Yemen) were the Jews so powerful and so organized, so conscious of their national unity. But it was precisely in Medina that Jewish resistance to the new "prophet" and the descendant of Ishmael finally crystallized. Here Mohammed, head of the community that is to link all the diverse elements in Medina into a common brotherhood, was occupied principally by religious matters. Fr. Moubarac has put it in sharp relief: "The 'prophetic' directs the 'political' in the evolution of the preaching in the Koran, and not the other way around."[13] (The entire passage is extremely interesting.)

This essay does not intend to develop all the arguments that support my position, namely, that Mohammed turned largely to the Jews of Mecca and, later to those of Medina, rather than to the pagan Arabs. Then, after he had been systematically spurned, he suddenly destroyed his adversaries and set himself to establishing the Abrahamitic Arab community.

Mohammed as Announcer to the Jews and Arabs of Mecca

As I remarked above, I accept as hypothetically true two essential propositions of the Muslim belief: the divine origin of the Koran's message and the genuine prophetic vocation of Mohammed; and I am studying both of them with a Christian key. At the same time, I do not accept the Muslim concept of the "book written in heaven" and given all at one time. Rather, I am convinced that the whole of the message preserved in the Koran does not represent the whole of Mohammed's apostolic work.

The call of Mohammed, as recorded for us in the Koran (no. 1, sura 96:1-5) and later broadened by tradition, does not seem to refer to a mission to Jews. Nor, at first sight, does the call seem to say to whom Mohammed much preach. It is clear, however, that the call comes from "the Lord who created Man . . . who taught by the Pen." The term *pen* points to God's teaching by means of Sacred Scripture, through which he "taught Man what he knew not," that is, revelation. Hence the call of Mohammed is tied in with the revelation already given by

God. Mecca contained not only pagan Arabs but Jews of the Sadducee tradition, who were to a large degree assimilated, especially through use of the Arabic language.

The first proclamation is the imminence of judgment and the existence of a future life after the resurrection. Neither the pagan Arabs nor the Jews, so entangled in material interests, gave a thought to judgment or accepted the belief in resurrection. The text alludes to the punishments God inflicted on the Thamudite people of Arabia, and may contain the "preaching" to the pagan Arabs (no. 7, sura 91:11–15). But I consider the following text (no. 8, sura 7) to be aimed at the Jews, who are personified in the man who refuses to believe in the judgment and to receive the orphan or feed the poor. The Jews always had disdain for Arabs in their contacts with them, as is seen in biblical and especially rabbinic literature. And the fact that the sura uses a word borrowed from the Hebrew (*mâ'ûn*, "refuge"), and presents those who pray as "full of ostentation," confirms my interpretation that we are dealing here with a Jew who practiced usury in Mecca (cf. no. 39, sura 104).

One indication of Mohammed's mission to the Jews is found in the visions — rather than oaths — that picture the "mountain of the fig, of the olives, Mount Zion and of the faithful land" (no. 10, sura 95:1–3). Muslim commentators and Orientalists have attempted different interpretations of these expressions, which they usually term "formulas of imprecation." "Hanna Zakarias" sees in them a proof that they came from the rabbi of Mecca who taught Mohammed: "Who else but the rabbi of Mecca could have sworn such solemn oaths by Sinai, by the book of Moses, by the temple?"[14]

Such grouping of terms and events is incomprehensible on the lips of anyone but a Jew. (Fr. Thery, who has written on this topic, is actually referring to no. 22, sura 52:1–4.) Mohammed has seen the image of elements that recall the history of Israel: the mount of the fig (*Bethphage*, "house of the fig"), the Mount of Olives, Sinai, and the land or city which is secure (the Holy Land or Jerusalem).

The fig was the symbol of the people of Israel, according to episodes in the gospels (Mk 11:12–14, 20–21, Mt 19:18–22). The gesture of Jesus was within the prophetic tradition of symbolic actions. The fig, symbol of Israel, remained untouched by Jesus' apostolate; it has not yielded fruits of faith and so it is cursed and dried up forever. Israel is set aside in the plan of God (cf. Lk 13:6–9, where the parable of the fig is referred to Israel). Hence, in this vision too, the fig is Israel's symbol.

The Mount of Olives is the witness of Jesus' (passing) triumph, on the eve of his passion, with his entry into Jerusalem. But it also witnesses the agony in the garden (Mk 14:26, Lk 22:39). Finally, it is eyewitness to the glorious ascension of Jesus to the right hand of the Father (Heb 2:9, Acts 1:12). But there is associated with it all the symbolism which, for a Jew, surrounds the olive. Jeremiah reminded faithless Israel that "the Lord once called you, 'a green olive tree, fair with goodly fruit'; but with the roar of a great tempest he will set fire to it, and its branches will be consumed" (Jer 11:16). The grafted olive tree is the image used by St. Paul to situate the mystery of the reengrafting of Israel into the olive tree (cf. Rom 11:17).

To Jewish ears, "Mount Sinai" evokes all of God's dealings with his people. The law, which comes forth from the Lord, corresponds to the earthly Jerusalem, which still remains the ideal of the Jews (cf. Gal 4:24–25). Jerusalem is also the "secure city" (*Amîn*), as pictured in Psalms 125:1–2; but the entire country, the Holy Land in its entirety, is the "secure" land, because God is its "protector."

A similar vision, evoking elements dear to the religious consciousness of Jewish hearers, is found in the introductory text of no. 22, sura 52:1–6, where the judgment stands at the close of Israel's history. I do not look on this text as more of an imprecation than the others, though it recalls that by which many Jews swore, in spite of the prohibition in the oral tradition, which Jesus repeated: "Do not swear at all, either by heaven . . . or by the earth . . . or by Jerusalem" (Mt 5:34–35). The "mountain" is Mount Sinai (v. 1); the "book inscribed in a parchment unrolled" is not, as Muslims interpret it, the heavenly model of the Koran but the Torah, given on Sinai and preserved in scrolls. The "temple visited" is not, as Muslim tradition and the Orientalists would have it, the temple in Mecca but the Temple of Jerusalem. This seems quite clear if one keeps in mind the full context of the preceding images. In any case, it is known that Mohammed had already decided on the practice of facing Jerusalem while praying (*qibla*); therefore Jerusalem was surely in his mind. I think we must interpret in the same manner similar expressions which have hitherto been referred to Mecca or the shrine of the Ka'aba. The subject is nearly always Jerusalem and the Jewish Temple.

The expression "the temple visited" refers to the oft expressed concept of both Testaments: the visitation of Yahweh. God visits the patriarchs. At the exodus he came to rescue Israel; at Sinai he came to give his law. But the punishments of God upon his people are also a "visitation of the Lord." The prophets looked upon events that had the nature of a judgment or punishment of God as special visitations. Most important among these were the first and the second destruction of the Temple. I think that verse 4 of sura 52 is a clear allusion to the destruction of the Temple at Jerusalem. There may also be an allusion to the most recent "visitation" God had made of the Holy City through the invasion of the Persians in the years 613–614 (cf. no. 76, sura 30:1–4/5)[15] Verse 6 evokes the miraculous passage over the Red Sea: "the swollen sea."

It is evident that all of the first part of this sura is directed to Jews who did not admit either the judgment or the future life. The second section is addressed especially to idolatrous pagan Arabs (vv. 29–49).

Another passage which seems clearly to refer to Jerusalem, and not to Mecca, is the following:

No! I swear by this land,
and thou art a lodger in this land
    [no. 40, sura 90:1–2]

The next verse reads "by the begetter, and that he begot." A traditional interpretation sees this as mention of Abraham and Ishmael. This is even more understandable if the city that is meant here is Jerusalem, the city of Abraham. The prayer we hear Abraham addressed to God, in the sura referred to as that of Abraham (no. 78, sura 14:38/35), "My Lord, make this land secure, and turn me and my sons away from serving idols," is historically situated in Jerusalem and the Holy Land. On the other hand, verse 40/37 can be understood as a prophecy of Abraham concerning Mecca and the shrine of the Ka'aba:

> Our Lord, I have made some of my seed to dwell in a valley where is no sown land by Thy Holy House; Our Lord, let them perform the prayer

"Some of my seed," then, refers to the progeny of Ishmael, the desert valley is Mecca, and the "holy house" is the shrine of the Ka'aba.

In verse 41/39 is a reference to the double descent, Israelite and Ishmaelite (Jewish Christians and Muslim Arabs). The two sons, Ishmael and Isaac, are explicitly named as though to cement the Arab-Jewish brotherhood.

Thus the land that is spoken of in the text (no. 81, sura 28:57) is not Mecca but the Holy Land. Indeed, all of the preceding context is concerned with the history of Israel and particularly Moses (a type of Christ). Verse 48 refers to the Jews, whom Mohammed invites to follow Jesus as Messiah, but who refused (v. 50). The "truth" that came to the Jews from God is Jesus Christ (v. 48). Verse 57 is usually thought of as spoken by the pagan Arabs and about the sanctuary in Mecca. But since the entire context is a discussion with Jews who believe in the Scriptures (cf. v. 53), I feel it must be ascribed to the Jews:

> They say, "Should we follow the guidance with thee, we shall be snatched from our land." Have We not established for them a sanctuary secure, to which are collected the fruits of everything, as a provision from us? But most of them know not.

The guidance here is the "way," Jesus Christ, and the land is Palestine. The entire theology of the Temple may be found in the words that follow. After the destruction of the Temple of Jerusalem, "the inviolate sanctuary," is Jesus Christ (cf. Jn 2:21–22). The Jews of Mecca think that, by following Jesus (the way), they would thenceforward be uprooted from their nation. God replies that henceforward they will have the New and indestructible Testament and fruits of all kinds (allegorically, the spiritual fruits of Jesus' work). The ignorance of the Jews regarding the mystery of Christ remains: "But most of them know not." The following verse alludes to the destruction of Jerusalem and the cities of Palestine by the Romans in A.D. 70 and, equally, to the devastation caused by the Persians during their conquest of Palestine in 613–614.

Still in the context of preaching to the Jews of Mecca, the "secure and inviolate sanctuary" is spoken of, because of which the people are attacked and despoiled (cf. no. 83, sura 29:67). This is still another reference to the destruction of Jerusalem and to the new sanctuary, Jesus Christ. Verse 68, "And who does greater evil than he who forges against God a lie, or cries lies to the truth when it comes to him?" may recall the text in John (8:44–50).

The other occasions also are always in a context of anti-Jewish polemics. No. 93, sura 2:118/124 from Medina), shows the Jews as wicked descendants of Abraham who receive no benefit from the messianic promises. In verse 129/125, the "house" is the Temple of Jerusalem, a meeting place for all humanity, and a place of "peace," of return. And Jerusalem is the place of the "great return" of all the people of Israel and all mankind at the last judgment. It was there that, with Ishmael, Abraham made the covenant with God. Abraham's prayer is for Jerusalem (the Promised Land) first of all. The apostle requested by Abraham is not Mohammed but Jesus Christ (v. 123/129), who will teach wisdom and will purify the descendants of Abraham (cf. Jn 8:56). Likewise, the context of verses 124/130–127/133 is aimed mainly at a Jewish audience. We are in Medina at the beginning of the preaching following the Hegirah, when Mohammed thinks the Jews of Medina are more ready to receive his message. "The members of this community have passed" (v. 128/134) is an expression which refers to the people of Israel as the people of God, who, after the destruction of Jerusalem, "have passed on," refusing to accept Jesus, and have received divine punishment.

It seems clear that all the Bible stories Mohammed used during the preaching at Mecca and later at Medina require a Jewish audience — people who already had some knowledge of them. But the entire history of Israel is recalled in such a way as to be a preparation for the story of Jesus.

In the Sura of the House of Imran we read:

> The first temple established for the people was that at Bekka, a place holy and a guidance to all mankind. [No. 99, sura 3: 90/96 (author's tr.)]

The Muslim interpretation, as well as that of Orientalists, considers *Bakkat* to be another name for Mecca. I feel, on the contrary, that this also is a clear allusion to Jerusalem's Temple, which the Jews considered to be the first temple for the people. Bi-bakka is the name of a place, meaning "of sorrow and tears." In the Bible we find reference to the "valley of tears" (Ps 84 (83):7). The "valley of Rephaim" was the last stop for pilgrims to Jerusalem.

"Dematerialization" of the Koran

Since this rereading of the Koran with a Christian key allows us to fathom its deeper meaning (*sensus plenior*), we must set about "dematerializing" many concepts that Muslim tradition interprets literally. Modern biblical criticism will be a great help in this process.

First, all the concepts that have to be dematerialized are already present in Semitic literature, and especially in the Bible. It seems to me that, starting with the concept of the "heavenly archetype," most texts of the Koran are poorly interpreted by Muslim exegetes. At any rate, the "mother of the Koran" and "the heavenly tables" are not the sole property of the Koran. Apocalyptic and rabbinical literature, as well as the Bible, talk about "tablets written in heaven."[16] No Catholic exegete ever thought that he had to take all these expressions literally, as books actually in Heaven, on real pages, inscribed in Hebrew or Greek or Arabic or Latin; but Muslim exegetes have thought so. It is our duty to help them go beyond such literal exegesis in order to clarify such concepts as inspiration, revelation, sacred book, etc. The construction of the Muslim theory on the "eternal archetype" of the Koran is parallel to, and perhaps dependent upon, the rabbinical theory of the everlasting Torah. Upon this concept depends the further theory of the verbal inspiration of the Koran, whose precise and perfect copy of the original Arabic is supposedly kept in Heaven.

Though it is true that certain expressions of the Koran, read literally, may support such a notion, one sees immediately, if the Koran is put back into the Semitic milieu whence it came, that these expressions are nothing other than Oriental and Semitic patterns of expression. They must be dematerialized. We have to remember that we Christians have gone through an evolution in our concepts of inspiration, from the "dictation" theory taught by Strabo and Bañez to present Catholic teaching.

Second, the distinction between the concepts of revelation and inspiration should be of help to Muslim theology in this process of dematerialization. Thus *Tanzîl* is the action of God communicating with men. This is taken in a material sense: that God literally sends down from Heaven the text of the heavenly book, communicating it at different periods of time to his messengers.[17] Because of this material conception of *Tanzîl,* the Muslim could never admit, for example, that the epistles of St. Paul might be inspired, because Paul wrote from Rome to the Corinthians or to the Colossians, and hence, since the writings do not come down from Heaven, they cannot be communications from God.

Third, when the Koran talks about the Torah, the gospels, the Zabûr (book of psalms?), Muslims understand a material, written book. *Kitab* (book) is always taken literally whenever the Koran speaks of the messengers, such as:

> We have given him the Book and made him a Prophet
> [no. 60, sura 19:13/12, 31/32]

It is Jesus himself who says: "God has given me the Book, and made me a Prophet," whereas, in speaking of the other messengers, the action of God is stressed. (Cf. no. 74:17–22, said of Moses; no. 69, sura 27:28–29, said of Solomon's letter; no. 91, sura 6:20, 89; no. 93, sura 2:50/53; etc.) I am inclined to think that it is a kind of investiture formula for a prophet: Receive the book, and give the book and wisdom. If so, then the word *kitâb* must be taken, in a parallel figurative sense, as *hikmah* (wisdom).

Thus it is useful to note numerous examples in Byzantine and Syrian iconography of Christ, the *Pantokrator,* in which the Lord is depicted holding a book which is lettered "Gospel" (*Evangelium*), as in the mosaic in the cupola of Daphni and in the apse of the cathedral of Cafalu (Italy). The child Jesus in the arms of the *panagia* Virgin of a mosaic in the church of Aghia Sophia in Istanbul also holds a book while in the mosaic of the basilica of Torcello he holds a *rotulus* or scroll. Even in Western iconography, Jesus holds the book in his hand: Christ the Master, in the cathedral of Chartres; the Christ of the tympanum of Vézelay; in Amiens; etc. In like manner, we often see the prophets and apostles holding a book as a symbol of their mission as heralds of the divine message.

All of this aids us in uncovering the figurative meaning of the word *to write* (e.g., in Jer. 31:33 and Prv 3:3, "to write upon the heart") and of the words *book, Torah, gospel,* and *Zabûr.* They do not correspond to such terms as *Pentateuch, Four Gospels, New Testament,* or *Book of Psalms.* The *suhûf* of Abraham and Moses, mentioned from the beginning of the preaching in Mecca (no. 16, sura 87:18–19), are not physical, inscribed pages. Ibn

Salâm, Ta'lâbî, Ibn Qotaiba, and other Muslim commentators speak of these *suhûf* as books. Ta'lâbî lists 48: 10 as revealed to Adam, 15 to Seth, 13 to Enoch, 10 to Abraham, etc. But all of this is the result of fantasy. Some Orientalists see allusions to apocalyptic works.[18] If we dematerialize these expressions, they convey the content of a special communication from God to Abraham and Moses, perhaps the promise of messianic salvation, or the covenant (cf. no. 15, sura 9:112/111). Mohammed must have known that the Torah in Jewish eyes, but especially in the eyes of a Sadducee, was not just the law written in the five books but, generally, the teaching of God to his people (Mosaic revelation), and I think it must be understood in this dematerialized sense in the Koran also. The Torah, as Mosaic revelation, existed before it was put into written form in the Pentateuch.[19]

In like manner, the word *law* did not mean the material book to the rabbis, or to St. Paul, or to the Koran; it meant the economy of the Sinaitic revelation. Parallel to this, the word *injîl* in the Koran does not, as Muslims usually think, mean a material, written book. Unfortunately, Christian Orientalists use the Muslim interpretation and thus lose the opportunity to point out one more historical error in the Koran, since Jesus did not write any books. Others think the expression refers to all the books of the New Testament. But the Koran has no intention of speaking of the books in the hands of the Christians. When it mentions a gospel or a book given to Jesus by God, and by Jesus to the apostles, it does not mean an actual, written text (the Four Gospels or the whole New Testament). This is only an allusion to the message and to the preaching of the evangelical revelation. The Koran's use of *gospel* or *book* should be compared to the like usage in Mark 1:15, but especially to its use by St. Paul as the perfecting of the law (cf. Rom 1:15–17, 3:21, 4:13; 1 Cor 15:1–2). The gospel was preached long before it appeared in the form of the Four Gospels.

Along with these concepts (we are but following the spiritual interpretation of various medieval and modern Muslim theologians) and the mystical tradition of Islam (Sufism), the concepts of the Koran concerning the kingdoms beyond the tomb, Paradise and Hell, must also be dematerialized.

Goldziher speaks, as do other Orientalists, of a "gnostic hostility to the Old Testament, and of Marcionite accusations of the forgery of Jewish and Christian Scriptures."[20] Although these accusations have been consistently repeated by most Orientalists, I think we may take a less harsh view. Though it is true that the Koran shows a defensive reaction toward the Jews (this is understandable), which perhaps moves to the offensive in Medina after the Hegirah, I have never discovered a single expression of Gnostic hostility to the Old Testament. As for Marcionite accusations of forgery, some misunderstandings will have to be cleared away.

The Accusation That the Texts Have Been Corrupted

At the close of the third period of Mohammed's preaching in Mecca, the Jews — among several accusations against Mohammed — repeated the charge that he was falsifying his pretended revelation (cf. no. 75, sura 15:103/101–107/105). In the answer to the accusation is the hint of something against the Jews:

> They only forge falsehood, who believe not in the signs of God, and those — they are the liars. [v. 107/105]

This insinuation becomes more and more precise in a polemic against Jews, and not against pagan Arabs:

> They measured not God with His true measure when they said, "God has not sent down aught on any mortal." Say: "Who sent down the Book that Moses brought as a light and guidance to men? You put it into parchments, revealing them, and hiding much; and you were taught that you knew not, you and your

fathers." Say: "God." Then leave them alone, playing their game of plunging.

This is a Book We have sent down, blessed and confirming that which was before it, and for thee to warn the Mother of Cities and those about her; and those who believe in the world to come believe in it, and watch over their prayers.

[No. 91, sura 6:91–92]

Here Mohammed's message stands in the same line as Mosaic revelation. The allusion to the Bible text on parchment rolls, which are shown to the people in the synagogues, is clear. There is also an accusation that the Jews hid part of the Bible's teaching. I think this must refer to the fact that the Jews "hid" (in the sense of not mentioning) the messianic prophecies concerning Jesus, which Mohammed was proclaiming to them. His message (the Koran), in fact, confirms the Scriptures that went before. It is his duty once more to warn Israel, Jerusalem, and as many as are around her (spiritually, the Jews) of the messianic office of Jesus Christ.

The expression "mother of the cities" (Ummah-l-Qurah), which commentators and Orientalists ordinarily refer to Mecca, seems, rather, to refer to Jerusalem. In fact, it is found in a context of polemics against the Jews of Mecca, where there is mention of Abraham and the prophetic line of his descendants. Mohammed, addressing himself to Jewish hearers, declares that it is his mission to remind them that they must reflect upon the Scriptures to recognize their proclamation of the coming of the Messiah, Jesus. For a Jewish audience, "mother of the cities" could not mean anything but Jerusalem (cf. no. 85, sura 42:5/7). In the Old Testament, Jerusalem is called "mother of the Jews" a number of times in connection with the image "Jerusalem, spouse of Yahweh." (Cf. Is 50:1: "Where is your mother's bill of divorce?" Jer 50:13, Hos 2:4, and Bar 4:8: "You have forgotten the eternal God, your Father, moreover you have saddened Jerusalem, your Mother.") Then follows the song of lamentation of Jerusalem, the "mother," who turns to the neighboring cities and to her "sons" (vv. 9–29).

In 4 Ezdras we read: "Since Zion, your Mother, has been afflicted" (10:9). St. Paul uses the same expression when he calls the heavenly Jerusalem "our mother," the mother of Christians, in opposition to the earthly Jerusalem, which remains the mother of the Jews. In rabbinical language, "mother of Israel" is the community itself, the people of Israel. The "land of Israel" is all of Palestine, of the Torah, but it is above all the holy city, Jerusalem.[21]

A correct interpretation of the message of Mohammed at the start of the period in Medina must note an intensified appeal to the Jews. We perceive an insistent recalling of the Mosaic covenant, the unfaithfulness of the Jews ("sowers of scandals"), and the destruction of Jerusalem, presented as an example of punishment for Israel's past sins as well as for its later obstinacy (no. 93, sura 2:38/40, 62/68). Some Jews "listen to the word of God only to change it knowingly later, after they have understood it well" (v. 70/75):

> Seeing there is a party of them that heard God's word, and then tampered with it, and that after they had comprehended it, wittingly?

There is no question here of altered written documents, as some have suggested, but rather a distorting or incorrect interpretation of the koranic text. This meaning is given to the text of no. 99, sura 3:72/78:

> And there is a sect of them twist their tongues with the Book, that you may suppose it part of the Book, yet it is not part of the Book; and they say, "It is from God," yet it is not from God, and they speak falsehood against God, and that wittingly.

Some would see this as an allusion to the oral tradition of the Jewish Talmud.[22] That some Jews would pervert the meaning of words does not imply, any more than the other texts, a direct falsification of documents but rather a distortion of the meaning (cf. no. 116, sura 5:45/41).

The accusation by Christians that the Jews had falsified the writings of the Old Testament was nothing new. On several occasions, from the time of Justin Martyr on, the fathers warn about use of the Jewish Scriptures. But the fathers extend this warning to Christian heretics, as well as Jews. St. Ephraim says that several sects in Syria had furthered the corruption of biblical texts. A like charge is found in St. Epiphanius: *"Sacras Litteras depravant, dum eas ad argumentum suum accomodare student"* (*Advers. Haeres.*, 1.I. t. 2, P.G. 41, col. 531), and especially in St. Jerome. It is also found sixty years after the death of Mohammed in the Council of Trullo.[23]

As for Jewish accusations of Christian distortion of texts, it is enough to recall that from the time of the so-called Council of Jamnia, after the destruction of Jerusalem, the use of the Alexandrine Septuagint was forbidden. In the controversy between Jews and Christians, the Jews continually reproach the Christians with false interpretation of the Old Testament.[24]

Still another misunderstanding has to be swept aside. The Koran is correct, and stands in the straight line of truth, when it casts suspicion upon the writings of Jews and the Christian heretics of Arabia with whom it deals. It is also true that to deduce from these expressions of the Koran that the Sacred Scriptures, both the Old and the New Testament, as found in the Christian churches, are textually corrupt is to go beyond the meaning of the Koran and to lack all critical spirit.

The People of the Book: **Ahl-al-Kitab**

For many centuries, Muslim tradition and Orientalists have ascribed the expression *Ahl-al-Kitâb,* "people or nation of the Scripture, or the Book," to both Jews and Christians. To disagree with this will seem rash to many, but I am more and more convinced that their ascription is mistaken and does not correspond to historical reality.

I am of the strong opinion that the term refers to a class or category of responsible people with whom Mohammed was carrying on discussion: interpreters of the Scripture, the class of doctors and rabbis. "Men of the book" would be the equivalent of the Hebrew expression *Soferim,* that is, the Scribes of Judaism, the class of interpreters and expounders of Sacred Scripture.[25] The Scribes were the men of the law, masters and teachers. They had great prestige and authority in the Jewish communities, ran the schools, and the like. They were often the highest authority in the community. Although Mohammed preached to the pagan Arabs, whether in Mecca or in Medina, he was conscious of having a special message for the people of Israel as well, and so his discussions were conducted for the most part with their leaders. If we analyze each case in which this expression is used, we will not conclude that both Jews and Christians are meant each time or that it necessarily refers to the entire Jewish community in every case. Hence the expression must be restricted to the Scribes and teachers of the Jews.

There is only one instance, in the final sura of the Koran (no. 116, sura 5:51/47), that we meet a parallel expression: *Ahl-al-Injîl,* "the people of the gospel." Here too, I think, we must understand them to be the leaders of the Christian community of Medina, who are arguing with Mohammed. There seems to be confirmation of this in the parallel expression *Ahl-al-Hadîth,* which does *not* mean "the people of the Sunna," that is, the orthodox Muslim people. The meaning is much more particular, referring to the masters of the spiritual life, who tried to remain faithful to tradition, to the Sunna, and tried to revive piety through a return to the teaching of the prophet.[26]

This restriction of the term *Ahl-al-Kitâb* to the leaders of the Jewish community — and its exclusion of the Christian community — allows us to view Mohammed's appeal to the Jews in a clearer light.

To think, as some Orientalists do, that when Mohammed was

at Mecca he had only vague ideas about the difference between Jews and Christians, and that he had begun to distinguish between them only at Medina, indicates a careless reading of the Koran. The text of the first sura from Medina (no. 93, sura 2:59/62) clearly recognizes the difference between Jews, Christians, and Sabaeans. The same distinction is found in another text, in which *Majusa* (Magi, Zoroastrians) are mentioned along with them (no. 109, sura 22:17). These Sabaeans, who are described as "monotheists and believers in the last judgment and in the future life" (cf. Heb 11:16), may be considered as Arabs who traced their descent from the tribe of Saba and who preserved Abraham's monotheism in the tradition of Ishmael. From the time of Mecca on, Mohammed knew exactly what differentiates Jews from Christians, which explains why he felt particularly impelled to preach the truths of the future life (resurrection and judgment, articles the Sadducees did not believe) and the messianic position of Jesus.

The Sowers of Scandal

We seem to meet the expressions "sowers of scandals" and "those who spread corruption" for the first time in the period of the first preaching in Mecca (no. 42, sura 89:11/12): *Alladhîna tagha'u fil-bilâdi.* The pronoun *Alladhîna* does not seem to allude, as many commentators think, to the various people just mentioned: Adhites, Thamudites, and the Pharaoh. Rather, it seems to be a clear allusion to the Jews: "those who show themselves proud in the land" (*al-bilâd* here, too, seems to be an allusion to the Holy Land and/or Jerusalem). "There they multiplied scandal. For this your Lord made the rod of punishment come down upon them" (v. 12/13). The punishment is the destruction of Jerusalem, which put an end to the Israelite nation.

A reference to increasing opposition from the Jews of Mecca, who sneeringly call Mohammed "the liar," appears in this text of encouragement, which he "received":

> Surely thy Lord knows very well
> those who have gone astray from
> His way, and He knows very well
> those who are guided.
> So obey thou not those who cry lies. They
> wish that thou shouldst compromise, then
> they would compromise.
> And obey thou not every mean swearer,
> backbiter, going about with slander,
> hinderer of good, guilty aggressor,
> coarse-grained, moreover ignoble,
> because he has wealth and sons.
> When Our signs are recited to him, he
> says, "Fairy-tales of the ancients!"
> We shall brand him upon muzzle!
>   [no. 51, sura 68:7–16]

Reading this passage, one is tempted to hear in it the echo of what St. Paul wrote in his first letter to the Thessalonians: "[the Jews] who killed both the Lord Jesus and the prophets, and drove us out, and displease God and oppose all men by hindering us from speaking to the Gentiles that they may be saved — so as always to fill up the measure of their sins" (1 Thes 2:15–16).

Mohammed is not a *reformer* of the Jews, as Blachère seems to claim by the title he gives the second part of sura 45:13/14–22/23. He is simply the announcer to the Jews of Mecca and Medina of the reality of the resurrection, the future life, and the arrival of the Messiah in the person of Jesus Christ. Here, we are in a concrete situation. The text is addressed to the Jews of Mecca, and has nothing to do with the text of no. 115, sura 9:5, which is concerned with a different circumstance and was given at Medina.

> Say unto those who believe, that they forgive those who do not look for the days of God. [Vv. 13/14–14/15]

The Jews who believe should forgive the Arabs, since God alone is judge. The Jews should be generous with the Arabs (we must remember their superior, disdainful attitude toward the sons of the "slave," the Arab Ishmaelites) ; God has been especially generous toward them:

> Indeed, We gave the Children of Israel
> the Book, the Judgment, and the Prophethood,
> and We provided them with good things,
> and We preferred them above all beings.
>
> [15/16]

The Hebrew division of Scripture is found here: Torah, Kethubin (the wisdom books), and Nabiyin (prophetic books) (cf. no. 91, sura 6:89). The foods referred to are the quails of the desert, and bring to mind all the kindness of God toward Israel.

> We gave them clear signs of the Command; so they differed not, except after the knowledge had come to them, being insolent to one another. [16/17]

This passage concerns the plan of God (the "command") ; hence it does not have to do with Mohammed's mission, as the Orientalists and Muslim exegetes would have it. Rather, it concerns the messianic mission of Jesus Christ. Israel, impelled by pride and envy, was divided when "KNOWLEDGE," that is, Jesus Christ (cf. 1 Cor 1:30), came into their midst.

The solution to the mystery of Christ will be presented to the Israelites and the Muslims on the day of resurrection:

> Surely
> thy Lord will decide between them
> on the Day of Resurrection touching
> their differences.
> Then we set thee upon an open way
> of the Command; therefore follow it,
> and follow not the caprices of those
> who do not know.
>
> [no. 73, sura 45:13/14–17/18]

Israel's response to this privilege and benefaction from God is ingratitude. Thus on two occasions God clearly showed his justice:

And we decreed for the Children of Israel in the Book: "You shall do corruption in the earth twice, and you shall ascend exceeding high." [no. 74, sura 17:4]

Verses 5 to 7, though variously interpreted, are in my judgment a recollection of an oracle concerning the two destructions of Jerusalem: at the time of the Babylonian captivity and by the Romans in A.D. 70.

The expression "sowers of scandal" is almost always associated with the defect of pride we find in several other texts, but not always with reference to the Jews (cf. no. 69, sura 27:49/48; no. 70, sura 18:93/94; no. 75, sura 16:90/88; no. 76, sura 30: 40/41; no. 79, sura 12:73; etc.). But the text of no. 86, sura 10:41/40, seems to refer to the Jews, since I think the whole context refers to the announcement of the messiahship of Jesus (vv. 38/37–46/45):

This Koran could not have been forged
apart from God; but it is a confirmation
of what is before it, and a distinguishing
of the Book, wherein is no doubt, from
the Lord of all Being. [38/37]

. . .
No; but they cried lies to that whereof
they comprehended not the knowledge, and whose
interpretation has not yet come to them.
Even so those that were before them
cried lies; then behold how was the end
of the evildoers! [40/39]

And some of them believe in it, and some
believe not in it. Thy Lord knows very well
those who do corruption. [41/40]

The Jews of our Lord's time always accused him of lying (cf. Jn 8:55, 10:20), and now the Jews call Mohammed a liar, who is announcing Jesus' messiahship to them: "that whereof they comprehended not the knowledge [the mystery of Christ], and whose interpretation has not yet come to them." The rejection of this announcement is still another scandal.

From the time of the first preaching in the city of refuge, Medina, after the expulsion from Mecca, Mohammed turned to the Jews of Medina. He thought they were more receptive to the announcement of both the resurrection and the messiahship of Jesus. To his astonishment, he was turned down again, and the struggle became more violent. The Koran has preserved a few fragments of this dialogue with the Jews, which condemns them even more definitely:

> God has set a seal on their hearts and on their hearing
>   and on their eyes is a covering,
> and there awaits them a mighty chastisement
> > [no. 93, sura 2:6/7]

Much earlier, Jesus had condemned the blindness of the Jews who refused to recognize him (Mt 15:14). St. Paul spoke of their blindness and of a veil that prevents them from seeing the mystery of Christ (Rom 11:25; 2 Cor 3:15).

> When it is said to them, "Do not corruption in the land!"
> they say, "We are the only ones that put things right." [10/11]

> Truly, they are the workers of corruption
>   but they are not aware [11/12]

> Those are they that have bought error
>   at the price of guidance,
> and their commerce has not profited them,
>   and they are not right-guided. [15/16]

> The likeness of them is as the likeness of a man
> who kindled a fire, and when it lit all about him
> God took away their light, and left them in darkness
>   unseeing,
>   deaf, dumb, blind —
> so they shall not return [16/17]
> > [no. 93, sura 2]

In addition, allusion is made here to the low price, the thirty silver pieces, paid by the Sanhedrin to Judas to get their hands on Jesus; and the "way of perdition" is sin, in opposition to the right way, or the "guidance" (*hûdah*), which is Jesus Christ (cf. Jn 14:6). The Jews, through their history, had kindled a light, the revelation of God, and when the Messiah came, "the Light of the World," God took the light away from Israel and Israel remained blind because the Jews did not follow Jesus (cf. Jn 8:12).

In this same sura (2), "sowers of scandals" is further applied to the Israelites, in the story of Moses (no. 93, sura 2:57/60; cf. no. 89, sura 7:160), and again to the Jews of Medina who oppose the preaching of Mohammed (no. 93, sura 2:201/205, 219/220).

We find this expression some forty times in the Koran, and for the most part in a context which deals with the Israelites or with the Jewish contemporaries of Mohammed. In the last sura it is clearly affirmed of the Jews, who have now refused to accept the message of the Koran (no. 116, sura 5:69/64):

The Jews say: "the hand of God is now closed!"
Let their own hands be closed and chained,
and let them be accursed for what they have said!
For on the contrary both hands of God are open and wide
and he bestows grace upon whomever he wills;
and surely that which has been revealed to you by your Lord
increases in many of them
stubborn rebellion and impiety:
we have raised up among them hostility and hate
until the day of the resurrection.

Each time that they will light a fire of war
God will put it out;
And they will make every effort
to sow scandal upon the earth
but God loves not the sowers of scandal!

"The Hand of God Is Closed"

If we are to understand the reactions of the Jews of Mecca and Medina to Mohammed's preaching, we must first understand their mentality and rabbinic teaching. Mohammed presented himself as a "spokesman for God," not only to his own people but also to the Jews who lived among the Arabs. Every Jew of that era was convinced that the "Spirit of God" did not manifest himself outside the Holy Land (Palestine) nor beyond the limits of the Jewish community. After Israel was divided, full revelation became impossible, and after the exile, prophetic revelation no longer existed. What *did* exist, to their mind, was prophecy of a lower kind. The community of Israel, and that living in Palestine, was an essential condition for the activity of the "Spirit." Some even thought that the action of the Spirit was limited to the city of Jerusalem. Other rabbis thought only Palestine was "sanctified." A person could experience the movement of the Spirit upon the high seas, and thus be a prophet (e.g., Jonah). But foreign lands were impure territories, and hence revelation there was impossible. Finally, the Spirit speaks not only when the chosen person is worthy but also when the community is worthy.[27]

Mohammed's claim to speak to the Jews in the name of God was unacceptable and inconceivable to them. He was not a member of the Israelite community; what was worse, he was an Arab descendant of Agar and Ishmael. According to talmudic tradition, Ishmael was not considered "seed of Abraham" but the "dog" which Abraham cannot save.[28] Furthermore, he was representative of the three principal sins: impurity, robbery by killers, and idolatry (*Genesis Rabba,* 63; Jalkut, 833). A rabbinic legend depicts the Israelites demanding their inheritance of the sons of Ishmael and of Ketura in the presence of Alexander the Great. (*Synedrin,* 98; *Genesis Rabba,* 61) Hence for centuries there had existed a national aversion, if not hatred, for the Arab by the Jew. Though the Jews of Mecca and Medina had business and social relations

The Meaning of the Koran   131

with Arabs, they were convinced that God could never charge an
"impure Arab" with teaching the chosen people.

The ordinary teaching of the rabbis was that prophecy had
ceased completely when the Temple of Jerusalem was destroyed
in A.D. 70. There were even those who taught that prophecy, as
an act of the Holy Spirit, had ceased with the death of the last
prophets (cf. Ps 74:9; 1 Mc 4:46, 9:27; Dn 3:38; Josephus
Flavius, *Antiquitates,* 13:1, 1). Thus it was in light of this way of
thinking that the Jews flatly told Mohammed: "The hand of God
is closed."

For many years previous to this time, rabbinic tradition had
ridiculed a certain "pneumatic" emphasis which appeared in the
primitive Christian community, conscious, as it was, of the Spirit's
active presence within it.[29] What effect could be produced by a
"son of Ishmael," who, if he did not claim to be a prophet sent
to the Jews but only to his own Arab people, nevertheless claimed
to bring the Jews the word of God (*Bath Qôl*)! As if to authenti-
cate his mission, Mohammed points to his visions of Sinai and
Jerusalem, and especially to the journey to the Temple (*Aqsa*)
(no. 74, sura 17:1).

But Mohammed is quite sure that the hands of God are not
closed; rather, both hands are wide open, and God grants his
grace to whomever he pleases. These words may be a distant echo
of those spoken by John the Baptist: "And do not presume to
say to yourselves, 'We have Abraham as our father'; for I tell you,
God is able from these stones to raise up children to Abraham"
(Mt 3:9). Confronted with the exclusivism of Jews and Christians
alike, Mohammed proclaimed the universality of the divine protection for all those who have been disinherited from the promise
of Abraham:

Say the Jews and Christians,
"We are the sons of God, and His beloved ones,"
Say: "Why then does He chastise you for your sins?
No; you are mortals of His creating;
He forgives whom He will, and He chastises
   whom He will."

[no. 116, sura 5:21/18]

This consciousness of being God's privileged ones is impressed upon Mohammed first by the Jews and then by the Christians of Medina as a reason for their refusal to believe him. This consciousness of "election" is sometimes emphasized just to offend and humble others,[30] and Mohammed reacts precisely against this offensive aspect. Mohammed remains and speaks of himself as the "prophet of the Gentiles," of the Arabs, the Ishmaelites, of the peoples whom the Jews (and Christians) of Mecca and Medina classed as excluded and abandoned by God.

Fr. Moubarac writes:

Mohammed is THE PROPHET OF THE GENTILES (no. 89— sura 7: 156/157–158). Perhaps this expression, related to Christianity, is the best rendering of the most beautiful, without doubt, title claimed by the apostles of Islam. But as he who is called the apostle of the Gentiles was not thereby detached from his own people, so also he who called himself their prophet did not restrict himself to his own. He communicated to them the revelation which was destined for them but which they had not received up to that time. This revelation is neither the Bible nor the Gospel, since the Koran is absolutely original. Yet it is equivalent to both because it represents the primitive revelation which Bible and Gospel had brought in their own times. The Koran re-edited it, not for all people in general, but rather for the sons of Ishmael especially, and in preference to other peoples who still had to wait. Isaac's people had to learn the language of Moses and Jesus, but they learned it with a pure Arabic accent. Thus the Koran comes forward as the heritage of all the believers.[31]

I should like to note an important fact. The rabbis admitted that although prophetic revelation ended definitively with the destruction of the Temple in A.D. 70, God was still able to communicate with his people through the "heavenly voice" (*Bath Qôl*). Literally, *Bath Qôl* means "daughter of a voice," that is, a supernatural voice, sometimes likened to the cooing of a dove (cf. Jn 1: 32). The "heavenly voice" was generally thought of as a personal inspiration, which did not involve the Jewish community; much less did it substitute for the Torah. We read in the Babylonian Talmud: "When the last prophets, Haggai, Zedhariah and Malachi died, the Holy Spirit ceased in Israel. Yet it was granted them to hear [the communications from God] by means of a heavenly voice (*Bath Qôl*) (Yoma, 9, b; cf. also Tosephta: Sotah, 13:2).

In the Koran, especially after the second period of preaching in Mecca, when the arguments and teaching of the Jews increased steadily, we often meet the imperative: *Qul,* or "Say!" Most of the injunctions of the "heavenly voice" seem to be aimed at the Jews (cf. no. 59, sura 15:89; no. 60, sura 19:76/75; no. 63, sura 43:81; no. 64, sura 72:1, 20, 21, 22, 26/25; no. 65, sura 67:23, 24 (26), 28, 29, 30; no. 66, sura 23:30/29, 86/84, 88/86, 90/88, 95/93, 99/97, 118, etc.). Notice that this expression occurs most often at the end of the third period of the Mecca preaching. It also appears in Medina, but not quite so often. To understand the connection between this formula of the Koran and the "heavenly voice" of the rabbis, we have to keep in mind the different reactions of the Jewish audiences in Mecca and Medina. In Medina, the arguments take a different tone; they are more pugnacious. Mohammed realized that the situation had changed, and so his language changed with it. God still has not closed his hand. His ways are quite different from man's ways. God sent a poor Jew to proclaim his word, and thus confound the wise of this world, when the apostle Paul talked to the philosophers of cultured Athens (cf. 1 Cor 1:27). And why should not a new gift of God come to some of Israel's sons, a gift difficult to discern? Once more God chooses an instrument which has neither nobility nor value in the eyes of the Jews. He does it deliberately, to leave them no room for boasting. Can he not raise up a son to Abraham from the stones of the desert and send him to vindicate the honor of Christ and the Mother whom the Jews have outraged (cf. Jn 8:41, 48–50), to challenge them to review the judgment they made on the Messiah, Jesus Christ?

God grants his grace to whom he wills, even to a son of Ishmael, a descendant of Abraham. Neither the privileges conceded to the Israelites in the past nor the gifts of mercy and grace

lavished upon the Christians have exhausted the infinite goodness
of God! The hands of God, both hands, are still open wide! (Cf.
no. 116, sura 5:69/64.)

Initial Presentation of the Mystery of Christ

Mohammed's Jewish audience imagined God in Heaven, sur-
rounded by his "council" (*sôd*) (cf. Ps 82:89, Dn 33:2–3, Is
40:1). Together with his council, God discussed the decrees which
concerned the running of the world. Amos announced that God
will do nothing before manifesting his *sôd* (divine plan) to his
servants and "prophets" (cf. Am 3:7). The true prophet could be
known from the false prophet because the true one has taken part
in the heavenly council (cf. Jer 23:18, 22, Jb 15:8, etc.). To understand and know the *sôd* — that is, the mysteries of God —
meant to have participated as "prophet" in the "council" and then
to have been deputed to unveil the divine decrees, and the treasures
of God, to men.

Now in many texts of the Koran it is repeated with a certain
insistence that Mohammed is not party to the "mystery of God,"
nor does he possess the "treasure of God." He is aware of the
limits of his mission:

> Say: "Surely I possess no power
> over you, either for hurt or for rectitude."

> Say: "From God shall protect me not
> anyone,
> and I shall find, apart from Him, no
> refuge,
> excepting a deliverance from God
> and His messages!"
>
> [no. 64, sura 72:21, 24/23]

Say: "I cannot obtain for myself
any advantage;
nor remove far from myself an injurious thing,
except in so far as God wills."

If I knew the "Mystery" [of God = *al-ghaiyeb*]
I should enjoy enough [spiritual] goods
and evil would not be able to strike me.
But I am only an ADMONISHER
and a MESSENGER of good news
to people who believe.

[no. 89, sura 7:188]

Say: "I am not an innovation among
the messengers, and I know not what
shall be done with me or with you.
I only follow what is revealed to me;
    I am only a clear warner."
[no. 90, sura 46:8/9]

Just as Noah told his people that he did not know the mysteries
of God (cf. no. 77, sura 11:33/31), Mohammed also expressly
denies knowledge of the divine mysteries and possession of the
"treasures of God":

Say: "I do not say to you, 'I possess
the treasuries of God'; I know not the Unseen
And I say not to you, 'I am an angel';
I only follow what is revealed to me."
[no. 91, sura 6:50]

Al-ghaiyeb is a key word in the Koran; literally, it means
"absence," "that which is hidden," "mystery," the "royal and
divine mystery." Hence it must be taken as the equivalent of the
Christian term *mystery*.

Keeping in mind this confession Mohammed made about the
"mysteries of God," we must place his presentation of the figure
of Jesus Christ in the general context of Mohammed's mission. It
is absolutely necessary to fix the situations in which the Koran's
texts on Jesus Christ and the Christians were uttered. Remember,

archical organization of the authentic, orthodox Church of Christ are not even referred to in the Koran. Hence it follows that the Koran deliberately limits itself to the actual, existent situation in the neighborhood of Mecca and Medina, where Mohammed's message was proclaimed. This fact is of capital importance for understanding why Christ is mentioned in the Koran. It appears that both Muslim commentators and Christian apologists have not weighed this fact sufficiently.

The Koran is the special "revelation" destined for the pagan Arabs, Ishmael's descendants. It is the beginning of a journey in the direction of God. It is the disclosure of the First Commandment to an idol-worshiping people and, at the same time, the initial step forward is comparable to the start of the Hebrew people's religio-social development in the Sinai desert under Moses' leadership. The psychology and religious content of the message from Sinai stands comparison with the Koran's message; very deep spiritual and psychological resemblances are not lacking. In both cases, God prescribes the law of obedience in a series of parallel events: the two visions (no. 57, sura 20:37; no. 30, sura 53:13), the miraculous confirmation (no. 57, sura 20:24; no. 30, sura 53:18; no. 74, sura 17:1; cf. no. 42, sura 89:20), the dilation of the breast (no. 57, sura 20:26; no. 5, sura 94:1). Both Moses and Mohammed are accused of using magic, and are labeled "sorcerers." Moses is called a magician (five times) because of the miracles he worked before Pharaoh (no. 49, sura 51:39; no. 58, sura 26:33/34; no. 80, sura 40:25/24; no. 87, sura 36:48/49; no. 89, sura 7:106/109). Mohammed is called a sorcerer twice, but the reason is not given (no. 61, sura 38:3/4, and no. 86, sura 10:2; both texts are identical). Also, the expression *Majnûn* (possessed) occurs eleven times in the Koran. It is applied to Moses twice (no. 49, sura 51:39; no. 58, sura 26:26/27), is used to describe Mohammed seven times (no. 18, sura 81:22; no. 22, sura 52:29; no. 51, sura 68:2, 5; no. 52, sura 37:35/36; no. 55, sura 44:13/14; no. 59, sura 15:6), and is used once of Noah (no. 50, sura 54:9).[32]

The religious, ethical, and social ideology of the Sinai desert is repeated in Mohammed's situation in Mecca and Medina. This is not true of the Israel of Christ's time, and much less true of orthodox Christianity of the seventh century. But the Koran is also an initial presentation of the mysterious figure of Jesus Christ to the Arabs, and most of all an appeal to the Jews of Mecca and Medina to recognize that Christ is the Messiah.

In the Koran itself, a mysterious evolution toward Christ can be traced. Towering over all the other biblical figures portrayed in the Koran are Jesus, the Messiah, and his Mother, the Virgin Mary. Mary is much more detailed in portrayal than Jesus. This fact seems clear: it is Mary who presents her Son; the figure of Jesus remains very vague. Hence we may say that there is only the hesitant beginning of a presentation of Jesus in the Koran, which should have been clearly brought out by Christians. It was not given to Mohammed to have knowledge of the mysteries of God, and so, to this very day, Islam is still blocked from making its journey to Christ.

What Kind of Christian Did Mohammed Meet?

It is not easy to get a clear picture of the Christian situation in Arabia in the seventh century, when Mohammed came on the stage of history. Daneus, in his commentary on the *De haeresibus* of St. Augustine, wrote that Arabia abounded in heresies — *"Ferax haereseon Arabia"* — as did neighboring Egypt. Indeed, from the fifth century on it was a favorite place of exile, used by Byzantine emperors for heretics or people suspected of heresy. But there are very few historical references to help us establish what the Christianity of Arabia, just before Mohammed's time, was like.

Eusebius speaks of Berillus, "bishop of the Arabs" of Bosra, a contemporary of Alexander Severus (222–235).[33] St. Jerome says that toward the end of his episcopal career, Berillus fell into the heresy of Modalism, and professed that the Word did not have a personality of its own before the Incarnation. St. Jerome is supposed to have seen letters that were exchanged between Berillus and Origen.[34] St. Epiphanius listed, toward the end of the fourth century, various heretical currents and sects that were floating about Arabia, such as the Audiani, whom Epiphanius reproached with anthropomorphism and the celebration of Easter on the Jewish Passover. They seem to have had monasteries in Arabia, but were headed for oblivion.[35] The Valesians, who are said to have been Arabs, mutilated their neophytes and rejected the law and the prophets; their headquarters was at Bacatha, near Philadelphia. There were also Elkesaites or Ebionites, related sects, and Antidicomarianites, who claimed that Mary had other children besides Jesus. At the other end of the scale were the women who offered sweets to Mary as a sacrifice and divine honors, as, "Mother of God."[36] Nestorius was exiled to Arabia in A.D. 435, was there but a short time, and was transferred to Egypt. It may be that he was not responsible for the spread of Nestorianism in Arabia. Nevertheless, about that time some bishops of Arabia lined up with the Nestorian doctrine. Several Monophysite sects were there too: the Phantasiasts; Paul of Beit Ukamin, nicknamed Niger, with his followers; the followers of John Philoponos; and some Cononites who held tritheistic beliefs.

It is also well to remember that the Christians of Arabia in Mohammed's time were mostly individual men without a following, who had preserved very little of authentic Christianity. We should not look for true, organized, Christian communities, with bishops and priests, at least not in Mecca or Medina, where Christians were probably rather ignorant and careless about their faith.[37]

The scant allusions to Christians in the Koran are not sufficient to identify them. As I said before, I exclude all the texts which speak of the "people of the book" because I am convinced they refer to Jewish learned men, to rabbis or Scribes.

Although we meet the expression "sons of Israel" in the suras of the Mecca period, there is no clear allusion to a Christian community. Nor is there explicit mention of Christians even where the Koran records the annunciation to Mary and the birth of Jesus (no. 60, sura 19:1–41/40). The entire context reveals that the story is intended to present the figure of Christ to the pagan idolators of Mecca and to the Jews who resided there. A late Muslim interpretation sees the Jews and the Christians, together, mentioned in the "Fatiha," the first sura of the Koran:

> Guide us in the straight path,
> the path of those whom Thou hast blessed,
> not of those against whom Thou arc wrathful,
> nor of those who are astray.
>
> [no. 46, sura 1:5–7]

According to this Muslim interpretation, those with whom God is angry are the Jews, and the Christians are those who have wandered from the right path.

There are some who claim to see a reference to Christians in the text of one of the last Mecca sermons:

> And do not drive away those who call
> upon their Lord at morning and evening
> desiring His countenance; nothing of their
> account falls upon thee, and nothing of
> their account falls upon them, that thou
> shouldst drive them away, and so become
> one of the evildoers.
>
> [no. 91, sura 6:52]

It is not clear from the context that these people are actually Christians. On the other hand, the same sura alludes to two communities which received the Holy Scriptures (v. 157/156) before the revelation reached the Arabs:

> This is a Book We have sent down, blessed;
> so follow it, and be godfearing; haply so
> you will find mercy;

lest you should say, "The Book was sent down
only upon two parties before us, and we
have indeed been heedless of their study"
>   [no. 91, sura 6:156/155–157/156]

These two communities (*ta'ifa*) are certainly the Jews and the
Christians. Thus also in sura 61 (no. 100), which is a polemical
passage countering the Jewish resistance to Mohammed's preach-
ing. It speaks of the origin of the two communities, Jewish and
Christian. The passage first recalls the resistance of the Jews to
Moses, then to Jesus' preaching, who in turn tells them Mohammed
would come to restore to him the honor the Jews refused him (cf.
Jn 8:50). Then the apostles are mentioned:

O believers, be you God's helpers, as
Jesus, Mary's son, said to the Apostles.
>   "Who will be my helpers
>   unto God?" The Apostles
>   said, "We will be helpers of God."
>   And a party of the Children of Israel
>   believed and a party disbelieved.
>   So we confirmed those who believed
>   against their enemy, and they became masters.
>   [no. 100, sura 61:14]

The apostles, Jesus' disciples, are God's "helpers." The expression
reminds one of St. Paul: "For we are fellow workers for God"
(1 Cor 3:9). A section of the sons of Israel who accepted Jesus
was "confirmed" by God, and emerged victorious. This is surely
an allusion to the beginnings of the Christian Church, though the
name, *al-Nassârâ*, is not given.

Sometimes Christians are explicitly named in the Koran, in
connection with the followers of monotheism (no. 93, sura 2:59/
62; no. 109, sura 22:17; no. 116, sura 5:73/69). They are criticized, as are the Jews, for their exclusiveness. The expression is
related as an opinion current among Jews and Christians rather
than as a doctrine of the Church.

And they say, "None shall enter Paradise
except that they be Jews or Christians."
Such are their fancies. Say: "Produce your proof,
    if you speak truly."
                                [no. 93, sura 2:105/111]

Rather than reflecting the dogmatic teaching of Christian ortho-
doxy, these texts present the attitude of individual Christians or a
group which showed signs of hostility to other Christians and the
Jews. The antagonism between Christians and Jews is one of
the barriers that halted Islam on its way to Christ, just as the
divisions among Christians stopped Islam from discovering the
true face of Christ (cf. Jn 17:21). Salvation is a pure gift of
God, which he bestows upon all those who do good, whether they
be Jews, Christians, or others:

Nay, but whoever submits his will to God,
being a good-doer, his wage is with his Lord,
and no fear shall be on them, neither shall they sorrow.

The Jews say, "The Christians stand not on anything";
the Christians say, "The Jews stand not on anything";
yet they recite the Book. So too the ignorant
say the like of them. God shall decide between them
on the Day of Resurrection touching their differences.
                        [No. 93, sura 2:106/112–107/113]

In this same sura (2), the text (vv. 169/174–171/176) does
not refer to Christians but to Jews. Mohammed was acceptable
neither to Jews nor Christians because both groups were unable to
comprehend the true meaning of his mission. They could not see
why Mohammed did not simply become a Jew or join one of the
Christian sects:

Never will the Jews be satisfied with thee, neither the Christians, not till thou followest their religion. Say: "God's guidance
is the true guidance." If thou followest their caprices, after the
knowledge that has come to thee, thou shalt have against God
neither protector nor helper.

And they say, "Be Jews or Christians and you shall be guided." Say thou: "Nay rather the creed of Abraham, a man of pure faith; he was no idolater."

[no. 93, sura 2:114/120, 129/135][38]

Who were these *an-Nassârâ*? They differed from the Jews when praying. The Jews turned their faces toward Jerusalem when they prayed; the Christians faced the Orient (cf. no. 93, sura 2:140/145). We also find criticism of exaggerated veneration of angels and saints, promoted by ignorant Christians (cf. no. 99, sura 3:73/79–74/80).

From these scanty details, it is not possible to give a confident identification of these Christians. The Koran's rejection of the expression "to take a son" (*ittakhâdha waladän*) can refer to the polytheist idolaters because of the tone and context of sexual generation, but it also reminds one of the Nestorian formula which spoke of a human person being taken into the divinity and becoming "Son of God." Likewise, the rejection of the Monophysite formula, "God is the Messiah, Son of Mary" (*Alläh hüwa al-Masîh Ibn Mariam*), does not, in itself, indicate a rejection of the orthodox formula. This rejected formula is not correctly rendered as "the Christ, Son of Mary, is God," because the word *Alläh* (God) is the subject of the sentence and not an attribute of *al-Masïh* (the Christ). To understand this nuance, we must remember the rules concerning the *communicatio idiomatum* (cf. no. 116, sura 5:19/17).[39] It is certain that there were some elements of Monophysite and Nestorian doctrine in Arabia, and these formulas lead us to think that the Christians in question must have been of these groups.

The same must be said about the rejection and condemnation of a trinitarian teaching which bears no relation to the orthodox Christian formula. There are indications during the Mecca period of an Arab reaction against Mohammed's invitation to consider Jesus an example to imitate:

And when the son of Mary is cited as an example, behold, thy people turn away from it and say, "What, are our gods better, or he?" They cite not him to thee, save to dispute [no. 63, sura 43:57–58]

Certainly some Mecca pagans and Jews, and perhaps some Christians, made use of the figure of Jesus to dispute with Mohammed. The echo of these discussions is heard in another Mecca sura, which contains a hint of a material conception of the Trinity that is far removed from the genuine Christian doctrine.

He — exalted be our Lord — majesty! — has not taken to Himself either consort or a son. [no. 64, sura 72:3]

This text, in connection with others (no. 66, sura 23:80/78–94/92; no. 67, sura 21:19–27; no. 116, sura 5:116), sheds an interesting light on the misconceptions held by the Christians with whom Mohammed was in contact. We have a statement and formulation of the tritheism which seems to have been professed by some Christian heretics in Arabia, who believed in a "trinity" composed of God (the Father), Mary, as a goddess and "wife" of God (the Holy Spirit), and Jesus (the Son of God and Mary).

In reference to this, it is useful to remember that the word *spirit* (*rûh*) is feminine gender in Semitic languages and hence can cause great misunderstanding. Thus some heretics took "Holy Spirit" for "mother of Jesus" by a misinterpretation of the words in Matthew's Gospel (3:16–17). At the baptism of Jesus the Holy Spirit appears in the form of a dove, and the heretics understood the words "This is my beloved Son, with whom I am well pleased" as spoken by the Spirit. Because *rûh* is feminine, the Holy Spirit was identified with the Virgin Mary, the *Theotokos*. St. Jerome tells how heretics fell into this same error by not attributing the words to God the Father.[40]

The fact, therefore, that Mohammed condemned such formulations of tritheism does not at all imply what Muslim theology and Christian apologetics erroneously thought: that Mohammed rejected the Christian dogma of the Trinity that there is one God in three Persons, or the dogma of the Incarnation of the second Person of the Trinity. The condemnation of these errors, professed by heretical Christians, cannot be stretched to condemnation of these Christian doctrines in their correct formulations. There is not the slightest hint of them in the Koran. It just does not mention them; and if it does not mention them, obviously it does not condemn them.

Eminent Position of Jesus in the Koran

Fr. Moubarac recognizes that a new analysis of the Koran's portrait of Jesus must still be made. There is a problem concerning Jesus in the Koran, and generations of Muslims, up to the present day, have been faced with it.[41] Much has been written about the place of Jesus and Mary in the Koran, but it may be that the real reason why Jesus is wrapped in mystery in it has still to be found. Jesus, as presented in the Koran, is qualified with the title "servant." This is especially true of the texts which argue with the Jews. I think that the aim of these texts is to present his messianic work in relation to the prophecies about the "servant of Yahweh" in Isaiah. The Koran counters the messianic triumphalism of some Jews by first presenting Jesus, not in the glory of Mount Thabor, to which only privileged ones were invited, but in the sweetness and meekness of the one who said: "— Learn of me; for I am meek and lowly of heart" (Mt 11:29).

The insistence — which might seem deliberate — with which the Koran emphasizes the humanity of Christ is not intended — as the Muslim commentators and anti-Muslim Christian apologists claim — to be a final and absolute denial of Christ's divinity. Jesus is described as *Issa, Ibn Mariam* — Jesus, Son of Mary — and must be seen in the light of the Koran's special purpose in "rehabilitating" Jesus in the wake of the blasphemies against him and Mary. Professor Massignon called attention, on more than one occasion, to the text of St. John that refers to the insinuation of the Jews that Mary conceived Jesus through fornication. The usual Christian exegesis is that, in biblical language, adultery refers to the unfaithfulness of Israel to God, her spouse. But it can be seen from the context that the Jews who were arguing with Jesus were boasting about their descent from Abraham: "Abraham is our father" (Jn 8:39). Jesus says to them: "If you were Abraham's children, you would do what Abraham did, but now you seek to kill me, a man who has told you the truth which I heard from God; this is not what Abraham did. You do what your father [i.e., the devil] did" (Jn 8:40). Because Jesus has thrown doubt upon their descent from Abraham, the Jews retaliate by an insult. They attack the reputation and honor of his mother. They said to him: "We have not been born of fornication; we have one Father, God" (Jn 8:41).

We have to remember also that both the Talmud and the Midrashes contain allusions to the spurious origin of Jesus. Krauss wrote: "The illegitimate birth of Jesus has always been a firm dogma of Judaism. Both the ancient and modern literature of the Jews clearly state it. . . . It remains a living truth in the mind of every Jew of simple faith because it was passed on to him by his parents as a fact."[42] Every Jewish source which speaks of Jesus tends to put him in a bad light by ascribing illegitimacy to him, the practice of sorcery with the help of the devil, and a shameful death. At Mecca, too, this blasphemy was current among the Jews. Mohammed — according to Jesus' promise in the gospel — is a man whom God has charged with rendering public witness to the Jews of Jesus' supernatural character, his holiness, and the holiness of his Mother. The Koran will register the fact of a curse upon those who have dishonored Mary, "for their unbelief, and their uttering against Mary a mighty calumny" (no. 102, sura 4:155/156).

If we read closely these texts concerning Jesus and Mary, and keep in mind also the rabbinic tradition concerning them, we begin to see a constant preoccupation to defend the figure of Christ and his Mother. An essential aspect of Mohammed's

mission is just this vindication of Christ's honor before the Jews
of Arabia, and more, before the Jews of this world. With this
in mind 'we may understand Jesus' prophetic vision of the
future in which he saw a 'bastard' son of Abraham intent upon
refuting the blasphemous accusation, 'Yet I do not seek my
own glory: there is One who seeks it and he will be the judge'
(Jn 8:50). The heavenly Father will do him justice, and in
the course of history Mohammed became an instrument of this
justice.[43]

Another thing to bear in mind when we reread the Koran in
the light of Christ, as I am attempting to do, is that it becomes clear
that this inchoate presentation of the mystery of Christ is meant
for the idolatrous Arab of the time, who up to then was cut off
from the gospel, and for the Jew of Arabia. Such a presentation —
considering the manner in which we think God goes about teaching mankind — had to be gradual. We also have to remember that
the apostle Paul wrote: "But I, brethren, could not address you
as spiritual men, but as men of the flesh, as babes in Christ. I fed
you with milk, not solid food; for you were not ready for it; and
even yet you are not ready, for you are still of the flesh" (1 Cor
3:1–3).[44]

On the other hand, we find in the very same Muslim tradition
authors such as Ibn Sîna and Ibn Rushd, who thought the Koran
is a prophetic instruction, preparing the way for a higher knowledge and intended for simple souls and the mass of the people.
If this theory is correct, the "revelation" in the Koran of the
mystery of Christ and of the mystery of God's interior life and
being cannot be more than rudimentary and elementary. We see
the very same thing in the New Testament, where Jesus uses this
step-by-step catechesis in dealing with his apostles. He does not
reveal everything to them at once, because the apostles could not
yet "bear" it (cf. Jn 16:12). Here we are confronted by the mysteries of God's ways, which men had better let alone!

The question could arise at this point: Why didn't God give
enough illumination to Mohammed's mind so that his preaching
would be protected from any deviation, especially in light of the

subsequent history of Islam and Christianity? We must remember, first of all, the part that God leaves to human freedom, even in the building of his kingdom. On the other hand, God has placed the task of being the sure guide, leading mankind to the fullness of the truth, in the hands of the Church, which alone possesses the fullness of the light — and even the Church does not arrive at this fullness all at once, nor is it always ready to give instant solutions to the problems of mankind. It should have been the task of the Church, through its sons, to assist the Muslims, starting with the Christian truths that are latent in the Koran and bringing them to light.

Muslim exegesis has not attempted to find a meaning for the position of Jesus in the series of biblical prophets given in the Koran. Is it really true that though the Koran recognizes a certain "order" among the prophets, it does not see any differences among them? In fact, the Koran *does* distinguish among them. The historical scenes it presents show a difference in importance among the characters it portrays. It is perfectly clear that Mohammed gave particular attention to the figures of Abraham, Moses, and Jesus. The statement placed on the lips of faithful Muslims notwithstanding, the Koran *does* see differences among the several divine messengers. The special place assigned to Jesus stands out with clarity.

I should like to call attention to the place Jesus seems to occupy in the lists of prophets. Geiger and other Orientalists have pointed out that the Koran's lists of prophets differ one from another and that it is very difficult to guess what significance, if any, this difference of order might have. Without rhyme or reason, most Orientalists attribute the succession of names to the ignorance of Mohammed. It seems to me, however, that if we take the name of Jesus as the central point of reference, and bear in mind the parallel structure, it is possible to discover a precise internal order in relation to Jesus Christ, who thus becomes the *center* about whom all the others revolve. Thus, in the Muslim profession of **faith:**

Say: "We believe in God
and in that which has been revealed to us,
and in that which was revealed
        to Abraham
and to Ishmael and to Isaac
and to Jacob and to the [Twelve] Tribes,
        and in that which was given to Moses,
        and to Jesus
and to the Prophets by their Lord,
without making any distinction among them,
and to Him we all give ourselves."

And whoever desires a religion
        different from Islam,
it shall not be accepted of him by God,
and he in the other life shall be among the losers.

                   [no. 99, sura 3:78/84–79/85]

This profession of faith concerns the "Islam" of Abraham as a religious attitude; it is total and trusting abandonment to the will of God. This must also be the meaning of the text "The true religion with God is Islam" (no. 99, sura 3:17/19).[45] This is the profession of faith the Muslim makes, in which, as in a first moment, he recognizes the essential element of the revelation; it is "complete submission to the will of God" — *Islam*. But, of course, it is possible that in this first moment it has not been clearly shown to the Muslim that there is a difference between the progressive revelations: from Abraham (his ancestor), to the covenant on Sinai, to Jesus. After the family tree of Abraham is listed, Jesus is situated between Moses and the prophets — not in chronological but in a symmetrical order that uses parallelism, centering upon Christ. Christ stands here as he did on Thabor, with the law (Moses) and the prophets on either side of him.

A sura of Mecca has another listing of the "Abrahamitic descendance" in which, nevertheless, we find the name of Noah inserted — who is expressly declared to have preceded Abraham — and Lot as well, who is named last:

That is Our argument, which We bestowed

upon Abraham as against his people.
We raise up in degrees whom We will;
surely thy Lord is All-wise, All-knowing.
And We gave to him Isaac and Jacob — each one We guided,
And Noah We guided before; and of his seed
David and Solomon, Job and Joseph,
                    Moses and Aaron —
even so We recompense the good-doers —
        Zachariah and John,
                    JESUS
        and Elias; each was of the righteous;
    Ishmael and Elisha, Jonah and Lot —
each one We preferred above all beings.

                            [no. 91, sura 6:83–86]

This text is found after the narration of Abraham's "testimony" on the existence and activity of God (no. 91, sura 6:74–83). In this list, Fr. Moubarac remarks, Abraham forms a triad with Isaac and Jacob, just as in the Sura of Mary (no. 60, sura 19: 50/49, 55/54–59/58). This triad corresponds to the one composed of Ishmael, Idrîs, and Dhû 'l-Kifl.[46] As elsewhere, the entire biblical line of prophets is presented as beginning with Abraham. But Noah, though he was anterior to Abraham, is inserted, along with Lot. The personages are presented in parallel groups of two: descendants of Abraham (*zuryiatihi*) who pass on the messianic promise which is fulfilled in Jesus, and "biblical prophets" who are outside the legal lineage of the people of Israel.

The characters of the Old Testament are "types" of the Messiah: Isaac and Jacob, David and Solomon are types of the Messiah king; Job and Joseph are types of the suffering Christ; Moses and Aaron are types of Christ as lawgiver and high priest. The two names from the New Testament are the immediate "precursors" and heralds of the Messiah. The five "biblical prophets" who are mentioned after Jesus are sent to those who are "excluded" from the lawful people of Israel: Elias, Ishmael, and Eliseus, who are connected with the resurrection of Christ as types. Elias, with Eliseus, works the miracle of raising to life. Elias brings back to life the widow's son (1 Kgs 17:17–24) and

Eliseus revivifies the son of the Sunamite (2 Kgs 4:32–37). Ishmael, almost dead from fatigue and thirst in the desert, revives through the intervention of the angel of Yahweh, who shows Agar a spring of water so that she can quench her son's thirst (Gn 21:14–19). Ishmael, the expelled one, "was sincere in his promise and a messenger prophet" (no. 60, sura 19:55/54–56/55) for the people who descended from him. Elias and Eliseus are prophets of the kingdom of Israel — an illegal kingdom in their time because of its schism from the kingdom of Judah. Their activity is in behalf of "excluded" people. Moreover, Elias is said to have been an Arab, if we believe a tradition recorded by St. Epiphanius, and this is why he is associated with Ishmael. Jonah, too, is a prophet sent to "excluded" people, the Ninivites. He too is a figure type of Christ's resurrection (Jon 2:1–3, 11, Mt 12:38–41). Lot, the nephew of Abraham, had been the first of Abraham's family to part with him (Gn 13:7–12), but Lot is in some sense a resurrected man because, through Abraham's prayer, he was enabled to escape death in the disaster of Sodom and Gomorrha (cf. Gn 19:29).

We can find a similar Christocentric interpretation in the list in the Sura of the Women, where the context is polemics against the Jews and the Koran defends the honor of Jesus and his Mother and the meaning of Jesus' death on the cross as a vicarious substitution:

In truth we have given you the revelation
as we gave it to Noah and the prophets
    who followed him;

and we gave it to Abraham
    to Ishmael and to Isaac,
    to Jacob and the [twelve] tribes,
        and to JESUS
to Job and to Jonah
and to Aaron and to Solomon
and to David we gave the Psalms

And so we sent Messengers
of whom we have already related to you the story

and Messengers of whom we have told you nothing.
  But with Moses God spoke aloud.

Messengers we sent announcers and admonishers,
  so that men would no longer have any argument
    to bring against God.
And God is sage and wise.
                    [no. 102, sura 4:161/163–162/165]

If we follow the rules of parallelism, this passage also shows
that the name of Jesus is at the center of the list and, at the same
time, at the center of a picture which sketches the four stages
and degrees of God's revelation: (1) the cosmic revelation, or
that of Noah; (2) the revelation to Abraham; (3) the revelation to
Moses (alliance with the people of Israel); and (4) the Christian
revelation (the new people of Israel, whose story is not related
by the Koran). If the order of the revelations is not chronological,
the insertion of Jesus between (3) and (4) is required by the
parallelism, according to degree.

Cosmic revelation is represented primarily by Noah. The prophets who came after him are not named here but elsewhere, where
they have to do with the pagan Arabs: Hüd, Sälïh, and Shu'aib.
Pre-Mosaic biblical revelation is represented by Abraham, the
father of believers, and is formed by the characters who inherited
the promise. Hence Ishmael is included here. Mosaic revelation
is of course represented by Moses, to whom God spoke directly.
Moses is named after the series of messianic types, in symmetry
with the name of Noah (six names before the name of Jesus and
six names after); Job and Jonah go together, because Job is a
prophetic type of the suffering Christ and Jonah is a prophetic
type of Christ risen from the dead. Aaron and Solomon are
coupled because Aaron is a type of Christ, the high priest, and
Solomon is a type of Christ as the divine wisdom and temple of
God (Solomon is the king-priest who built the Temple in Jerusalem). David, a prophetic type of Christ as king and prophet,
and singer in the psalms of Christ's royalty, is joined with Moses,
a type of Christ as lawgiver and judge.

Christian revelation is implicit in the expression "messengers of whom we have told you nothing." The story of Christ, his apostles, and Christian origins is absent from the Koran. Those for whom the Koran is intended are just barely at the first glimmerings of some knowledge of Christ. It is reserved to Christians to supply what the Koran did not proclaim.

A Christian Reading of the Koran Discovers Christ in the Full Meaning of the Texts

It has been regarded as legitimate for Muslim exegetes to give full rein to their imaginations, which has resulted in fantastic interpretations of a text. This being so, I feel justified in attempting, in the light of Christ, and basing myself upon the hypothetically sacred origin of the Koran, to bring out all that there may be in the Koran about Christ, reading the text in its "fuller sense."

> In truth we revealed it [made it come down]
>   on the Night of Destiny.
> Whatever may be the Night of Destiny?
> The Night of Destiny is more beautiful than a thousand
>   months.
> There descend Angels and the Spirit
>   with the permission of God,
>   to settle every thing.
> Night of Peace even to the coming of the dawn.
>   [no. 29, sura 97: 1–5]

The usual interpretation of Muslims and Orientalists sees this sura as describing the "night" in which the Koran was communicated, all at once, to Mohammed. But this descent of the complete

Koran in one night contains a contradiction, which exegetes get around by saying that God took it back again into Heaven and then revealed it anew, but this time in sections, one at a time. Because this "explanation" is based upon the theory that the Koran was an actual, physical book, written in Heaven, I cannot accept it. This is one more place where we have to "dematerialize."

The night of *Qadr* is Christmas night, when Christ made his visible appearance upon earth. This is the night of "power," during which the divine decree was carried out: "the mystery which was hidden from ages and generations" (Col 1:26, Eph 1:4–14). The Semite's mind — and this includes the Bible, of course — sees night as the time of darkness, or ignorance and unbelief (Rom 13:12; 1 Thes 5:5). It is also the time of affliction and sorrow (Is 21:12). It is the time of death: "Night comes, when no one can work" (Jn 9:4). But *this* night is the only one of its kind; it is the night of destiny, and more beautiful than a thousand months. During it the angels descend, which immediately calls to mind the angels at Bethlehem (Lk 2:13). The Koran calls Jesus "a Spirit from the Lord" (no. 102, sura 4:169/171). Jesus is witnessed to by the "Spirit of Holiness" (no. 93, sura 2:81/87, 254, 253; no. 116, sura 5:109/110). Hence the phrase makes sense if we read it as referring to the descent of the Spirit of holiness with Jesus on Christmas night. The phrase "with God's permission," which is found in other texts of the Koran where the subject is Jesus' activity (no. 99, sura 3:43/49), must be seen as the full adherence of the human will of Christ to the divine will (Jn 4:34, 5:30, 6:38), as that perfect obedience to the Father which earned the exaltation of the Son's name (Phil 2:7–11).

Min kullu Amren, which some translate "to establish everything," granted its wide range of meanings (—*Amr* = "command," "order," "divine plan or decree"), can be understood in the Pauline sense that the whole plan of creation is fixed and founded upon Christ. And the "night of peace" is that night when peace was heralded by the angels to all men with whom God is pleased (Lk 2:14).

The Koran recites the story of the birth of Jesus in another passage (no. 60, sura 19:22–34/35); but here we have a personal vision or revelation to Mohammed which calls up the tremendous mystery of God's goodness to men. Other passages of the Koran also refer to this night of destiny, or rather night of the birth, and Muslim exegetes and Orientalists explain them as the night of the Koran's descent. But this reinterpretation in the light of Christ allows me to refer them to Christ's birth:

H. M.

[By means of] the Most Clear Book

In truth we have revealed it
in a BLESSED NIGHT
that men might be warned

In that night every wise order was decreed.
[no. 55, sura 44:1–3/4]

The "most clear book" is not the Koran. When we dematerialize this passage, as we do for the vision of Ezekiel (2:9), the book is a symbol of the gospel revelation: of God's Word, who on Christmas night manifested himself to mankind. Christ enters the world to alert men and to witness to the truth. Nor is the plural *We* merely the majestic plural; it is the *We* of the three divine Persons. The sura goes on, and becomes an argument with the Jews of Mecca. It runs thus: If now, at this time, the preaching of the prophet Mohammed is a new call of God to his people, the fact that the Jews rejected the message of Christ in times past gives reason to think that they are about to do the same thing this time.

But how can the Warning aid them,
when a clear Messenger already came to them!

And still they disdainfully turned their
shoulders and said:
"Crazy Imposter."
[no. 55, sura 44:12/13–13/14 = Jn 10:19–21]

The "clear messenger," the explicit apostle, was Jesus, who had clearly revealed his mission and nature before the Sanhedrin. Verses 6/7–8/9 seem to be an echo of Jesus' witness before that judgment seat (cf. Mt 26:64); a first chastisement was the destruction of Jerusalem (vv. 14/15–15/16). And the unfaithfulness of the Jews of Jesus' time was but a repetition of that of their forefathers, as the story of the exodus shows, in spite of the fact that God had "chosen" Israel (vv. 16/17–31/32). In the person of Jesus, God gave them still another evident proof of his love for men (v. 32/33). His resurrection is the cause of all men's rising from the dead. And still the Jews of Mecca refuse to believe it! (vv. 33/34–42).

"Knowledge has come to them." Like the "night of destiny," many other expressions have to be rethought according to their "full sense." For instance, the expression "knowledge has come to them" should be understood of the Jews. "Knowledge" here is Jesus Christ, in the meaning taught by St. Paul: "Christ Jesus, who has become for us God — gives wisdom and justice and sanctification, and redemption" (1 Cor 1:30); "But we speak the wisdom of God, mysterious, hidden, which God foreordained before the world" (1 Cor 2:7); and "Christ Jesus, in whom are hidden all the treasures of wisdom and knowledge" (Col 2:3).

During the Medina period the polemic against the Jews becomes more evident. Mohammed has the task of telling them that Jesus was the Messiah and that, to the present, the sons of Israel have not accepted him — no more than they received the gospel preaching in the New Testament.

In truth we gave to Moses the Book
And we made the other Messengers follow him in succession,
and we gave to Jesus, the Son of Mary
evident proofs
and we confirmed him with the Spirit of Holiness.
But then every time that
a messenger brings you commands you do not like,
you proudly rebel

and some of them you call liars, and some you kill? [81/87]

But they (i.e. the Jews) say:
"Our hearts are not circumcised!"
On the contrary, God has cursed them for their misbelief
for the little they believe! [82/88]

When a book reached them (i.e. the announcement of the gospel)
from God who confirmed that which they already had,
while formerly they were calling for victory over the impious,
when what they already were well acquainted with,
They rejected;
May God curse the deniers! [83/89]

What a terrible bargain they made of their souls,
renouncing that which God had sent,
jealous because God reveals his grace
to whom he wills from among his servants;
they have thus incurred wrath upon wrath,
the deniers shall have shameful torment. [84/90]

And when it is said to them:
But believe in that which God has revealed!
They reply: "We believe in what was revealed to us!"
denying that which came after,
whereas it is but the Truth
which confirms that which they already have.

Say, then, to them:
"Why then, if you are believers, as you say,
did you kill the Prophets before?" [85/91]

[no. 93, sura 2]

This text, and similar ones, directly concerns the Jews' rejection of Christ's message. Muslim commentators and Orientalists see in it a reproach to the Jews of Medina for not having acknowledged Mohammed and accepted the Koran. But I am convinced that here, too, we have to use a Christian key to read the text. In fact, after recalling the revelation given to Moses and the other prophets of the Old Testament (v. 81/87), Jesus, the son of Mary, is explicitly mentioned: "We have confirmed him with the

Holy Spirit (cf. Mt 3:16, 4:1, 12:8, Acts 4:27, 10:38, etc.). We must read the expression "Holy Spirit" in the sense it is used in the texts quoted from the New Testament.[47] The phrase "we gave Jesus . . . the clear signs" is also found elsewhere (cf. v. 254/253) and is, as it were, an answer to what was demanded of Jesus (cf. Lk 11:15–16, Mt 16:1, Mk 8:11). We find the repetition here of Jesus' accusation of the Pharisees, that they were swollen with pride (cf. Lk 11:43) and were killers of prophets: "Therefore I send you prophets and wise men and scribes, some of whom you will kill and crucify, and some you will scourge in your synagogues and persecute from town to town" (Mt 23:34). Mohammed saw some of the "signs" when he was carried by night from the temple of Mecca to the Temple of Jerusalem, where he was shown two crimes of the Israelites which brought down on them two punishments. The first was the murder of the prophet Isaiah, and this as avenged by the destruction of the first Temple and the Babylonian exile. The second was the condemnation and crucifixion of Jesus Christ, punished by the destruction of the second Temple and the dispersal of Israel (cf. no. 74, sura 17). The charge of prophet-killing recurs often in the preaching in Medina (cf. no. 93, sura 2:58/61; no. 99, sura 3:20/21, 108/112, 177/181, 180/183; no. 102, sura 4:154/155; no. 116, sura 5: 74/70).

There is no question here of rejecting the Koran. Mohammed is talking about the Jewish rejection of Jesus and his message in the New Testament, which confirmed the scrolls of the Old Testament in the hands of the Jews. Jesus, the Messiah, had won the victory over unbelievers, the victory so longed for by the patriarchs of the Old Testament. Israel's sin is that she did not welcome Jesus. The shameful bargain whereby the Jews sold their own souls is an explicit reference to Judas, who handed Jesus over for thirty pieces of silver (v. 84/90). Thirty silver pieces was the price of a slave (Mt 26:14–16, 27:3–10), which is seen by New Testament writers as the fulfillment of the prophecy of Zechariah. Thus they sold their souls in this cheap bargain, rejecting their Messiah and the message of "that one of his Servants whom he filled with his grace" (cf. Jn 1:17), Jesus Christ, the "servant of Yahweh." This is the great crime in Israel's history, and it drew down upon her God's curse, "anger upon anger."

Jesus Is the Truth: **Al Haqq**

The context of the question put to the Jews, "Do you believe in him whom God has sent down?" refers to the preaching of Jesus and the apostles contained in the New Testament, which is the fulfillment of Israel's messianic expectation. "We believe only in what was sent down on us." This answer is Israel's refusal to receive Jesus and the New Testament as revealed Scripture.

The Koran seems clear here, in that we first have the sentence *wa ikfurûna bimâ warâ'ahu,* which I interpret as "they are unbelieving"; that is, they do not accept the Scriptures which came after him (*warâ'ahu*). The pronoun refers to Jesus Christ, because, in the second sentence, *wa HUWA al-haqqu musaddiqan,* "and HE is the truth confirming the truthfulness of the messages [prophecies] in their possession" (v. 85/91), *al-Haqq,* "the Truth," is not an abstract concept but a person, Jesus Christ, who is explicitly named in the preceding verse (81/87). We should take note of another and astonishing fact. Certain texts at times replace *al-Haqq* with the name of Jesus. When this happens, the texts glow with an entirely new light, and we seem to hear Jesus saying: "I am the truth." Let us take the Gospel statement that the Word, the Truth, enlightens every man who comes into this world (cf. Jn 1:9). This same Word also shone on the author of the Koran. That light can be found in most of the texts which use the expression *bi-l Haqq,* or *al-Haqq,* and we read it as Christ. The "day of truth," judgment day (no. 26, sura 78:39), is also, according to the Koran, the day of explicit disclosure of the mystery of Christ. Then all men will know exactly who Jesus Christ is.

I think the entire context authorizes this Christological interpretation of the expression "Truth marking the veracity of the messages they possess in the Old Testament."

Mohammed is directed to ask the Jews the same question that Jesus asked of their ancestors: "Why do you murder God's prophets?" (cf. Mt 23:34). This passage should be read while keeping in mind the great speech of the martyr, Stephen, before the Sanhedrin (Acts 7:1–55).

That is why I think the words of verse 95/101 do not refer to Mohammed and the Koran but to Jesus and the New Testament:

> And when a Messenger of God came to them, who confirmed the revelation given them, they took no account of the book of God as though they had known nothing.

In sura 3 (no. 99, sura 3:57/64–77/83) is a text concerning the progeny of Abraham, and the background is a controversy with the Jews of Medina. Abraham was prior to both the law of Moses and the gospel.

> Ha, you are the ones who dispute on what you know; why then dispute you touching a matter of which you know not anything? [58/65]

The subject is the promises of blessings upon Ishmael which God made to Abraham. Mohammed now has the mission to redeem them in favor of his people outside the pale, in the name of Abraham and in face of the niggardliness of the Christians and the Jews: "God knows, while you do not know; Abraham was neither a Jew nor a Christian, but was *hanif,* and a man conformed to God (*muslim*) and he was not among the idolaters" (60/67).

Once again, the prophet who is spoken of is not Mohammed but Jesus Christ, who is the one most closely connected with Abraham and whom Abraham had desired to see (cf. Jn 8:57–59). During this polemic the subject under discussion is primarily the mystery of Christ. The appeal to the "people of the book" (i.e., to the Jewish Scribes who represent the Jewish community of Medina) becomes ever more insistent. Denunciation is made of the excessive veneration and exaggerated importance given the cult of angels and patriarchs (v. 74/80). (Cf. Jn 9:28: "We are disciples of Moses"; nevertheless, the Jews reject Jesus in the name of Abraham and Moses.) The covenant and the messianic promise are brought up:

> Then there shall come to you a Messenger confirming what is with you — you shall believe in him and you shall help him [75/81]

It is Jesus, once more, and not Mohammed, who is the prophet or messenger spoken of. One must believe in him.

Jesus brought a new law and new wisdom. He asked his apostles to be his "witnesses" (Acts 1:21–22, 23:11, etc.). "Bear witness so, and I shall be with you among the witnesses." Put these words of the Koran on the lips of Jesus and at once Matthew's text comes to mind: "So everyone who acknowledges me before men, I also will acknowledge before my Father who is in heaven" (Mt 10:32), as well as those other words of Jesus: "Behold, I am with you all days even unto the consummation of the world" (Mt 28:20). All of this refers to Jesus, not to Mohammed. Jesus is the great witness (cf. Jn 1:18, 8:38). His whole life, and especially his death, was a witness to the truth (1 Tim 6:13, 2:6–7).

After Jesus Christ came, those who did not receive him are thus described: "Whosoever turns his back after that — they are the ungodly" (76/82). The same interpretation must be made of other texts. For example, in no. 101, sura 57:26–27, the command "Believe in his Messenger" is not about Mohammed but about Jesus Christ and Mohammed's announcement of the mystery of Christ to the Jews.

In a similar way, a Christological interpretation must be given to other expressions in the Koran in order to uncover their fuller meanings, especially those that relate to New Testament expressions. For example, the word *huda* (direction, way, or guide; the promise of salvation given to Adam and Eve in the garden) is pointed to by the use of this word in no. 57, sura 2:121/123:

> Away from here all of you! You shall be enemies one to another! Surely there shall come from me a GUIDE and whoever follows my Guide, shall not go astray, nor shall he be unhappy any more.

The account of the preaching to the *Ginn* (looked upon as mysterious goblins) can be viewed as an "Arab" version of the descent of Jesus to Limbo to preach to the spirits of the kingdom beyond the tomb (cf. 1 Pt 3:19–20, Eph 4:9). The term *hudy,* meaning direction, points to Jesus, who is the way which must be followed (cf. Jn 14:6, 8:12; no. 64, sura 72:13). Moses was given the Scripture to direct it toward the Messiah. No. 66, sura 23:51/49–52/50, and no. 69, sura 27:78/76–79/77, say that Mohammed's preaching "relates to the Children of Israel most of that concerning which they are at variance; i.e. the coming of the Messiah." The word *innahu* does not refer to the Koran but to "that upon which they are divided," Jesus, who is "Direction and Mercy for the believers."

Just as with *hûdah,* "direction," *al-Haqq,* "truth," and *ar-rahmat,* "mercy," the expression *an-Nûr,* "light," is found in many texts to designate the person of Jesus, light of the world, etc. (cf. no. 107, sura 24:34, where God is the light). The lamp, light from light, is Jesus Christ; it is in a vessel of glass (cf. 2 Cor 4:7), which may be an image for the humanity of Christ in which the divinity dwells (cf. Col 2:9). Christ is the star (cf. no. 30, sura 53, 1) and the blessed tree is Mary, who is symbolized in the olive tree (cf. Ps 51:10, Eccl 24:19; no. 66, sura 23:20). The oil is a symbol of Christ, "which shines though no fire lights it, Light from Light." Throughout this theme on light the deep Christological sense can be found hidden in it. Only a Christian key gives that sense (cf. no. 100, sura 61:8; no. 101, sura 57:12–13; no. 111, sura 66:8; no. 115, sura 9:32). In verse 30 the statement "the Messiah is the son of God" is in a context which suggests the Nestorian meaning of the statement, namely, that of adoration of Christ as a god distinct from God the Father, as some deity who is separate from and standing beside God.

The Crucifixion, Death, and Resurrection of Jesus

The reality of the crucifixion and death of Jesus is essential to the Christian faith, since it is inextricably bound up with the resurrection (cf. 1 Cor 15:3–5, 12–17). W. M. Watt writes that this has special interest for Christians because the Koran denies the ugly fact of Jesus' death on the cross. He says that the Muslims still believe that this denial is valid in spite of the contrary testimony of the historical tradition. The first intention of the Koran was to deprive the Jews of the victory they claimed was theirs in Jesus' death. But as it is now understood, the text goes much further than that.[48]

Muslim tradition, Massignon says, after the year 150 of the Hegirah maintained that the Koran most certainly teaches that Jesus was not crucified. Instead, God miraculously put a "double" in his place. Because of this interpretation, all Christian apologists were firm in concluding that the Koran could not possibly be of divine origin; this error was too blatant. Further, all the Orientalists read the texts on the crucifixion of Jesus in the same sense as Muslim tradition, though they differ on how this explanation of a Christian doctrine arose. Many Orientalists saw Docetism at the root of the error.[49] Fr. Moubarac observes, with acuteness, that the Koran knows nothing of metaphysical distinctions between nature and person. It simply testifies to the oneness of God in the manner of Israel's prophets. And the whole of the discussion about the Incarnation turned upon these distinctions. So we must begin a reexamination of the Koran with this fact before us. The denial of the crucifixion must be studied with focus upon the word *yaqinan,* "they did not really kill him." The Muslims, for their part, must not cling forever to an opinion which has been accepted as "traditional and orthodox." Here again, as elsewhere, there is room not exactly for evolution of a dogma but for an interioriza- tion of the data of religious history.[50]

I feel that this reexamination should be attempted. For if we begin with the hypothesis that the Koran may actually be of divine origin, it is not possible for it to contain such a clear contradiction of historical data and Christian revelation. One text which seems to me to affirm very distinctly the reality of Jesus' death is part of the Sura of the Family of Imran:

> And the others (the Jews) laid snares;
> And God, of all the snare-layers is the best!
>
> When God said:
> "OH, JESUS, I SHALL CAUSE YOU TO DIE,
> AND THEN I SHALL RAISE YOU UP TO ME,
> and I will purge you of the unbelievers,
> and shall place those who have followed you
> high above the unbelievers
> until the day of the Resurrection;
> Then shall you all return to Me
> and I shall judge between you of your disagreements."
>
> [no. 99, sura 3:47/54–48/55]

It is a well-known fact that whenever the characters and actions of the men in the Bible and in the Koran are compared, the Koran puts emphasis on God's activity rather than man's. For example, the Bible presents Adam as the namer of the animals (Gn 2:19– 20), but the Koran says that God taught Adam the names of things (no. 93, sura 2:29/31). In Genesis it is Abraham who intercedes with God to obtain pardon for Sodom (18:23 ff.); but in the

Koran, God refuses to discuss matters with Abraham and so he is obliged to bow before the all-predetermining will of God (no. 77, sura 11:77/74–78/76). The same thing is seen in the history of Joseph (no. 79, sura 12).

What is behind these contrasting attitudes? The Jewish attitude developed out of rabbinic Judaism, which holds, as an absolute, the necessary and complete freedom of man: man does not need God, either to save himself or to avoid evil, and he reaches God by his own powers. St. Paul fought this attitude of self-sufficiency, bringing out the frailty of man, the powerlessness of the Mosaic law itself, and the necessity for the intervention of God's grace. This is the atmosphere in which the Koran moves; its thought is Pauline. The weight is upon the work of God, to whom everything is under absolute domination.

Let us return to the text which concerns the death of Christ (no. 99, sura 3:48/55), which comes about by the will of God (cf. Phil 2:8). Romans and Jews alike are but instruments that God manipulates for his own purposes. It is in this meaning that we must take the words which God the Father addresses to Jesus — in the first person singular, not the plural *We*: "Oh, Jesus, I shall cause you to die." This text, therefore, speaks clearly of Christ's death as the work of God and not of men. The statements in the same text: "I shall raise you up to Me," "I shall place those who have followed you high above the unbelievers . . . then shall you all return to Me," are expressions which need reinterpretation in the light of St. Paul's thinking. Bear in mind, however, that the texts of St. Paul show Jesus returning all things and all beings to God. It is Jesus who "delivers the kingdom to God the Father" (1 Cor 15:23–24). Not so in the Koran. All the activity which brings all things back to God is the work of God himself. This is always in opposition to the Jewish persuasion of man's sufficiency to work out his own salvation and return to God.[51]

The Red Heifer

Another text in the Koran has been completely overlooked in the discussion of Jesus' death and resurrection. Tabarï, and after him the Muslim exegetes, think it refers to an event from the time of Moses. The koranic narration, the Orientalists say, is an echo of the prescriptions of Deuteronomy for the case of a man who has been murdered and whose murderer is unknown (cf. Dt 21:1–7). Blachère feels he must admit that the Koran's account breathes a quite different spirit from that of Deuteronomy.[52]

> And when you killed a man
> and argued about him,
> and God made manifest what you were concealing,
>
> at which time We said to you:
> "Strike him with a part of her."
> Thus GOD RAISES TO LIFE THE DEAD
> and shows you his SIGNS
> so that you may comprehend.
>
> But consequently your hearts became hardened,
> and became like the rocks,
> rather, even harder;
>
> for there are rocks from which the rivers disgorge,
> and others split open and out comes the water,
> and others crumble for fear of God;
> but God is not oblivious of what you are doing.
>   [no. 93, sura 2:67/72–69/74]

First of all, sura 2 is called "The Cow," taking its title from the story of the red cow (vv. 63/67–66/71) and the Jews of Medina. It reminds them of the command to sacrifice a red heifer. The regulations are found in Numbers 19:1–10. Now all Christian tradition, from the fathers to the later theologians, has always seen in the sacrifice of the cow, or red heifer, as a type or figure of the suffering and death of Jesus, the sacrifice of the New

Covenant. Further, I am convinced that the text of the Koran, immediately following this reminder of the heifer sacrifice commanded by Moses, refers to the death and resurrection of Jesus Christ (vv. 67/72–69/74).

The Koran is not arguing over the meaning of Jesus' death, as it does in the text of no. 102, sura 4:156/157; it simply registers the fact: "and when you killed a MAN and argued about him." These words must be read in the light of the Gospel of St. John (11:46–53): "And God made manifest that which you were concealing." The resurrection of Jesus was supposed to remain hidden from the people of Jerusalem, and this is why the Sanhedrin paid the guards to keep quiet (Mt 28:11–15). The sentence which the Koran gives as an order from God, namely, "Strike him with a part of her," refers to the direction to sprinkle the blood of the heifer seven times over the outside of the sanctuary tent (Nm 19:4). But here it takes on the meaning which the Epistle to the Hebrews gives the rite: "But when Christ appeared as a high priest of the good things to come, he entered once for all through the greater and more perfect tabernacle not made by hands [i.e., not of this creation], nor again by virtue of blood of goats and calves, but by virtue of his own blood, into the Holies, having obtained eternal redemption. For if the blood of goats and bulls and the sprinkled ashes of a heifer sanctify the unclean unto the cleansing of the flesh, how much more will the blood of Christ" (Heb 9:11–14). "Thus God RAISES TO LIFE THE DEAD and shows you his Signs so that you may comprehend" (68/73). Here, too, the Muslim needs the Christian to help him grasp the real meaning of the Koran. Apropos of this, the Koran itself directed Mohammed to ask the help of those who had received the Scripture before him:

> If you are in doubt about that which we have made come down upon you; question those who recite the [revealed] Scripture before you. [no. 86, sura 10:94]

A Christian is in a position to show how this text is concerned with the resurrection of Christ, of the Man whom the Jews killed and whom God has raised from the dead (cf. Acts 2:22–24), so that he became the "sign" and the principle of resurrection for all mankind (cf. Jn 11:25; 1 Cor 15:12–28).

The reproach of the Koran concerning the unbelief of the Jews, "but consequently, your hearts became hardened, and became like the rocks, rather even harder," is an echo of the speech of the martyr Stephen before the Sanhedrin (Acts 7:51). Further, "the rocks" suggests the miracle Moses worked at Meriba, which comes just after the prescriptions concerning the sacrifice of the heifer (Nm 20:1–13): "And Moses lifted up his hand and struck the rock with his rod twice; and water came forth abundantly." Now if the fathers of the Church saw a prophetic figure of the sacrificial death of Christ, slain outside the walls of Jerusalem (cf. Jn 19:17, Heb 13:11–12), in the prescriptions concerning the slaying of the red heifer outside the camp, and if they saw in the rock from which Moses sought water (following the interpretation St. Paul gave [1 Cor 10:4]) Jesus Christ as "a spring of living water" from whose heart flow torrents of grace (cf. Jn 4:13–14, 7:37–39, Rv 21:6, etc.), and if Christ is the living source of the sacraments and grace, there were other rocks which God made a wonder to men, and which, the Koran states, "have crumbled for fear of God" (cf. Mt 24:1–2, 21:5–6). I see in this passage a clear though mysterious testimony to the death and resurrection of Christ and the destruction of Jerusalem and its Temple.

The Text Which Seems to Deny the Death of Christ on the Cross

This highly controversial text is found in the Sura of the Women (no. 102, sura 4:156/157) in a strongly polemical setting, which must not be lost sight of. The passage is speaking to the Jews of

Medina "who refuse faith in God and his messengers" and demand that "a book be sent down to them from heaven; and God
had contracted with them a most firm covenant on Sinai" (vv.
149/150–153/154). It then lists the accusations for which, according to the Koran, the people of Israel have been cursed:

So then, because they have violated the Covenant
and have disowned the Signs of God
and have killed the prophets wrongly
and have said: "Our hearts are uncircumcised!"
(but it is God rather who has sealed the unbelief,
so that but few of them believe)

and again for their unbelief
and for having spoken a horrible calumny against Mary:

and for having said: "We have killed the Christ,
Jesus Son of Mary, the Messenger of God!"
WHEREAS THEY NEITHER KILLED HIM NOR
    CRUCIFIED HIM.
ALTHOUGH SOMEBODY WAS DELIVERED TO THEIR
    EYES LIKE TO HIM

(and in truth those whose opinion on this matter differs
are certainly in doubt),
nor have they any knowledge about this matter,

although they follow a conjecture,
IT IS CERTAIN THAT THEY DID NOT KILL HIM!

But God raised him up to himself;
and God is powerful and wise;

and there is no one of the People of the Book
who will not believe in Him, before his death,
and He on the day of resurrection will be testimony
against them

[no. 102, sura 4:154/155–157/159]

The Koran accused the Jews of Medina of having violated the
covenant of Sinai; they also denied the manifest signs of God's
intervention in the world and, among these signs, they particularly
denied Jesus and Mary; they even denied the mission of Mo-

hammed himself. They murdered the prophets (an accusation which has already been repeated a good number of times in the Koran, echoing Jesus' words. (Cf. Mt 23:29–38, Rom 11:2–6; no. 93, sura 2:58/61, 85/91; no. 99, sura 3:20/21, 108/112, 177/181, 180/183; no. 116, sura 5:74/70.)

"Our hearts are uncircumcised" seems to be a sentence used by the Jews themselves to mock those who disdained them (Jer 4: 4, 9:26), and St. Paul had called for "circumcision of the heart" (Rom 2:25–29). St. Stephen condemned the leaders of the San-hedrin as men who were uncircumcised of heart and killers of prophets (Acts 7:51–53). In punishment, God has sealed up their hearts, and there are few believers among them. This remark of the Koran parallels St. Paul's saying: "But their minds were darkened; for to this day, when the Old Testament is read to them the selfsame veil remains, not being lifted to declare the Christ in whom it is made" (2 Cor 3:13–14). The Koran adduces a second accusation after that of unbelief: the calumny against the honor of Mary the Mother of Jesus, the glory of Israel and Jerusalem.

The argument the Jews used to prove that Jesus was a false Messiah was based upon his shameful death on the cross. The Jews had always stoutly maintained that to say, as the Christians did, that *Jesus crucified* was their Messiah was a sacrilegious affront to God's providence and an insult to human intelligence. And, as a matter of history, we see St. Paul, prior to his conversion, repelled by the exaltation of Jesus crucified as Messiah by the Christians. His Israelite conscience was formed by the text of Deuteronomy: "for a hanged man is accursed by God" (21:23). But after his conversion, Paul uses the same text as a point of reference when teaching the doctrine of the saving death of Jesus in his letter to the Galatians (3:10–13; cf. 2 Cor 5:21).

C. G. Montefiore thought that the Sadducees, with the help and support of other rabbis (Scribes), along with the Romans, were responsible for the death of Jesus.[53] As I remarked previously, the Jews of Mecca and Medina had remained faithful to the creed and practices of the Sadducees, as did the Jews of Ethiopia. Thus it is easy to believe, with this fact before us, that they would look upon Jesus as a political agitator and a dangerous disturber of the uneasy peace with their Roman overlords (cf. Jn 11:48).[54] Chwolson was convinced that the Sadducees alone were the ones who plotted Jesus' death.[55]

Herford says that the Talmud has nothing at all to say about the Romans' part in the execution of Jesus and puts it wholly and squarely upon the Jews.[56] Hence it is quite clear that the manner of Christ's condemnation and death carried a double taint: (1) crucifixion, because of its horror and shame, was the most abhorred form of death, and (2) it had a special curse upon it, inflicted by the Torah (Dt 21:23; cf. Gal 3:13, Acts 5:30, 10:39). Still, it must be remembered that Deuteronomy does not speak directly of people condemned to crucifixion; it has to do with criminals who were exposed to the public and fixed to a post, and this after their death. No Jew in his right mind could conceive of the Messiah ending this way; the very thought offended God.[57] Hilkiah, a rabbi of the Amoraic period, had this to say of the Christian belief: "Those people are crazy liars who say that God had a son and that he allowed him to be put to death. Is it possible that the God who would not permit Abraham to kill Isaac would have allowed his own son to be put to death without destroying the whole world and reducing it to chaos?"[58]

Jewish thinking in Medina must be kept in mind in order to understand the Koran's limits and the true meaning of its statements. For these Jews, the death of Jesus is as certain as anything can be and, as far as they are concerned, the decisive and final argument that proves him a false messiah. But the Medina Jews know for certain that their forefathers in Palestine had killed him: "We killed the Christ, Jesus Son of Mary; the Messenger of God." The only logical conclusion was that he could not possibly have been the Messiah, as Christians wanted them to believe.

The statements of the Koran, "whereas they neither killed him nor crucified him, although somebody was rendered to their eyes like to him," do not refer to the *fact of the crucifixion and death* of Jesus. These statements deny that the *true perpetrators* of the deed were *Jews!* The koranic statement must be read and understood in the light of Christian dogma on the meaning and worth of the death of Christ. The death and resurrection of Christ are the proof of his divine mission. But they are even more the great mystery of God's mercy, which has a cosmic meaning, and cannot be produced by men. Therefore the death of Jesus was not the result of the trial and condemnation of a supposed criminal, brought about by the religious authorities of Israel ("We killed the Messiah") and by the Roman authorities. It was an event preordained by God and executed by "diabolical powers," which used men as mere tools to carry out the affair. The text must be interpreted against the background of Pauline thought. If the Jews are "the enemies of the cross of Christ" (Gal 6:12–14, Phil 3:18), the crucifixion of Jesus is the effect of the machinations of the powers and the "princes of this world." Christ's death is part of the divine plan of incarnation and redemption: the glorification of the Son of God. It is "the wisdom of God, mysterious, hidden, which God foreordained before the world . . . which none of the rulers of this world has known; *for had they known it, they would never have crucified the Lord of glory"* (1 Cor 2:7–8).

Furthermore, the death of Christ was not caused by the condemnation of Jews and Romans. It was Jesus' free and spontaneous self-immolation. No one, except the Father and Jesus himself, could have disposed of his life. A number of times Jesus had shown that he had the power to escape the snares of those who wanted to kill him (cf. Mt 2:13–21, Lk 4:29–30, Jn 7:30–32, 8:59, 18:4–9). "For this reason the Father loves me, because I lay down my life, that I may take it up again. No one takes it from me, but I lay it down of myself. I have power to lay it down, and I have power to take it again. Such is the command I have received from my Father" (Jn 10:17–18; cf. no. 99, sura 3:47–54).

Hence, in light of this gospel text and the Christian dogma on the free and spontaneous self-immolation of Jesus, we must read and interpret the koranic text thus: No! It was not the Jews who killed and crucified Christ; he gave himself freely. Even after his death, during the hours that preceded his rising, Christ remained alive in some manner, in the sense expressed by the Roman liturgy for Holy Saturday: "I have become like a man who needs no help, free among the dead."

It may also be interesting to note a detail which is sometimes forgotten in the West: the peculiar nature of Christ's death. His death was not a death in the usual sense, as when we talk about the death of human beings. This, of course, is because of the permanence of the hypostatic union. For this reason, Oriental artists, from the fifth to the beginning of the ninth century, almost always represent Christ as alive on the cross. Christian thought concentrated particularly on the divinity of Christ, and the general belief was that he could not die completely, as we do, unless there was not only a separation of soul from body, but also a separation of the body from the divine nature — which was not the case. Hence to show Christ as dead was to show only the human remains of Christ. Many Oriental authors maintained that when Jesus breathed his last, his body, though separated from the soul, remained in some way "living" through the hypostatic union.[59]

Passing on to the other statement of the Koran, "although somebody was rendered to their eyes like to him," we should continue to see reflections of Pauline thought. St. Paul saw death as the "wages of sin" (Rom 6:23). For love of us, Jesus made himself "sin" (2 Cor 5:21), "a curse" (Gal 3:13). The "double," which became the object of divine justice, is "sin," as personalized by St. Paul; it is the whole humanity of the "old man" which was crucified, that the sinful body might be destroyed (Rom 6:6). All of humanity was condemned upon the cross, and Christ set aside the decree of condemnation, nailing *it* to the cross (Col 2:14).

We can readily admit that Mohammed probably did not fully grasp the deep meaning of the words he felt compelled to utter. Nor did Muslim exegetes and modern Orientalists penetrate their meaning any more than he did. The Christian key, however, gives the inner sense that is really there.

Even the words that immediately follow, "and in truth those whose opinion on this matter [i.e., on the reality of Christ's death] are certainly in doubt, nor have they any knowledge about this matter, although they follow a conjecture," must be read in the light of John's Gospel, which notes: "There arose a division among the Jews because of these words" (10:19). The knowledge that the Jews of Mecca and Medina lacked in order to grasp the meaning of the manner of Jesus' death can be supplied only by the Church. The *fact* is that his death was not the work of Jews: "it is certain that they did not kill him." His death was but a phase in the process of glorification which God gave him:

But God raised him up to himself;
and God is powerful and wise [156/158]

I read the lines just after this, "and there is no one of the People of the Book who will not believe in Him, before his death" (157/159), as offering hope to every Jew. Before death, every Jew will make an explicit or implicit act of faith in Christ. They who have believed in Christ will, on the day of resurrection, be witnesses against the obstinate.

My interpretation of these famous verses of the Koran eliminates the necessity of looking for Docetism, etc., in it.

Do not say: "Three" (no. 102, sura 4:169/171).

Many of the texts of the Sura of Women are polemics aimed at the Jews. "People of the book," as I have shown above, is an expression that describes the leaders of the Jewish community (though at times it refers to the community as a whole). It is never used to describe the Christian community. Christians are called An-Nassära and are rhetorically addressed as "people of the gospel."

Once again, we must read the text which seems to deny the doctrine of the Trinity and the divinity of Christ as addressed to the Jews of Medina and not to Christians.

O People of the Book [i.e., Scribes and rabbis]
Do not be fanatics about your religion
and say not of God other than the Truth. [169/171]

Certainly the Messiah, Jesus Son of Mary,

IS THE MESSENGER OF GOD, HIS WORD (*kalimat*),

WHOM HE PLACED IN MARY,
A SPIRIT PROCEEDING FROM HIM.

Believe then in God and in his Messengers!
Say not: "Three"! It is enough and will be better for you!
For God is one God! May He be exalted!

That a son belongs to Him! To Him belongs
that which is in the heavens and upon the earth!
He alone is enough to protect us. [169/171]

The Messiah did not disdain to be
a SERVANT OF GOD, and neither the angels more
    close.
Those who find it an indignity to adore Him
and are proud
He shall assemble together before Him [171/172]
                    [no. 102, sura 4: 169/171–171/172]

First, we must take notice here of a grammatical point. The
conjunction *innama* is usually considered as exclusive: "The Messiah . . . is only" or "is nothing but . . ." But I think that it
should be considered a re-inforcing declarative with *ma*. So I
translate: "Certainly the Messiah, Jesus Son of Mary, is the Messenger of God." I do this because the text is meant for the Jews
("O People of the Book"), who refuse to recognize the messiahship of Jesus and his mission. The Koran proclaims to the Jews
and the pagans of Medina the excellence of Jesus, Word of God
and Spirit, proceeding from God.

These expressions, which contain the germs of Christian teaching on the divinity of Christ, could not have been understood in
their full meaning either by Mohammed or his audience. Once
again we must use the Christian key to unlock the deeper meaning.
The Jews are invited to believe not only in God (many of them
have already been condemned as unbelieving materialists) but in
his messengers as well, among whom is Jesus. "And say not:
'Three.' " When the messiahship of Jesus was introduced with the
formula "He is a Word and a Spirit proceeding from God," the

Jews of Medina jeered at Mohammed (and the Christians), throwing in his face the remark that there are now three Gods instead of one! The text is a reproach of this sneering twist that they gave to the formula. It has been said with justification that the Koran makes judgment on the manner of speaking of the mystery of God but does not pronounce directly upon the mystery of the Trinity. Its hearers were just not prepared for this. Once they had accepted Jesus as Messiah and one sent from God, they could be initiated by degree into the realization of who he is and the knowledge of God's inner life which is revealed to us by the Son (Jn 1:18).

Hence to claim — as have all Muslim theologians and all Christian apologetics for thirteen centuries — that this text repudiates the Trinity is to take it and similar texts out of context — the context of the Koran — but more especially out of the context of its surroundings. We all know, from talmudic and rabbinic literature up to present-day theologians, the unanimity with which Judaism has rejected the Trinity. With few exceptions, it does not even bother to examine the doctrine. It is denied, a priori, as incompatible with Jewish monotheism. Saadia Ben Joseph (882–942), one of the few who attempted a study of the Trinity by using Christian material, reproached the heretical Jew, Hiwi of Bakh, for having "Christian" ideas and for dividing God into *three*.[60] J. H. Hertz denounced the Judeo-Christians for "having darkened the sky of the monotheism of Israel by teaching the new doctrine of God's having a son, identifying a man born of a woman with God, and proclaiming the doctrine of the Trinity."[61] Kohler wrote: "The absolute unity of God, fundamental and central belief of Judaism, became a matter of life and death for the synagogue the moment the Christian church placed Jesus, its Messiah, upon the throne of God, whether as his son or as his equal."[62]

The Christian doctrine of the Trinity has often been ridiculed by Jews by the telling of various stories which always end with the number three.[63] In Mecca, too, they mocked Christians by calling out: "Three, three, three." So the Koran reproves this, since, in fact, the mystery of the Trinity does *not* mean three Gods, or that two other beings are associated with God: "Say not: 'Three'! It is enough and will be better for you! For God is one God! May He be exalted!" I translate the phrase *An iakuna lahu waladu* as "that a Son may belong to Him."[64] The meaning, which we can find expressed elsewhere, as well as in the Koran, is that if God owns everything in Heaven and on earth, he could also have a Son. "Say: 'If the All-merciful has a son, then I am the first to serve him' " (no. 63, sura 43:81).

The Messiah did not disdain to present himself as the "servant of God." Rather, he is actually the "servant of Yahweh," of whom Isaiah speaks. Because he accepted humiliation in his quality as servant, the Father has exalted him, giving him a name before which angels, men, and demons bend (cf. Phil 2:9–11). "Those who find it unworthy to adore Jesus, and refuse him honor on account of their pride, as did Iblis once, the chief of the Angels," he will assemble before him to judge them (cf. vv. 170–172). The Koran is alluding to the sin of the angels, which was supposed to have been their refusal to adore Adam. A Christian tradition, passed on chiefly by the Oriental fathers (and surely echoed here in the Koran), has it that the angels sinned by refusing to adore Christ the God-Man, who was presented to them in a vision so that they might make an act of faith in the incarnation, acknowledge their dependence on him, and so receive grace and an eternally glorious life.[65] This most recent proclamation of Jesus' messiahship, made by Mohammed, is a reminder that God's gift is for all men:

O men!
To you has already come the "proof"
on the part of your Lord,
and upon you we have made most clear Light descend!
As for those who believe in God
and cling to Him with confidence,
He shall make them enter into his Mercy
and his grace, and shall guide them to Himself
by a straight path.

[no. 102, sura 4:174–175]

It is not just the Jews, but all men who are addressed here. The proof of the goodness of God has come into the world, and it is Jesus Christ, the most clear light. Enter into Christ, who is the mercy of God (cf. no. 60, sura 19:21; no. 77, sura 11:61/58; no. 99, sura 3:6/8) and his grace! (cf. no. 93, sura 2:207/211). Jesus is the straight way which leads to the Father!

In the chronologically final Sura, the argumentation with the Jews seems to have reached its culminating point. The Koran invites them to practice not only the Torah but also the gospel, and this is laid down as a condition for admission to the divine banquet to which Christ invites

Say: O People of the Book!
For what other thing can you blame us
except for believing in God,
and in that which He has revealed to us,
and in that which He revealed before us? [64/59]

But if the People of the Book believed and feared God
We would purify them of their wickedness
and we shall make them enter gardens of delights! [70/65]

And if they put the Torah into practice and
the Gospel, and that which has been revealed to them
by their Lord, they would enjoy the fruits
which they have above their heads and under their feet. [70/66]

and they are wicked who say:
"God is the third of THREE"!
There is no other divinity, only God is the Unique.
and if they do not stop saying such things
a cruel punishment will touch those
who thus blaspheme. [77/73]

Will they never turn finally to God
asking his pardon?
God is indulgent, He is clement. [78/74]

The Messiah, Son of Mary,
was he not perhaps the Messenger
before whom the Apostles passed
and his Mother was a holy one,
and they both ate food?

Look how we explain clearly to them the "Signs"
and look how they go far from the True. [79/75]

Those among the Sons of Israel who were wicked
were formerly cursed by the mouth of David
and of Jesus Son of Mary,
because they were rebels and prevaricators. [82/78]
[no. 116, sura 5]

Once again we see the condemnation of Jews who calumniate
the Christians and blaspheme God by the gibe: "God is the third
of Three." If the entirety of the mystery (*al-ghaiyeb*) of God's
inner life has been revealed neither in the Old Testament nor in
the Koran's preaching, still the Jews have no business laughing
at things they do not understand, ascribing to the revelation of
Jesus, the gospel, something he never taught, namely, that he
and his mother are two divinities together with God (cf. no. 116,
sura 5:116). In verse 79/75 I deem the *mâ* to be interrogative,
not negative, and translate accordingly. Since the whole context is
directed toward the Jews who do not believe that Jesus is the
Messiah and who insult the honor of his mother, the Koran
reasserts that Jesus was a genuine messenger from God, before
whom the other messengers pass in review in order to honor him,
and his mother was a saint. They were actual people, not
phantasies.

In these texts, when they are read with the Christian key, is an
introduction to the mystery of Christ, but, at the same time, one
is put on guard against false interpretations of the Trinity and the
incarnation, contained in Monophysite and Nestorian formulas.

Awaiting the Return of Christ

A thread of expectation runs throughout the Koran. Mohammed
is constantly invited, together with his followers, to "wait," to

have "patience" ,(cf. no. 33, sura 70:5; no. 89, sura 7:69/71; no. 86, sura 10:21/20, 102; no. 91, sura 6:159/158; etc.). Islam, as it were, is straining toward the general judgment. Indeed, the conclusion of the Koran (no. 116, 5:108/109–120) presents a kind of picture of the judgment. Jesus appears as the Son of Man. Verses 109/110–120 are a presentation in outline of the earthly life of Jesus seen as "true man."

St. Augustine shows in his *De Trinitate* (lib. I, c. 12) the how and the why of Jesus' appearance at the last judgment, as judge, in his "Figure of a Servant" and "Son of Man." It is so that, Augustine says, he may be seen by good and bad alike. The bad are unable to see the "form of God," the divinity of Christ, by which he is equal to the Father. Christ has received from his Father the power of judgment insofar as he is Son of Man; and the preaching of the Koran gave Islam an initial knowledge of the Son of Man.

St. Augustine says "When the Word made himself flesh, he removed from mortals any excuse for remaining in the shadows of death. The warmth of the Word has penetrated this same shadow"; He writes further: "Believe in Christ born in the flesh and you shall reach the Christ born of God, God in God."[66]

Islam's position today, it seems to me, is privileged in its confrontation with Israel and its relationship to the Church, and this both historically and theologically. While Israel continues to deny the historical Christ, Islam, led by the Koran, recognizes Jesus as the Messiah and vindicates the honor of his Mother. The Muslim, already a believer in the Christ born of God and the flesh, will more easily believe in the Christ who is born of God and is God of God. This beginning of a knowledge of Christ can serve as the point of departure for a further unveiling of the unfathomable riches of the mystery of Christ. But to the Christian who has seen deeper into the fullness of the mystery, this initial and deficient knowledge of Christ has always seemed just another heresy pertaining to Jesus. Yet is it not a fact that imperfect knowledge is expressed in vague, incomplete, and obscure formulations? That is why it is the business of the Christian to turn the full light of revelation upon the Koran, to reread it accordingly, and to place in proper relief all those elements which find their deepest meaning in the Christian mystery. In this case, the message of the Koran, which I have hypothetically considered authentic, would take its place in the divine plan.

Some of the fathers of the Church seem to have envisaged the possibility that, outside of Scripture and Christian tradition, God, through his infinite goodness, may have sent messengers and writings to peoples who have not been mature enough to comprehend more than various preliminary elements of supernatural revelation. Thus they would be set on their way toward a later reception of its fullness. Hence I think we may classify the Koran as part of a supernatural economy which is relative and provisional but, nevertheless, acts as an instrument of salvation for a section of mankind still involved in paganism, not yet ready to receive the gospel, and, in a mysterious manner, working with the work of Christ and his Church. Professor Massignon pointed out this preparatory function of Islam when he wrote:

> Moving beyond the descendants of Ishmael, the Muslim religion, bursting forth from Yemen and Oman as far as the Sahara and the Gobi deserts, has brought to far-off places a new community of believers in the one God of Abraham. Starting in Medina, Islam, using the Koran, popularized the taste for a monotheistic revelation among so many people to whom the idea of the Living God of Abraham and the rewards and punishments of the next life had not yet arrived. In Persia, it extinguished forever its sacred fire, to light with Abraham's faith the road to the hereafter. It introduced the Indians to the notion of a personal God and broke the caste system. It extended open arms and the invitation to share in the patriarchal blessing given to the excluded, to the Turks, the Mongols, the Chinese, Indonesians, Malaysians, Berbers and Negroes. With the monotheism of the Bible, it gave them at the same time some simple acquaintance with Jesus Christ and Mary.[67]

Islam remains, to this day, a preparatory economy, a catechumenate oriented toward the full mystery of Christ. This is why it preserves intact the spirit of the Old Testament, with its vision of earthly happiness and its tendency toward restoration of a temporal kingdom of God upon earth, and why it still tolerates a moral inferiority that God once allowed, as in Old Testament times (polygamy, war, etc.). In its role as a provisory and passing dispensation, a catechumenate, the Koran leads each Muslim to making an act of supernatural faith in the one, true God of the Bible.

I really do not think that this fact can be denied — certainly not after the explicit statements of Pope St. Gregory VII in his letter to Sultan Anzir. The Pope declared that the God worshiped by the Muslims is the one, true God whom the Christians adore, *"licet diverso modo"* (*P.L.* 148, c. 450–451). For this reason, I cannot understand why, here and there, a few Catholic authors still say such things as "Allah, the deity of the Koran, was the tribal god of the Arabs."

This supernatural faith in the one, true God, Lord, Creator, and Rewarder (cf. Heb 11:6), contains the rudiments of faith in Jesus Christ — a faith barely seen in the hazy passages of the Koran. It is, however, a faith which is able to give life to supernatural hope in divine justice and in the unlimited mercy of God, who distributes his graces and pardons. The whole Koran is centered upon God and his name. God plays the lead part. His holy name is mentioned more than 10,000 times. He is everywhere present, everywhere exerting his power. The Koran seems prepared to strip every creature of its natural powers in order to protect the transcendence and majesty and absolute dominion of God.

Some Christian apologists, as well as some Orientalists, like to point out how arbitrary the God of the Koran is. They forget that the Koran is reacting against a rabbinic exaggeration which made God, in some way, dependent upon the law. The Koran means to remind the Jews that they must recognize God's place *above* the law.

Islam Has neither Priesthood nor Sacrifice

This fact stands alone in the religious mentality and religious climate of the Semites, and the comparative history of religions seeks to find reasons for it. How did it happen that Islam, a Semitic religion which has many points of contact with both Judaism and Christianity, is the only Semitic religion that has no sacrifice and priesthood? And this in spite of the fact that the entire background of Islam's birth is the pre-Islamic Arab tradition, which had *both?* Precisely because this is inexplicable, it is, for me, just one more proof that Islam has a supernatural origin. At the same time, it shows the internal capacity and the necessity for Islam to integrate and complete itself in the supreme Christian economy. Just because Islam *did* come after Christianity, it could have neither sacrifice nor priesthood. After the incarnation and the sacrifice of Calvary, there could no longer be any genuine sacrifice except that of the cross, nor any priesthood except that of Jesus.

To discover and make an exact estimate of Muslim *pietas,* that profound religious sense with which the Muslim nourishes the theological virtues, and to understand how he strives continuously toward a conscious worship of God, one should read the profound and revealing study of Muslim devotion by Constance Padwick, *Muslim Devotions — A Study of Prayer-Manuals in Common Use.*[68] This book may come as a surprise, but a pleasant one, to many Christians, and particularly to theologians. It will help them see the Muslim in his truly humble search for God.

Thus understood, Islam, the Abrahamitic mystery, aided by the love of true Christians, may rediscover its character as a provisory and relative economy; but, even more than that, it may discover its internal orientation toward the mystery of Jesus, from whom will come the knowledge of the mystery of God, of those treasures of *al-ghayyeb* which remained hidden from the prophet Mohammed.

Reevaluation of the Religious Personality of Mohammed

A duty imposes itself upon every Christian who desires to engage in brotherly dialogue with the Muslims. Except for a few modern instances, Christians, and particularly Western Christians, have assailed Islam. Their weapons have been utter disdain for the Koran, its holy book, the word of God to every Muslim, and, more serious yet, defamation of the man whom each Muslim generation has revered as "the Prophet of God to the Arab people."

To make reparation for this is a simple obligation of justice. But it is likewise an indispensable condition for opening one's mind to understanding the Abrahamitic mystery of Islam. *"Amor dat novos oculos."* To achieve objective evaluation of the true greatness of Mohammed's religious personality and his mission, we have to bear in mind at all times the historical, geographical, and human conditions in which his mission was born and developed. In a sense, this reevaluation and rehabilitation, unfortunately, has already been done — by the wrong people. Starting in the eighteenth century, the Rationalists took a new look at Mohammed, but their aim and spirit was an indirect attack upon Christianity.

We must take up this study of Mohammed's personality once again, viewing him with Christian eyes, and try to form an impartial and, as far as possible, complete judgment of his religious experience and his message. And here is a fact worthy of notice: to this very day, the Church has never made an official and direct judgment of the person and work of Mohammed.

The judgment made by Pope Innocent III in his letter to all the faithful, *De negotio Terrae Sanctae,* might seem to be the Church's condemnation.[69] It is not, however, an infallible definition. It is a judgment based on false ideas that circulated in the Middle Ages; it reflects the mentality of the time. The Pope's application of the text of Revelation is, moreover, a product of that time.

Historical reality has failed to confirm this application of the "vision" concerning the beast. Islam is still with us, and today we know that this judgment upon the person and "bad faith" of Mohammed was mistaken. This same medieval mentality is also behind the judgment of the great Franciscan theologian, Alexander of Hales, upon those who think well of Mohammed and look upon him as an instrument and a messenger from God: *"Illi autem qui venerantur Mohametum quasi Sanctum Dei, per hoc intendentes Deo placere, quasi esset Nuntius Dei, pro apostatis sunt reputandi."*[70]

In the formation of any judgment, it is clear that every Christian has an obligation to keep before him certain principles which demand justice and charity. *"Quid perdo, si credo quod bonus est?"*[71] *"Cum enim hoc datur quod Dei est, sanctum dat etiam non sancta conscientia."*[72] Further, St. Thomas teaches us: *"Dubia judicia de malitia alterius, semper sunt in meliorem partem interpretandum. . . . Et ideo ubi non apparet manifesta indicia de malitia alicuius, debemus eum ut bonum habere, in meliorem partem interpretandum quod dubium est."*[73]

The judgments made by Catholic authors, up to the present, are for the most part full of prejudices which turn out to be quite unjust. Fr. Lammens S.J., though a great Orientalist, to whom much is owed for his invaluable researches, never developed the slightest sympathy for Mohammed and his followers. He did not love them. We have to say the same thing about the pages of "Hanna Zakaria," which are full of resentment, not to say hatred, of Mohammed. The various Catholic encyclopedias are equally impregnated with prejudice against Mohammed and his mission: the article "Mahomet" of H. Leclercq[74] and the article "Coran" of P. Palmieri,[75] which is followed by Professor Casanova's "Mahomet,"[76] though it renders a milder verdict. Thus we see a certain progress in Catholic circles from 1908 (Palmieri) to 1926 (Casanova). The article "Mahomet" by Fr. Powers S.J. is almost wholly dependent upon the judgments of Fr. Lammens.[77]

New avenues, leading to more satisfying answers to the problem of Islam, were opened by the works of Professor Louis Massignon on Muslim mysticism, and especially by his great work upon the Muslim martyr, Ibn Mansur al-Hallâj.[78] The saintly Abbé J. Monchanin's article, "Islam et Christianisme," could be the starting point for finding an adequate answer to the problem of Mohammed's mission.[79] Other works in the same line of thought are also valuable contributions — the more valuable because based on personal experience — those of the Moroccan Franciscan (and former Muslim) Fr. John Abd-el-Jalil, of Abbé Ledit, Fr. Moubarac, Fr. Anawati O.P., Louis Gardet, and others.

It must be freely admitted that Mohammed, seen from the perspective of a thorough study of the Koran, emerges as one of the great religious souls of non-Christian mankind. He responded to a call (no. 1, sura 96:1–5). He was made aware of the absolute primacy of the divine initiative in the life of every man. His response was primarily an act of faith. He introduced his people, the sons of Ishmael, to faith in the God of Abraham, thus fulfilling the ancient promise of God to Abraham of a special blessing for the son of the slave girl Agar and her offspring. He was fully conscious of his mission as a messenger to the sons of Israel as well; he was to proclaim to them the messiahship of Jesus Christ and to defend the honor of Mary. In his own person, he was the first of his people to cast himself into the arms of God and thus become the "first Muslim." He was the first to admit that he is a weak man, as is every man, and subject to passions. He was obliged to confess that he did not have miracle-working charismas. He did not understand the mysteries of God. Though he declared that he was neither a saint nor an intercessor, he was nevertheless a witness, the herald of God's judgments.

Massignon writes:

The secret of this soul, consecrated to such a destiny, remains hidden from us. We cannot afford to take seriously the hypothesis of al-Ghazali, who maintained that from the very beginning Mohammed was "one passionately in love with God," wandering about in the wastelands of Mount Hira, drunk with the desire for union, for Sura 53 is devoid of any outcry of mystical love. Nevertheless, one cannot deny, as have many

Orientalists who were misled by the self-interested arguments of the *foqaha* (Muslim jurists), the sincere and lasting vehemence of his devotion, his severe discipline, those frequent and voluntary prayers he poured forth nightly. This man, like all real leaders, was hard on himself. The very diversity of Muslim mystics' "meditations" upon the interior life of Mohammed is evidence of how mysterious this aspect remains.

Massignon continues:

Let us but take into account that which his public life bears witness to: the evidence of his firmness of will, his mastery of himself, moderation and prudence, meekness and gentleness, patience and providence, all the active qualities of a leader in war and a statesman, and all of these under the discipline of a deep faith. Let us not confuse this, without proof, as do certain neo-Muslims of India, with the heroic personal practice of the Sermon on the Mount. It is an ideal that the Koran does, however, record, and in praise, not in reprobation.[80]

The whole Christian tradition, through the centuries, has been content to emphasize Mohammed's "ferocity and sensuality." Even though Mohammed appeared long after the proclamation of the gospel, Mohammed and Islam — spiritually, qualitatively, and morally — remain fixed in an "era which may be considered analogous to that of the patriarchal law of the Old Testament." (Massignon)

Mecca and Medina are the starting points of a religious journey, a march in God's direction, very much like that of the people of Israel, starting at the foot of Sinai. And so, as regards Mohammed's morality, it behooves us to use moderation — that same moderation the fathers of the Church used when they spoke of, and justified, the polygamy and wars of extermination and genocide carried on in God's name by the patriarchs and holy men of the Old Testament. As were Gideon, David, and Solomon, Mohammed also could have been a man of God, notwithstanding, here and there, a fierce and warlike deed in vindication of God's honor — deeds analogous to the massacres which are presented as ordered by God in the stories of Exodus or the books of Judges and Kings. In spite of his polygamy, and his sensitivity to feminine charm, Mohammed could have been a man of prayer and worship of God, as were the "holy king David, harp of the Holy Spirit," and the wise Solomon, whose harems were much larger than that of Islam's prophet. Only one who understands the mentality of the Semite can appreciate the profound longing for a male line of descent.[81]

This reevaluation must also take into account the constant and lively veneration and respect for Mohammed which has tenaciously gripped the hearts of Muslim populations over the centuries. This restitution to a man of his good name is an act of justice; but it is more. It is an act of gratitude to divine Providence for what it has brought about by the mysterious mission of this "son of Abraham, raised from the stones of the desert," whose mission is only beginning to be seen by Christians for what it was.

"Amor dat novos oculos"

With the eyes and heart of a soul filled with love for Christ, all those who undertake the study of the holy book of Islam and the figure of its prophet will realize that the Lord and his mercy make their presence felt in the message of the Koran and in Mohammed's soul. "All that is good and just in the Koran cannot reveal its deepest meaning or its perfect fulfillment except in our Lord Jesus Christ." (Pius XII)

PART FOUR

VATICAN COUNCIL II, DIALOGUE BETWEEN CHRISTIANS AND MUSLIMS, AND CONCLUSION

Vatican Council II and the Muslim Religion

THE NEW SPIRIT IN DEALING WITH THE MUSLIM WORLD

It is true, in the course of centuries many dissensions and hostilities have arisen between Christians and Muslims. Often Church historians and other Christians have blamed only the Muslims. It is difficult for a Christian to look back impartially on so many judgments concerning Muslims given throughout the centuries, especially with regard to two very sensitive points in the Muslim soul: The Person of the Prophet Muhammad and the sacred character of the Qur'än. We must admit that throughout a period of thirteen centuries — allowing for a few exceptions — the Church has always viewed Islam in its deficiencies and negatively. The Church has made hardly any effort to discover the deep religious character of the Muslim religion.

We must affirm today that the Christians of the West had seen the rapid spread of Islam throughout the Mediterranean basin including the conquest of Sicily and Spain. It was similar to the victory of the Greco-Roman expansion over the "Syrian" civilization begun with Alexander the Great.[1] In the eleventh century the young forces of the religious and cultural Christian rebirth reacted to the Muslim expansion more through an instinct for preservation than by a purely evangelical vision. Medieval Christianity responded with armed Crusaders against the belligerent efforts of Islam, and the Crusades have left down through the centuries an inheritance of mutual misunderstanding between East and West. The medieval mind had many confused and inaccurate ideas concerning the origin and person of Mohammed and was incapable of discovering the authentic religious values in Islam. Mohammed was the continual object of personal ridicule on the part of Christianity. The apologetic work of Peter the Venerable stagnated for centuries the opinion of Christians regarding the image of the Arab prophet and his religion. Islam was considered the fruit of diabolical forces on a political and military plane which only the sword could defeat. It was the most anti-Christian force that the Church would ever encounter in her history.[2]

After the call of Blessed Urban II for the First Crusade, it became common parlance in Christianity to designate the Muslims as "a people without God . . . an impious people . . . dogs . . . chaff destined for eternal fire." Unfortunately, this vocabulary — far from charitable — was used for centuries by Christians, and even appeared in papal documents. In order to justify her actions, the Church, conscious of her divine mission, sometimes was stern with those who dishonored her with their scandalous lives, by their spirit of schism, and by the spread of new, dangerous, and false doctrines. However, she still bears the responsibility of having closed for centuries, to millions of souls, access to the Gospel because of the lack of charitable understanding and respect for the Muslim conscience.[3]

We must admit that in recent years a new avenue has been opened for the purpose of overcoming the misunderstanding and hostility to which the Declaration of Vatican Council II alludes.

In the middle of the last century a new stage in the study of Islam had begun. European Orientalists undertook a more direct and less biased study of the historical and religious phenomenon known as Islam under its multiple aspects.

This whole new movement, along with other factors, has altered the attention on the part of the Catholic Church. Islam came to be considered above all and strictly for its religious values. In the past it would seem that Christian apologists were satisfied in placing in relief the negative aspects of Islam in the development of society.

Immediately after the war, following the lead of the Egyptians, many Muslim nations wanted to enter into diplomatic relations with the Holy See. For the holy pontiff, Pius XII, by his actions favoring peace and helping so many victims of the war, had awakened a true admiration even in the Muslim world. On the occasion of the presentation of the credentials by his excellency Omar Taher Bey, the new minister of Egypt to the Holy See (October 17, 1947), the *Osservatore Romano* spoke of "the beginning of a new era in the relationship between the Catholic Church and the Muslim world." In fact, after Egypt, diplomatic relations were established with Lebanon, Syria, Pakistan, Indonesia, Iran, and under the pontificate of John XXIII, with Turkey. Pope John, who had previously lived in the Muslim world and who had a high regard for the religious qualities of such a sincerely pious people, wanted that the words in the prayer of consecration to Christ the King which were offensive to the Muslims be suppressed: "Be you King also of those who are still involved in the darkness of idolatry or of Islam." Whereas it is true that the Protestants preceded the Catholics in the study of Islam up to the beginning of this century, Catholic religious orders made a tremendous contribution in recent years to Islamic Studies by organizing some Study Centers.

ISLAM CONSIDERED PRINCIPALLY AS A RELIGION

Before the Crusades, we find in papal documents a letter of Pope St. Gregory VII to the Muslim Prince Anzir which the "Declaration" of Vatican Council II cited. Assuming the importance of the document, I believe that it is well to report it in English:

> Gregory, Bishop, Servant of the Servants of God, to Anzir, King of the province of Sitifense of Mauritania, in Africa, health and apostolic benediction.
> Your Majesty has sent us letters this year seeking that we

should ordain a bishop according to the norms of the Christian constitutions. We have voluntarily complied because it seems to us that your request is just and most worthy. After you had sent gifts to us, you have also freed some Christians who were your slaves out of reverence for St. Peter, Prince of the Apostles, and for love of Us, promising, at the same time, to free more of them.

This generosity could not have been inspired in your heart except by God the Creator of all things without Whom we cannot do anything good, in fact, not even think of Him; He Who enlightens every man who comes into this world was the One Who illuminated your mind to make this decision. In fact, the Omnipotent God, Who desires all men to be saved and that none be lost, approves nothing higher in us after love of Him than the love of man for man that he should do unto others as he would want done unto himself.

We must exchange charity such as this more particularly among ourselves than towards other people, the reason being that, although it is in a different manner, we believe and we confess the one, true God and it is He Whom we praise and venerate every day as the Creator of all ages and Ruler of the world. As the Apostle says: He is our peace. He Who out of two things has made the only one . . . God is our witness that we sincerely love you to the glory of God and we wish you good things and prosperity in this present life and in the future, and that the same God lead you, after a long sojourn in this life, to the bosom of our blessed and most holy Patriarch Abraham to whom we pray with our lips and our heart.[4]

This letter seems to have been ignored for many centuries by "Christian apologists" who often, up to recent times, had insisted that "Alläh," the God of whom the Qur'än speaks and whom the Muslims adore, was not the God of biblical revelation. Furthermore, this letter affirms not only explicitly that Christians and Muslims adore the same God in a different manner but also that the distribution of supernatural illuminating grace which came from Jesus Christ also resides among pious Muslim souls. Throughout the letter the Pope seems to treat the Sultan Anzir as a "religious man" and considered Islam as a religion.

POPE PAUL VI AND DIALOGUE WITH ISLAM

This important attitude of considering Islam as a religion rather than as a culture or political system would seem to me to be the same spirit we explicitly find in the letter of our Holy Father Paul VI.

The Pope, in his first encyclical "Ecclesiam suam" of August 6, 1964, had invited all men of good will to dialogue with the Catholic Church. In his encyclical he presented a vision of all humanity centered in Christ and in His Church marked by diverse "approaches." The first wide and all-embrasive circle includes all humanity. In the second circle he recognizes all those who adore the one and true God: the Jews, who remain even today the people of Israel, and the Muslims, heirs also of a common father of believers: Abraham. In the third circle our separated Christian brethren are found. It seems to me that it is worthwhile to report the words regarding the Muslims:

> Then we see another circle around us. This, too, is vast in its extent, yet it is not so far away from us. It is made up of those who adore the one, supreme God whom we too adore.
>
> We mean the children, worthy of our affection and respect, of the Hebrew people, faithful to the religion that we call that of the Old Testament. Then, the adorers of God according to the conception of monotheism, *the religion of the Muslims especially,* deserving of our admiration for all that is true and good in their worship of God. And also the followers of the great Afro-Asiatic religions.[5]

Here Paul VI presents a vision of all non-Christian religions without pretending to give any specific judgment on them. It is significant that a certain hierarchical order is found. Judaism has a very particular relation with the Church; and after Judaism among other monotheistic religions (Sikhism and perhaps ancient Confucianism) the Muslim religion has a special place. Paul VI does not give the reasons for the special place he gives to Islam but we find this emphasis both in the Constitution on the Church and, even more detailed, in the conciliar Declaration on non-Christian Religions.

After the classification of the various religions, the Holy Father believed it opportune to declare that the appraisal of the true and authentic religious values contained in each of these should not entice us to be unassuming or indifferent:

> Obviously we cannot share in these various forms of religion, nor can we remain indifferent to the fact that each of them, in its own way, should authorize its followers not to seek to discover whether God has revealed the perfect and definitive form, free from all error, in which He wishes to be known, loved and served. Indeed, honesty compels us to declare openly our conviction that there is but one true religion, the religion of Christianity. It is our hope that all who seek God and adore Him may come to acknowledge its truth.
>
> But we do, nevertheless, recognize and respect the moral and spiritual values of the various non-Christian religions, and we desire to join with them in promoting and defending common ideals of religious liberty, human brotherhood, good culture, social welfare and civil order. For Our part, We are ready to enter into discussion on these common ideals, and will not fail to take the initiative where Our offer of discussion in genuine, mutual respect would be well received.[6]

After the explicit clarification of the unique and transcendent validity of Christianity, the Holy Father succinctly enumerates, in relation to the other religions, the possible areas for common collaboration: in the field of religious liberty, that of the community of man, cultural recognition, good works in the social and civil order. These are various areas which were already referred to by Pope John XXIII who had asked for the collaboration of all men of good will in his encyclical letter *Pacem in Terris*.

VATICAN COUNCIL II AND THE MUSLIM RELIGION

It is not easy to see and to foresee today all the valid and important consequences of the work of renewal promoted by

Vatican Council II. In this article I can only limit myself to outline a few aspects of those things which are new avenues treated by the Council for a mutual understanding of Christians with the Muslim world. That which the Council has left us in its "Declaration on the Relationship of the Church to Non-Christian Religions," especially with regard to Islam, must be considered as a consequence of long investigation within the last sixty years. I feel that it would be useful to outline some conclusions of this investigation before attempting a deeper analysis of the Council's text.

The letter *Ecclesiam suam* of Pope Paul VI prepared the great conciliar document which is the dogmatic constitution *De Ecclesia.* Chapter 2 of the Constitution speaks of the "People of God." In this chapter we find the sacramental ontological basis of all ecclesiology, which goes beyond the encyclical of Pius XII *Mystici Corporis;* and, avoiding a vocabulary too juridical, the Council emphasized the biblical notion of the "People of God." This expression is not only a biblical one but also historical insofar as it views the Church not statically but in its dynamic becoming, destined to assemble all humanity which by right is instituted in Christ. After having spoken of the various persons who "belong" to the Church and are incorporated in it, either perfectly or imperfectly, as the "People of God" through Baptism, faith, etc., the Council has accentuated the manner in which those who have not yet accepted the Gospel of Christ find themselves "included" in the "People of God." By a singular privilege Judaism is recognized as: "The people to whom the covenants and the promises were given and from whom Christ was born according to the flesh" (Rom 9:4–5). On account of their fathers, this people remain most dear to God, for God does not repent of the gifts He makes" (cf. Rom 11:28–29).

Secondly, the constitution explicitly speaks of the Muslims who also enter into the plan of Salvation:

> But the plan of salvation also includes those who acknowledge the Creator. In the first place among these there are the Muslims, who, professing to hold the faith of Abraham, along with us

adore the one and merciful God, who on the last day will judge mankind.[7]

These few lines do not pretend to describe the Muslim religion; in fact, the presentation of the Muslim faith as presented here is very limited. Instead, it is obvious that the Council has attempted to treat the essential religious elements of the monotheistic Muslim faith. Islam is a religion and the Council considers it as such. It is a religion centered around the God of Abraham, recognized as the Creator. And even more than that, the God adored by the Muslims is the one, true, and merciful God of biblical revelation Whom we adore and Who will come to judge resurrected humanity. It is these essentially religious elements that the "Declaration" presents in a broader context.

DECLARATION ON THE RELATIONSHIP OF THE CHURCH TO NON-CHRISTIAN RELIGIONS

On October 28, 1965, Paul VI signed the "Declaration of the Ecumenical Vatican Council II on the relationship of the Church to non-Christian religions." The date was significant for the same Holy Father deigned to single it out in his homily "It pleases Us." He referred to the fact that "it occurs on the feast of the Holy Apostles Simon and Jude, in whose honor the word of the Lord was just dedicated, with the reading of the Gospel just heard, in which words the joy of the apostolic mission was promised and not its facility. In spite of the difficulty that is encountered and the suffering which it reserves, whoever exercises this apostolic mission learns a lesson. It pleases Us also that this is verified on the anniversary of the election of Our venerated predecessor John XXIII to whose inspired idea We owe the convocation of the Council."[8]

The word of the Lord to which the Pope made reference was "proclaimed" in the Gospel of the Mass which was related by St. John the Evangelist in the Discourse at the Last Supper. Jesus had clearly presented the difficulty of the apostolic mission, which is joined to the continuation of the salvific activity of Jesus, more particularly in His sufferings, in His passion, and in His death (cf. Jn 15:17–25). These words of Jesus — in the will of the Holy Father — must be present to all who apply themselves to the study and the realization of the solemn documents which the Holy Father and the Council Fathers promulgated by their apostolic authority. The documents are not only the declaration *Nostra aetate* concerning non-Christian religions but the three conciliar decrees: (1) *Christus Dominus,* on the pastoral office of bishops; (2) *Perfectae caritatis,* on the renewal of religious life; (3) *Optatam totius,* on the ministry and formation of priests; together with the declaration *Gravissimus educationis,* on the Christian education of youth.

The pastoral office of bishops is to continue the work of sanctifying humanity, to the glorification of the heavenly Father, according to the apostolic mandate left by Jesus Christ. This pastoral activity finds effective cooperation in the priestly ministry and in the total dedication of those consecrated souls in religious life. In this panorama of an activity aimed at the sanctification of humanity, the Church sees at a divine glance the immense parts of humanity which have an approach to God through religions which are non-Christian, "by which men search for God, groping for Him that they may by chance find Him."[9]

The maternal glance of the Church is fixed on those parts of humanity to which a full knowledge of the mystery of Christ and the means of salvation have not yet reached. This glance is fixed by the Council in its declaration on the relationship of the Church to non-Christian religions.

It has been justly noted that for the first time in the history of conciliar documents we find "Declarations." The promulgation of some "declarations" (three in number: besides the two mentioned before — on Christian education and on the relationship of the Church to non-Christian religions — the declaration on religious liberty) has been one of the innovations introduced by Vatican Council II. It may be asked what force do these documents have. According to the most accepted opinions we are treating of documents that express the "feeling" of the Church on certain important questions. Naturally, these documents presuppose a teaching which can be found more explicitly enunciated in doctrinal documents as the "constitutions"; but with the "declarations" the Council wishes to establish guidelines of a practical nature.

The material of the "Declaration on the Relationship of the Church to non-Christian Religions" was originally at the beginning of Chapter 4 of the Decree on Ecumenism. The declaration was refused more than twice and after the second session it became a separate text. It was Cardinal Bea who presented it to the Counciliar assembly on September 25, 1964, and passed it for discussion from the 28th to the 30th of September. The debates were centered on the section concerning Judaism. In fact, at the very first discussion, when this material was offered as a part of chapter 4 of the schema on Ecumenism, no one spoke of anything else except the Jews. The reaction of certain factions remained absorbed in old considerations of anti-semitism, and the bishops of Arabic countries, who feared a political misinterpretation of the Declaration, as if it would contain a reference to the Israeli state, continued debates almost completely concerning the Hebrew people. This explains why the other religions were not taken up directly as subjects of discussion. Someone has noted that the theme and the spirit was totally new and that the majority of the Fathers were not prepared to discuss similar topics.

The declaration is presented in five brief paragraphs:

(1) A *preamble*: It relates the process of unification which all mankind is tending toward today; therefore the Church examines with greater attention the nature of its relationship to non-Christian religions. She wishes to examine these things in order that men may have before them all that they have in common: their common origin from God and their common eternal destiny. The Church can also give an answer to many questions concerning the human condition, etc.

(2) The second paragraph, after having emphasized the religious sense innate in man which many times arrives at a knowledge of a Supreme Being, points to the two great religions of the

Far East: Hinduism and Buddism, and "to other religions to be found everywhere which strive variously to answer the restless searchings of the human heart by proposing 'ways' which consist of teachings, rules of life, and sacred ceremonies."

(3) The Muslim religion, as already stated in the Constitution on the Church, is considered specifically and this is so precisely because in its religious nature it does not belong to that group of religions from the Far East, but is an addition and is also related to the religion of the Bible.

(4) The fourth article is concerned with Judaism and wishes to bring to mind the links by which the people of the New Testament are spiritually bound to the lineage of Abraham.

(5) The fifth paragraph, finally, affirms the universal brotherhood of all men which excludes every discrimination in those things which concern the dignity of man and diminishes their rights. It bids all Christians — according to the admonition of the Apostles Peter and Paul — and ardently implores them to "maintain good fellowship among the nations," (1 Pt 2:12) and if it is possible as far as in them lies to keep peace with all men (cf. Rom 12:8) so that they may truly be sons of the Father Who is in heaven.

THE VIEW OF THE CHURCH ON ISLAM

The third paragraph, which is the view of the Church on Islam, presents the authentic elements in the Muslim religion.

Upon the Muslims, too, the Church looks with esteem. They adore one God, living and enduring, merciful and all-powerful, Maker of heaven and earth and Speaker to men. They strive to submit wholeheartedly even to His inscrutable decrees, just as did Abraham, with whom the Islamic faith is pleased to associate itself. Though they do not acknowledge Jesus as God, they revere Him as a prophet. They also honor Mary, His virgin mother; at times they call on her, too, with devotion. In addition they await the day of judgment when God will give each man his due after raising him up. Consequently, they prize the moral life, and give worship to God especially through prayer, almsgiving, and fasting.[10]

We should not seek in these words of the Council a theological interpretation of so important a religious fact as Islam is. The Declaration maintains a practical level with the intent of opening a dialogue with the Muslims also; and it was not even a remote attempt to present a theology of the religions of the world. The above notwithstanding, it seems to me that the elements emphasized as characteristic of Muslim spirituality merit to be considered as points of departure in order to initiate our dialogue with the Muslims. And the following are presented as the essential aspects of the Muslim faith:

1. The Muslims adore the one, true, living, and sustaining God, Creator of heaven and earth.
2. Their spiritual attitude before God is to be completely submissive to His supreme will, just as did Abraham, "with whom the Islamic faith is pleased to associate itself."
3. The Muslims venerate Jesus Christ and honor His most holy mother Mary.
4. They believe in the future life awaiting the last judgment "when God will give each man his due after raising him up."
5. They are bound to a moral law and give worship to God through prayer, almsgiving and fasting.

These five points which the Declaration presents as authentic elements of the religious spirituality of the Muslim soul deserve to be examined one by one as constituting "the glance of esteem which the Church has for the Muslims, and also topics of mutual dialogue."

I do not pretend here to explain these various topics in detail. I wish to limit myself to a few considerations and suggest some avenues of research for a major theological reflection. As I have previously indicated, a preliminary need for dialogue is to abandon all the prejudices accumulated for centuries in Christian consciences against the Prophet Mohammed and the Qur'än. We can never penetrate the spirituality of the Muslim world if we do not understand the religious personality of the Prophet of Islam. In order to penetrate the secret of Mohammed's soul it is necessary, in addition, to have a certain familiarity with the Qur'än.

> Precisely because they did not sufficiently frequent the Qur'än (Professor Louis Massignon wrote) many Europeans studied Muslim thinkers from the outside, without entering into the heart of Islam itself; not having known how to become a sincere guest of this "Community" — ever alive — after thirteen hundred years that its members wished to live together, they (Europeans) were not able to gather either the radiant structure or the central interdependence of the lives which their patient erudition divided.[11]

If this is true for those who study the lives and the spirituality of many Muslim mystics, it is particularly true with regard to those who study the personality of Mohammed. The same must be said for the sincere and sympathetic study of the Qur'än.

THE WORSHIP OF THE GOD OF ABRAHAM

The Church in the conciliar documents has understood that the God worshiped by the Muslims is the living and true God of the revelation to Abraham. The fact that the "Declaration" cites the letter of Pope Gregory VII is significant. One can no longer, it seems to me, speak of Islam as a "natural religion" in the sense that the God Whom they worship is the God "arrived at by the faculty of human reason," and not the God of biblical Revelation.

It is true that the essence of the religion of Mohammed and the Muslims is the proclamation of the absolute divine transcendence. But the monotheism of the Qur'än cannot be reduced to a pure affirmation of the natural order as that of a "natural theodicy." The attitude of Mohammed and of the Muslims before the mystery of God is not a simple "philosophical" attitude but essentially a religious one. He and his followers did not arrive at God through a process of rational proofs, but rather discovered the God of Abraham under the impulse of supernatural grace.

This truth, it seems to me, is confirmed by the explicit acknowl-

edgment made in the "Declaration" concerning the relationship between the religion of Abraham and that of the Muslims, in the
passage quoted earlier: "They [the Muslims] strive to submit
wholeheartedly even to His inscrutable decrees as did Abraham
with whom the Islamic faith is pleased to associate itself." It
is this condition of absolute dependence on God Mohammed
experienced in his early youth as an orphan and throughout his
life. Man cannot pretend to be anything: all that he has, all that
he is, is a pure gift of God. God, therefore, appears as the supreme
and absolute liberty that claims continual adoration and the confession of divine omnipotence.

Perhaps it is too superficial to speak about the God of the
Qur'än as a "capricious arbitrator" and to speak about the
"fatalism of the Qur'än" without regard to its profound sense of
divine transcendence and liberty. This absolute will exacts as an
answer on the part of man complete dependence and total un-
conditional surrender of himself to the Lordship of God. *Islam*
means precisely "total submission"; *Muslim* means "he who is
submissive to God." As the Qur'än says: "Abraham was the first
Muslim" (submissive to God.)

This relationship to Abraham is explicitly expressed by every
Muslim at the end of his prayer:

> O God call down blessing on Muhammed
> and on the family of Muhammed
> As thou didst call down blessing
> on Abraham and on the family of Abraham.

"Through this *tasliya* the Muslim faith links itself," Professor
Massignon wrote, "to the prayer of Abraham, who is called the
founder of the Muslim community (Sura 22:77), and consequently
superior to Mohammed according to some ancient scholars. It [the
Muslim faith] thus points to a supernatural source, giving it, one
could almost say, a theological foundation: the last incorruptible
part of the paternal legacy to Ishmael, finally rediscovered and venerated with a jealous exclusivism."[12]

PRESENTATION OF THE MYSTERY OF CHRIST

I have attempted a "Christian reading" of the Qur'än, that is, a reinterpretation of the sacred book of Islam in the light of Christ, applying to it, in addition, the methods of biblical criticism. I see the message of the Qur'än as intended for the Jews of Mecca first, then for those of Medina and for the Arab pagans, descendents of Ishmael.

The Qur'än is a "revelation" destined for the pagan Arabs who are the descendents of Ishmael, as well as a witness to the Messiahship of Jesus for the Jews of Mecca and Medina. It is the beginning of an avenue to God; the discovery of the first commandment to an idolatrous people and, at the same time, the first presentation of Jesus. Under certain aspects this initial march is comparable to the beginning of the religious-social development of the Hebrew people in the desert of Sinai, under the guidance of Moses. Between Moses and Mohammed profound psychological and spiritual similarities exist. The religious content and the social ethics of the Sinaitic message are similar to those of the message of the Qur'än. It is to this desert situation that the Qur'än speaks, not to that of the Israelites in Palestine at the time of the coming of Jesus and even less to that of orthodox Christianity of the seventh century.

But the Qur'än is, in addition, an initial presentation to the Arabs of the mysterious personage of Jesus Christ; and, above all, it is a calling back of the Jews of Mecca and Medina in order to recognize that Christ was the Messiah. Jesus, the Messiah, and His mother, the Virgin Mary, are the personages that dominate the Qur'än by their excellence among all other biblical figures. The Qur'anic references to Mary are much more articulate than those to Jesus. In the Qur'än there is, admittedly, only an initial presentation of the mystery of Christ which must be exemplified to the Muslims by the apostolic activity of the Christians.

Rereading the Qur'än "in the light of Christ" makes it clear that this initial presentation of the mystery of Christ was destined for the idolatrous and pagan Arabic people until now closed to the Gospel, for the Jews of Arabia, and perhaps for the millions of "pagans" in other parts of the world who have not yet arrived at a notion of the personal God of biblical revelation. This presentation, according to the "divine pedagogy," must be gradual, as St. Paul says (1 Cor 3:1–3). It should have been the task of the Church to help the Muslim — beginning with the Christian truth, implicit and latent in the Qur'än — to come to a full understanding of the mystery of Christ.

I believe that there is more Christian truth in the Qur'än than usually recognized by Christians. While Israel continues to reject the historical Christ, Islam, as presented in the Qur'än, recognizes Jesus as the Messiah and vindicates against Israel the honor of His most Holy Mother. The Muslims already believe in a Christ born of the flesh, and one day they may more easily believe in a Christ born of God — a God from God. This initial acknowledgment of the mystery of Christ must be the point of departure for a more profound discovery of the unfathomable riches of the mystery of the Incarnation.

THE LONGED FOR RETURN OF CHRIST AND THE RESURRECTION

The Declaration of the Council also states: "[The Muslims] believe in an after-life, await the last judgment, when God will give each man his due after raising him up." Mohammed, answering the divine call, was not only the herald of Abraham's monotheism to the Arab people, the cantor of the greatness of God in creation, the proclaimer of the messiahship of Jesus Christ to the Israelite community of Mecca and Medina, but also "the prophet of the last judgment" who preached the last judgment, the resurrection of the dead, and a future life. The themes of the resurrection of the dead and of the final judgment, re-echo the apocalyptic biblical pronunciations, and are continually heard, especially in his preaching in Mecca. Therefore, there is in the Qur'än an accent on "awaiting." Mohammed is continually invited, along with his followers, "to await," "to be patient" —

because Islam is like an expectation toward the day of the final judgment.

In fact, the conclusion of the Qur'än, contained in Sura 5 (the last in chronological order), presents for us the scene of the last judgment. There Jesus appears as the "Son of Man." The verses 109/110–120 are a schematic representation of the earthly life of Christ, the true and perfect man. And God is presented in the Qur'än as the Supreme Judge. (Fr. Moubarac uses in his definition of Islam the term "Monotheistic Eschatology.")

Jesus is the "Sign" and the "Knowledge" of the "now," of the final judgment (sura 43:61). Muslim tradition speaks about the end of time as the supreme manifestation of the justice of God, of His triumph over Satan, and of Jesus' victory over the anti-Christ. The same tradition is not definite with regard to the "Divine Justice," which some attribute to Jesus' return to earth as *Mahdih*, "The Guide."

As I have stated elsewhere, I feel that precisely because of this eschatological vigilance of the final resurrection and because of the expectation of the second coming of Jesus Christ as Judge, we must arrive at the conviction that — through the Virgin Mary — Islam is intimately directed and orientated toward Christ as the "cathecumenate of the sons of Ishmael."[13]

THE COMMUNITY OF GOD IN A PATH TOWARD HIM

The entire message of the Qur'än is a "recall for a return to God." This call is constantly repeated: "And you will all return to Him." Human life, according to the Qur'än as well as to the Bible, is nothing else but a "path toward God" (cf. sura 1:2, 8; 2:142, 213; 3:51; 96, 101; 5:16; 6:39, 87 etc.). The Muslim must belong "entirely to God." ("I did not create angels and men other than that I should be worshipped!")

The "Declaration" says that the Muslims "have an esteem for the moral life and render worship to God, above all, by prayer, fasting, and almsgiving." Islam, centered about the faith of the

God of Abraham, has brought to the masses of humanity which did not yet receive the message of the Bible, the directives of the God of Revelation. The first and principal duty of every man, according to the Qur'än, is that of proclaiming the unity of God by means of the shahâda: "There is no other divinity except God." Except for the profession of faith, presupposed always as sincere, the religion of the Qur'än leaves the conscience to the rule of natural law and to the entirely personal interior movement of grace. Islam has not assumed the task to fathom the intimacies of the heart but instead it recalls the divine sanctions that are necessary for the social traces of sin. In fact, the "commandments of Sinai" are found in the Qur'än although their formulation is not exactly the same as in the Bible. God's commandments which the Qur'än presents to us may be reduced to twelve:

1. to proclaim the unity of God (shahâda);
2. to respect one's mother and father;
3. to be good toward one's neighbor and the weak;
4. to give alms to the needy;
5. not to kill new-born babes for fear of poverty;
6. not to fornicate;
7. not to kill;
8. to respect the goods of orphans and widows;
9. to keep one's promises;
10. to give just due, that is, not to steal;
11. not to curse;
12. not to be proud.[14]

The "right path," the "way of God," the means by which one must "return to Him" consists in the fulfillment of these divine precepts. The end of this path is the last judgment, which follows the resurrection, when the just will be presented as those who have fulfilled the precepts of the Lord.

In connection with this concept of God as the end of human life and in relation to the various duties or precepts formulated by God in His law, we can also find in the Qur'än a doctrine of sin, seen as a transgression of divine ordinances, disobedience to the command of God, revolt against God, and ingratitude. The worst sin is that of refusing to recognize God as one and to associate with Him other beings in adoration. In fact, Islam has been concerned primarily with the external aspect of one's act, and not always with the internal intention. For this reason it punishes only the social aspects of sin, and tends to minimize the reality of original sin and the significance of intent. It punishes adultery but not the impure desire; it punishes fraud and cheating but not lying; it punishes detraction and calumny but not envy. So the responsibility of the agent is reduced to external imputable acts.

This "extrinsic" structure of Islam demonstrates the religious antimony inherent in the very nature of the religion of the Qur'än. There is lacking a living doctrinal authority and the sacramental action of the priesthood which is found in the Church of Christ and prefigured in the authority of the "synagogue" and in the "levitical priesthood" of the Old Testament. In Islam the tension between personal prophetic inspiration and the external law cannot find an equilibrium; and the history of the conflict between the doctors of the law and the mystic sages confirms this tragedy.

Because of this deficiency of "interiority," the Muslim society is continually tempted to succumb to formalism, phariseism, and juridicalism that extinguishes the flame of the spirit. Hence, there is a tendency to reduce the spiritual to the temporal and the values of faith, which are "above reason," to the level of reason, etc.[15]

These deficiencies and these temptations proceed from the fact that Islam remains, in a certain sense, the "original religion of Abraham," before Sinai and before Pentecost. Yet, the Spirit of God has not ceased to raise up through the centuries generous and holy souls who fixed their minds upon the holiness of the biblical characters presented in the Qur'än, especially upon the character of Jesus, and allowed themselves to be transported by grace to union with God.[16]

CONCLUSION

The following words, found in this same declaration seem very significant:

> Although in the course of the centuries many quarrels and hostilities have arisen between Christians and Muslims, this most sacred Synod urges all to forget the past and to strive sincerely for mutual understanding. On behalf of all mankind, let them make common cause of safeguarding and fostering social justice, moral values, peace, and freedom.[17]

In paragraph 3 of the "Declaration on the Relationship of the Church to non-Christian Religions" the directive is given to enter into a dialogue with the Muslim world upon a strictly religious plane.

I have made an effort to deal with the five points that the Council has emphasized as the authentic elements of the spirituality of the Muslim, elements which can be taken as a basis for a reinterpretation of the sacred book of Islam.

The "dialogue of salvation" may help the Muslim people to continue on their march toward the Lord Jesus Christ, a march which had begun with Islam itself, but which had been arrested for centuries.

The dialogue is nothing but a beginning. Both sides need preparation with prayer and study. "It is necessary before speaking to listen to the voice and more so the heart of man . . . It is necessary that we become brothers . . . The climate for a dialogue is friendship" (Paul VI, *Ecclesiam suam*). "Love gives new eyes," St. Augustine used to say.

St. Bonaventure, New York   FR. GIULIO F. BASETTI-SANI O.F.M.

FOOTNOTES

Part One

1. G. Basetti-Sani, *Louis Massignon: Christian Ecumenist — Prophet of Inter-Religious Reconciliation* (Chicago, 1974).

2. L. Massignon, "Le Signe Marial," *Rhythmes du Monde,* no. 3 (1948), pp. 12ff.

3. J. Abd-el-Jalil, *L'Islam et Nous* (Paris, 1947), *Breve Histoire de la Littérature Arabe* (Paris, 1947), *Aspects intérieurs de l'Islam* (Paris, 1949), *Marie et l'Islam* (Paris, 1950); Y. Moubarac, *Abraham dans le Coran,* (Paris, 1958), *Pentalogie Islamo-Chrétienne* (Beirut, 1972–73), vols. 1–4.

4. Y. Moubarac, *Abraham dans le Coran — L'Histoire d'Abraham dans le Coran et la naissance de l'Islam.*

5. Y. Moubarac, "Etapes d'une voie spirituelle d'aprés l'Histoire d'Abraham dans le Coran et ses correspondances dans la vie de Muhammad," in *Abraham dans le Coran,* pp. 179–185.

6. L. Massignon, *La Passion de Hallâj martyr mystique de l'Islam* (new ed.; Paris, 1975), 3:213–217, 300–306, 326.

7. *Nouvelle Revue de Science Missionnaire* (Beckerin, Switz.), 10 (1954): 180–193, reproduced in *Muslim World* (Hartford, Conn., Oct. 1956), pp. 345–353, and in *World Dominion* (London, Oct. 1957), pp. 239–246.

8. C. Ledit, *Mahomet, Israel et le Christ* (Paris, 1956).

9. J. Montchanin, "Islam et Christianisme," *Bulletin des Missions* (St. André lez Bruges), 17 (1938): 10–23.

10. See G. Basetti-Sani, "Muhammad è un vero Profeta?" *Renovatio* (Genoa), 10, no. 4 (Oct.–Dec. 1975): 412–455.

Part Two

1. See Montgomery Watt, *Bell's Introduction to the Qur'ân* (Edinburgh, 1970), pp. 57–58.

2. Papiae, 1539.

3. *L'Alcorano di Maometto, nel quale si contiene la dottrina, la dottrina e le leggi sue* (Venice, 1547). See J. Kritzeck, *Sons of Abraham* (Baltimore, 1965), pp. 67–68.

4. A. J. Arberry, *The Koran Interpreted* (London, 1955), 1:14.

5. London, 1930 (Mentor Book, N.Y.).

6. R. Bell, *The Qur'ân. Translation with a Critical Re-Arrangement of the Surah* (Edinburgh, 1937–39), 2 vols.

7. Arberry said: "Disciples of the Higher Criticism, having watched with fascinated admiration how their masters played havoc with the traditional sacrosanctity of the Bible, threw themselves with brisk enthusiasm into the congenial task of demolishing the Koran. . . . The most extreme representative of this school of thought, which once tyrannised over Koranic studies in the West, was no doubt the late Dr. Richard Bell. . . . It is against this excess of anatomical mincing that I argue the unity of the Sura and the Koran" (*The Koran Interpreted*, 2:10, 11, 12).

8. R. Blachère, *Le Coran* (Paris, 1947), 2:xv.

9. Moubarac, *Abraham dans le Coran*, pp. 91–95.

10. Abd-el-Jalil, *Aspects intérieurs de l'Islam*, pp. 30–31.

11. Kritzeck, *Sons of Abraham*, pp. 33–40.

12. Moubarac, *Abraham dans le Coran*, pp. 173–174.

13. Y. Moubarac, *Les Etudes d'Epigraphie Sud-Semitique et Naissance de l'Islam* (Paris, 1957).

14. E. Sayous, *Jesus Christ d'apres Mahomet ou les notions et les doctrines musulmanes sur le Christianisme* (Paris–Leipzig, 1881).

15. Tor Andrae, *Mohammed — The Man and His Faith* (New York, 1955); Italian translation by Francesco Gabrieli: *Maometto, la sua vita e la sua fede* (Bari, 1934), p. vii (English edition, pp. 112–113).

16. *Bell's Introduction to the Qur'ân*, pp. 7–9.

17. R. Blachère, *Le Problème de Mahomet* (Paris, 1952), pp. 22, 62–63.

18. G. Widengren, *Muhammaed, the Apostle of God and His Ascension* (Uppsala, 1955).

19. H. J. Schoeps, *Theologie und Geschishte des Judenchristentum* (Tübingen, 1949).

20. Moubarac, *Abraham dans le Coran*, pp. 146, 148.

21. H. C. Puech, *Le Manichéisme. Son Fondateur, sa doctrine* (Paris, 1949).

22. T. Boman, *Hebrew Thought Compared with Greek* (London, 1960); J. Barr, *The Semantics of Biblical Language* (London, 1961); A. R. Crollius, *The Word in the Experience of Revelation in the Qur'ân and Hindu Scriptures* (Rome, 1974), pp. 37ff.

23. L. Massignon, *Les Langues sémitiques et le mode de récueillement que elles inspirent*, in Opera Minora, 2:570–580; idem, *La langue arabe et la valeur de la parole humaine en tant que témoignage*, Opera Minora, 2:581–587.

24. L. Massignon, *Les "Sept Dormants" apocalypse de l'Islam*, in Opera Minora, 3:104–118.

25. L. Massignon, *Les Trois Prières d'Abraham* (Tours, 1935), p. 52.

26. L. Massignon, *Elie et son rôle transhistorique, Khadîr en Islam,* in Opera Minora, 1:148.

27. T. Sabbagh, *La Métaphore dans le Coran* (Paris, 1943); C. Torrey, *The Commercial-Theological Terms in the Koran* (Leiden, 1928).

28. A. Bausani, *Il Corano* (Florence, 1955), n. 31, p. 695; Watt, *Bell's Introduction to the Qur'ân,* p. 81.

29. Moubarac, *Les Etudes d'Epigraphie Sud-Semitique et la Naissance de l'Islam.*

30. *Abraham dans le Coran,* p. 174.

31. Bausani, *Il Corano,* pp. i–iv; H. A. R. Gibb, *Mohammedanism* (Oxford, 1954), p. 49; *Bell's Introduction to the Qur'ân,* pp. 30–55, 86–107.

32. L. Massignon, *Situation de l'Islam,* in Opera Minora, 1:16.

33. Montefiore and Loewe, *A Rabbinic Anthology* (New York, 1963), pp. 10–12. For the use of the first person plural, see P. Koury, *Paul d'Antioche, évêque melkite de Sidon* (Beirut, 1964).

34. Moubarac, *Abraham dans le Coran,* pp. 16–20.

35. For a treatment of the priestly functions of the "Kahinin" in pagan Arabia, see *Bell's Introduction to the Qur'ân,* pp. 18, 21, 77–79, 154.

36. R. Blachère, *Introduction au Coran* (Paris, 1947), pp. 161–181; *Bell's Introduction to the Qur'ân,* pp. 77–79.

37. Tor Andrae, *Mohammed,* pp. 48–51; R. H. Charles, *Eschatology* (New York, 1963), pp. 173–184. In *Bell's Introduction* we read: "There is just a little in the Qur'ân to support the hypothesis adopted by Tor Andrae that Muhammad actually heard voices; but the fact that the revelations took the form of words might be held to show that Muhammad was closer to the auditory than to the visual type of inspiration" (p. 19).

38. Massignon, *Les Trois Prières d'Abraham,* pp. 43–44, and *The Church Teaches,* (Herder, 1961), p. 133.

39. Massignon, *La Passion de Hallâj,* 3:137, n. 8.

40. Abd-el-Jalil, *Aspects Intérieurs de l'Islam,* p. 126.

41. Tor Andrae, *Mohammed,* pp. 86–90; Blachère, *Le Coran,* pp. 133–134, 349–351; J. Bowman, "The Debt of Islam to Monophysite Syrian Christianity," *Nederlands Theologish Tijdschrift,* 19 (1964–65): 177–201.

42. L. Massignon, *Essai sur les origines du Lexique technique de la mystique Musulmane* (Paris, 1954), pp. 142–143.

43. Abd-el-Jalil, *Aspects Intérieurs de l'Islam,* p. 39; Moubarac, *Abraham dans le Coran,* pp. 136–137.

44. Bell, *Introduction to the Qur'ân,* pp. 121–128; Gibb, *Mohammedanism,* pp. 37–43.

45. Moubarac, *Abraham dans le Coran,* pp. 15–29, 119–148; "Moïse dans le Coran" and "Elie le Prophète," in *Pentalogie Islamo-Chrétienne,* 2:127–156, 157–174.

46. Y. Moubarac, *L'Islam* (Castermann, 1962), pp. 24–28, 52–63.

47. For example, Abdoul Masih al-Ghaliviry, *Les miracles de Mahomet* (Harissa, 1937), p. 365.

48. M. Guidi, "Storia della Religione dell'Islam," in Tacchi-Venturi, *Storia delle Religioni* (Turin, 1936), 2:6.

49. Gibb, *Mohammedanism*, p. 73; Fazlur Rahman, *Islam* (New York, 1968), pp. 75–95.

50. S. Schechter, *Aspects of Rabbinic Theology* (New York, 1961), pp. 205–207.

51. Crollius, *The Word in the Experience of Revelation in the Qur'ân and Hindu Scriptures*, pp. 144–155; Fazlur Rahman, *Islam*, p. 26.

Part Three

1. J. Jomier, *The Bible and the Koran* (New York, 1964), pp. 29, 34, 86, 113, 114, 115.

2. Pius XII, Dec. 31, 1952, *Acta Apost. Sedis*, 45 (1953): 99; Paul VI, Mar. 29, 1964, *Acta Apost. Sedis*, 56 (1964): 394. Vatican Council II, *Decree on the Church's Missionary Activity (Ad Gentes)*, n. 11: "Let them [all Christians] be familiar with their national and religious traditions, gladly and reverently laying bare the seed of the word which lies hidden in them. . . . Christ himself searched the hearts of men, and led them to divine light through truly human conversation. So also his disciples, profoundly penetrated by the Spirit of Christ, should know the people among whom they live, and should establish contact with them. Thus they themselves can learn by sincere and patient dialogue what treasures a bountiful God has distributed among the nations of the earth. But at the same time, let them try to illumine these treasures with the light of the Gospel, to set them free, and to bring them under the dominion of God their Savior."

3. E. Dermenghen, *Vies des Saints Musulmans* (Algiers, 1943), p. 70.

4. René Guenon and Frithjof Schuon.

5. Gibb, *Mohammedanism*, pp. 96–97; Fazlur Rahman, *Islam*, pp. 39–40.

6. *Summa Theologica*, II–II, q. 173, a. 2: "Sciendum tamen quod quia mens Prophetae est instrumentum deficiens, ut dictum est, etiam veri Prophetae non omnia cognoscunt quae in eorum visis aut verbis aut etiam factis Spiritus Sanctus intendit."

7. "Hanna Zakarias," *L'Islam entreprise juive*, 1:19.

8. *Abraham dans le Coran*, pp. 51–62.

9. W. Leslau, *Falasha Anthology*, Yale Judaica Series (New Haven, 1951), vol. 6.

10. S. Goitein, *Jews and Arabs* (New York, 1955), p. 51; Kritzeck, *Sons of Abraham*, pp. 35–36.

11. Margolis and Marx, *A History of the Jewish People* (New York, 1962), p. 260.

12. J. Klausner, *Jesus of Nazareth* (London, 1925), pp. 216–222.
13. Moubarac, "Moïse dans le Coran," in *Pentalogie Islamo-Chrétienne*, 2:142, n. 17.
14. H. "Zakarias," *L'Islam entreprise juive*, 2:34.
15. C. Ledit, *Mahomet, Israel et le Christ* (Paris, 1956), p. 24.
16. See Book of Jubilees, 18:18, 19:9, 33:10; Testament of the Twelve Patriarchs, 5:4, 7:5, etc.; Book of Henoch, 81. According to the Bible, certain "books" are in Heaven: the "Book of Truth" (Dn 15:21), the "Book of Reckonings" (Jer 17:1, Mal 3:16, Ps 56 (55):9, Dn 7:10, Lk 10:20, Rv 20:12, the "Book of Life" (Is 4:3, Dn 12:1, Mt 10:32, Rv 3:5, 13:8, 20:5).
17. Anawati and Gardet, *Introduction à la Théologie Musulmane* (Paris, 1948), pp. 23, n. 3; 26–27, 29–31.
18. J. Jomier, *The Bible and the Koran*, pp. 31–35.
19. S. Schechter, *Aspects of Rabbinic Theology*, pp. 116–117; H. J. Schoeps, *The Jewish Christian Argument* (New York, 1963), pp. 40–52.
20. I. Goldziher, *Le Dogme et la Loi de l'Islam* (Paris, 1958), pp. 12–13.
21. *Pesikta Rabbati*, 26, 132: "my Mother Sion"; *Targum H. L.*, 8, 5: "Sion which is the Mother of Israel"; etc.
22. H. Speyer, "Yahûdî," in *Shorter Encyclopedia of Islam* (Leiden, 1953), p. 639.
23. Hefele and Leclercq, *Histoire des Conciles*, 3: pt. 1, p. 571.
24. Schoeps, *The Jewish Christian Argument*, pp. 20–35, 183, n. 35; J. Jocz, *The Jewish People and Jesus Christ* (London, 1962), pp. 50–52.
25. M. Adler, *The World of the Talmud* (New York, 1963), pp. 21–31; Montefiore and Loewe, *A Rabbinic Anthology*, pp. 279, 444, 497, 709, 713; Ibn Ishaq, *Life of Muhammad* (London, 1955), pp. 7, 85, 93–95, 136, 139, 197, etc.
26. Massignon, *La Passion de Hallâj*, 1:108–109. Abû Hurayra said explicitly that the "People of the Book" (the rabbis) read the Tawrat in Hebrew and interpreted it in Arabic to the Muslims (I. Goldziher, *Etudes Islamologiques* [Leiden, 1962], p. 263).
27. Montefiore and Loewe, *A Rabbinic Anthology*, p. 16; W. D. Davies, *Paul and Rabbinic Judaism* (London, 1962), pp. 206–207.
28. *Nedarim*, 2, 2; *Exodus Rabba*, 5; *Genesis Rabba*, 45, etc.
29. Talmud of Babylon, *Baba Bathra*, 12a.
30. Schechter, *Aspects of Rabbinic Theology*, pp. 340–347.
31. Moubarac, *Abraham dans le Coran*, p. 144.
32. Massignon, *La Passion de Hallâj*, 3:39, 213.
33. *Historia Ecclesiastica*, VI, 20, P.G., 20, c. 571.
34. *De viris illustribus*, c. LX, P.L., 23, c. 598.
35. *De Haeresis*, LXX, 10–15, P.G., 42, c. 355–374.
36. Ibid., LXXVIII–LXXIX, P.G., 42, c. 700–756.
37. H. Lammens, "Les Chrétiens à la Mecque à la veille de l'Hégire," *Bulletin de l'Institut Français de Archéologie Orientale* (Cairo, 1918), p. 229.

38. The last line might read: "No! We are of the descendance of Abraham who was a Hanif, and no idolater." M. Watt, "The Christian criticized in the Qur'ân." *The Muslim World* LVII (1967), 197–201.

39. I. Di Matteo, *La Dività di Cristo e la dottrina della Trinità in Maometto e nei polemisti musulmani* (Rome, 1938), p. 11. See also R. C. Zaehner, *Inde, Israël, Islam — Religions mystiques et Révélation Prophétiques* (Paris, 1965), pp. 255, 314–333.

40. *Commentarium in Isaiam Prophetam,* 1.XI, c; 40, P.L., 24, cc. 404–405; *Commentarium in Micheam,* 1.II, c. 7, P.L., 25, c. 1221–1222.

41. Moubarac, *L'Islam,* p. 62; Abd-el-Jalil, *Marie et l'Islam,* pp. 64–77; Zaehner, *Inde, Israël, Islam,* pp. 305–333.

42. S. Krauss, *Das Leben Jesu nach juedischen Quellen* (Berlin, 1902), quoted by J. Klausner in *Jesus of Nazareth* (Boston, 1964), pp. 47–54.

43. Massignon, *Les Trois Prières d'Abraham,* p. 47.

44. Cf. Denzinger and Schonmetzer, *Enchiridion Symbolorum* (33d ed.; New York, 1963), n. 771, p. 246.

45. Moubarac, *Abraham dans le Coran* ("La religion d'Abraham est l'Islam"), pp. 103–118.

46. Ibid., pp. 26.

47. For its traditional Muslim interpretation, see O'Shaughnessy, *The Development of the Meaning of Spirit in the Koran* (Rome, 1953).

48. *Muhammad at Medina,* (Oxford, 1956), 317–318.

49. Bell, *Introduction to the Qur'ân,* p. 183; Gaudefroy Demombynes, *Mahomet* (Paris, 1956), pp. 428–429. Tor Andrae, in *Mohammed* (pp. 112–113), sees traces of Manicheism rather than Docetism. Blachère, *Le Coran,* p. 965.

50. Moubarac, *L'Islam,* p. 164, n. 10.

51. L. Baeck, *Judaism and Christianity* (New York, 1961), pp. 169–185; A. Marmorstein, *The Doctrine of Merits in the Old Rabbinical Literature* (London, 1920), pp. 41–49.

52. *Le Coran,* p. 747, n. 68.

53. C. G. Montefiore, *The Synoptic Gospels* (London, 1927), p. 382.

54. Klausner, *Jesus of Nazareth,* pp. 152ff., 349–355.

55. D. Chwolson, *Das letzte Passamahl Christi und der Tag seiner Todes* (St. Petersburg, 1892), p. 96. "A learned and detailed investigation of the circumstances of Jesus' trial and condemnation. In it Chwolson attempted to prove that Jesus was sentenced to death by the Sadducean High Court and that therefore the Pharisees and masses of Jews bear no guilt."

56. R. T. Hertford, *Christianity in Talmud and Midrash* (London, 1903), p. 83; J. Parkes, *The Conflict of the Church and the Synagogue* (New York, 1961), p. 46.

57. J. Jacobs, *"Jesus,"* in *Jewish Encyclopedia,* 7:166; M. J. Lagrange, *Le Messianisme* (Paris, 1909), p. 239.

58. Agada, *Bereshit,* 31, quoted by Schoeps in *The Jewish Christian Argument,* p. 23.

59. L. H. Grondijs, *L'Iconographie byzantine du Crucifix mort sur la*

Croix (Utrecht, 1945); Massignon, *Les Trois Prières d'Abraham,* pp. 45–46.

60. J. Guttman, *Philosophies of Judaism* (New York, 1964), pp. 68, 417.

61. J. H. Hertz, *Affirmation of Judaism* (London, 1927), p. 17.

62. K. Kohler, *The Origins of the Synagogue and the Church* (New York, 1929), p. 140; see also his "Christianity" in *Jewish Encyclopedia,* 4:54–55.

63. Montefiore and Loewe, *A Rabbinic Anthology,* pp. 12, 452, 491, etc.

64. Blachère, *Le Coran,* p. 968.

65. G. Basetti-Sani, "Satana nel Corano," *Sacra Doctrina* (Bologna, 1973), no. 72, pp. 587–653.

66. *Enarr. in Psalmo,* 123, n. 2, P.L., 37, c. 1641; *In Ps.* 18, n. 7, P.L. 36, c. 135.

67. L. Massignon, *L'Homme Parfait en Islam,* in Opera Minora, 1:114–115; idem, *Les Trois Prières d'Abraham,* pp. 14–15.

68. C. Padwick, *Muslim Devotions. A Study of Prayer-Manuals in Common Use* (London, 1961).

69. *De Negotio Terrae Sanctae,* P.L., 216, c. 818.

70. Alexander of Hales, *Summa Theologica,* n. 775 (Quaracchi, 1930), 3:760.

71. St. Augustine, *Super Psalmum,* 147, n. 16, P.L., 37, c. 1924.

72. St. Augustine, *Contra litteras Petiliani,* 1.3, c. 8, n. 9, P.L., 43, c. 453.

73. *Summa Theologica,* II–II, q. 60, a. 4.

74. H. Leclercq, "Mahomet," in *Dict. Archéol. Chrètienne et Liturgie,* 10:cc. 1160–1176.

75. P. Palmieri, "Coran," in *Dict. Théol. Catholique,* 3:c. 1839.

76. P. Casanova, "Mahomet," in *Dict. Théol. Catholique,* 9:cc. 1573–1590.

77. P. Powers, "Mahomet," in *Dict. d'Apologétique et de la Foi Catholique,* 3:cc. 74–87.

78. Massignon, *La Passion de Hallâj* (2d/ed.; Paris, 1975), 4 vols.

79. Monchanin, "Islam et Christianisme," pp. 10–23.

80. Massignon, *Essai sur les Origines du Lexique tecnique de la Mystique Musulmane,* pp. 143, 144–145; idem, *La Passion de Hallâj,* 3:213–217, 300–306, 311–323.

81. Ibn 'Arabi, *La Sagesse des Prophètes* (Paris, 1955), pp. 182–197. For a new evaluation of Mohammed among Christians, see W. A. Bijlefeld, "A Prophet and More than a Prophet?" *Muslim World* (1969), pp. 1–28, and J. E. Royster, "The Study of Muhammad. A Survey of Approaches from the Perspective of the History and Phenomenology of Religion," *Muslim World* (1972), pp. 49–70.

Part Four

1. Cf. A. J. Toynbee, *Civilization on Trial and the World and the West,* (Meridian Books, 1958), pp. 164–165, 246–247.

2. Petrus Venerabilis, *Summula contra sectam Saracenorum, sive Ismaëlitarum,* P.L., 189, c. 651-659.

3. *Synodalis Concio Urbanis Papae Ilae,* in Mansi: Coll. Conc. t. 20, cc. 821–824. The more common designation found also in pontifical documents is that of "Enemies of the Cross of Christ," and "the most wicked Arab people." Cf. Norman Daniel, *Islam and the West* (Edinburgh, 1960).

4. Migne, *Patrologia Latina* t. 148 cc. 450–451; cf. G. Basetti-Sani O.F.M. *Mohammed et S. Francois,* Ottawa, 1953, p. 217, n. 11.

5. Paul VI, *Ecclesiam suam,* The American Press, n. 111, p. 54.

6. *Ibid.,* n. 111, 112, pp. 54-55.

7. *Dogmatic Constitution on the Church,* c. 2, n. 16, *The Documents of Vatican II,* Walter M. Abbott, S.J. general editor (New York, 1966), p. 34.

8. Homily of Paul VI, on October 28, 1965.

9. The Decree *Ad Gentes,* on missionary activity in *The Documents of Vatican II,* pp. 584–630.

10. *Declaration on the Relationship of the Church to non-Christian Religions,* no. 3, p. 663.

11. L. Massignon, *La Passion d al-Hallaj, martyr mystique de l'Islam* (Paris, 2ed., 1975), t. 3, p. 10.

12. L. Massignon, *Les trois prières d'Abraham,* II, p. 15; Y. Moubarac, *l'Islam,* pp. 79-80. For the calling down of blessing (*tasliya*) on Abraham cf. C. Padwick, *Muslim Devotions* (London, 1961), pp. 167ff.

13. G. Basetti-Sani O.F.M., *Mohammed et S. Francois,* pp. 210–11.

14. Cf. G. Basetti-Sani O.F.M.: "I Comandamenti di Dio nel Corano," in *La Seuola Cattolica,* t. 81, 1953, pp. 329–349.

15. L. Massignon, *Les trois prières d'Abraham,* II, p. 43. D. M. Donaldson, *Studies in Muslim Ethics* (London, 1953). We give the French original of the passage of Massignon referred to: "La pratique de la religion islamique n'est appréciée qu'*ad extra* pour la "faciliter"; — par une mansuétude qui n'est pas sans laxisme, le contrôle canonique vise l'acte plus que l'intention, l'observance plus que l'obéissance, le temporel plus que le spirituel; les jugements intimes et les actes commis en privé échappent à sa juridiction. Déjà le Qor'an accorde au prophète des privilèges, *rokhas,* mitigations toutes salomoniennes, et assez laxistes, dans la vie conjugale. L'Islam ne juge qu'an for externe, ne punit que la trace sociale des pêches . . ."

16. Cf. C. E. Padwick's, *Muslim Devotions,* quoted in note 22. E. Dermenghem, *Vies des Saints Musulmans* (Alger, 1943). G. C. Anawati — L. Gardet, *Mystique Musulmane* (Paris, 1961). R. A. Nicolson, *The Mystics of Islam* (London, 1970).

17. *Declaration on the Relationship of the Church to non-Christian Religions,* n. 3, p. 663.

THE AUTHOR

Fr. Giulio B. Sani O.F.M.

Curriculum Vitae

Fr. Giulio B. Sani O.F.M., Professor of Christian and Islamic Theology. Born in Florence (Italy), January 6, 1912.

EDUCATION

1928-31: Franciscan Seminary, Florence, Italy: Philosophy
1931-35: Franciscan Seminary, Arezzo, Italy: Theology
1935-36: Oriental Studies in Cairo (Egypt)
1936-37: Institut Catholique de Paris (France), Ecole de Langues Orientales
1937-39: Pontifical Institute of Oriental Studies, Rome, Italy
1952-54: Facultés Catholiques de Lyon, France (Holy Scripture and Dogmatic Courses)
1960-61: Dropsie College, Philadelphia, Penna: Comparative Religion

DEGREES

a) "Licentiatus Laureandus" in Oriental Ecclesiastical Studies at the Institutum Orientalium Studiorum, Rome, July 1939
b) "Licentiatus Laureandus" in Theology, at the Facultés Catholiques de Lyon, France, June 1954
c) "Lector Generalis Orientalium Studiorum," of the Franciscan Order, 1947
d) "Diploma" in Coptic Language: Ecole des Langues Orientales in the Institut Catholique de Paris, France, June 1938
e) "Diploma" in Arabic Language: Scuola di Lingue dell'Impero, Rome, June 1939

f) Orals for Ph.D. degree in Comp. Religion passed: Dropsie
     College 1961

TEACHING APPOINTMENTS

1939-52: Professor of Theology, Philosophy, and Islamic Insti-
          tutions in the Franciscan Oriental Seminary of Ghiza,
          Egypt
1952-55: Professor of Patrology and Church History in the Sem-
          inaire des Missions Franciscaines, Lyon, France
1951 Jan: Course of six lectures on "Christian and Islamic East"
          at the Catholic University of Milan, Italy
1955-56: Research on Islamic Theology in the Institut Domini-
          cain d'Etudes Orientales," Cairo, Egypt
1957-58: Honorary Research Assistant in the Institute of Islamic
          Studies at McGill University, Montreal, Canada
1959 Feb.-March: Course of five lectures on "The Religions of
          Africa" at the University of Florence, Italy
1965-68: Research, lectures (Compar. Religion) St. Bonaventure
          University, N.Y.
1968   Six lectures on Islam at the Institute for Advanced
          Religious Studies, Notre Dame University, Indiana

          Currently stationed in Italy, Lecturer on Christian-
          Muslim relations in the Middle East

ACTIVITIES

Director of Studies in the Franciscan Oriental Seminary in Ghiza,
    Egypt from 1939-52
President of the Franciscan Oriental Seminary, Ghiza, Egypt 1946-
    48
Editor of "Kyrilliana" — Melanges d'Etudes Historiques, Theolo-
    giques et Liturgiques at the occasion of the Centenary of St.
    Cyril of Alexandria (444-1944) in 1947
"Delegate of the Italian Catholic Commission" for the emigration
    of Italian families from Egypt to Australia, and "Social Assistant
    of Emigration" in the Italian Consulate at Port Said, in 1956
1956-57 in Brazil, delegated by the "Intergovernmental Committee

for European Migration" of Geneva, to execute and establish the "Father B. Sani Plan" which involved placing the Italian worker's families in the migration from Egypt to Brazil and also in Uruguay and Argentina.

LANGUAGES

Italian, French, Latin — thorough familiarity
Arabic, Coptic, Classical Greek, Portugese, Spanish — competent knowledge
English — thorough familiarity, but heavy accent

PUBLICATIONS

Books: "Mohammed et Saint Francois" (in French), Ottawa 1959, vi, 284pp., also English edition by Franciscan Herald Press

"Introduzione allo Studio de Corano" (Italian), Brescia 1967

"Il Corano Nella Luce Di Cristo," Rome, 1972

"Louis Massignon, Christian Ecumenist" (English), Franciscan Herald Press, 1974

Articles on theology, history, and problems of Christian and Moslem Orient in:

A) *Encyclopaedies*: a) "Dictionnaire d'Histoire Ecclesiastique" (Paris-Louvain); b) "Enciclopedia Cattolica" (Citta del Vaticano); c) "I Grandi del Cattolicesimo" (Roma); d) "Roma," (Rome), etc., etc.

B) *Periodicals*: a) Archivum Franciscanum Historicum (Florence); b) Cahiers d'histoire d'Egypte (Cairo); c) "Muslim World, The" (Hartford, Conn.); d) Nouvelle Revue de Science Missionnaire (Beckerin-Suisse); e) Orientalia Christiana Periodica (Rome); f) Oriente (L') Christiano e l'Unita della Chiesa, (Rome); g) Oriente Moderno, (Rome); h) Rayon d'Egypte (Cairo); i) Scuola Cattolica (Milano); j) Studi Francescani (Firenze); k) Voce del Nilo (Cairo); l) World Dominion (London); Concilium (Louvain); Revue d'Histoire Ecclesiastique (Louvain); Le Missioni Cattoliche (Milano); World mission (New York).